ISBN: 978129035173

Published by:
HardPress Publishing
8345 NW 66TH ST #2561
MIAMI FL 33166-2626

Email: info@hardpress.net
Web: http://www.hardpress.net

RACE ORTHODOXY
IN THE SOUTH

RACE ORTHODOXY IN THE SOUTH

AND OTHER ASPECTS OF THE NEGRO QUESTION

BY

THOMAS PEARCE BAILEY, Ph.D.

FORMERLY: ASSOCIATE PROFESSOR OF EDUCATION IN THE UNIVERSITY OF CALIFORNIA;
UNIVERSITY EXTENSION LECTURER FOR THE UNIVERSITY OF CHICAGO; SUPERIN-
TENDENT OF SCHOOLS OF MEMPHIS; INVESTIGATOR FOR THE NEW YORK
BUREAU OF MUNICIPAL RESEARCH; DEAN OF THE DEPARTMENT
OF EDUCATION AND PROFESSOR OF PSYCHOLOGY AND EDU-
CATION IN THE UNIVERSITY OF MISSISSIPPI

NEW YORK
THE NEALE PUBLISHING COMPANY
1914

TABLE OF CONTENTS

APPENDIX

RACE ORTHODOXY IN THE SOUTH

A. The Race Problem and Race Prejudice.

I. A FOOLS' PARADISE FOR NEGROES

(This paper was used as a test of public opinion in magazine circles. The editor of a very high-grade journal wrote the author in a manner that expressed deep interest in the paper; he asked for permission to keep the paper longer and to send it to a "friend who knew Southern Conditions." The editor afterward returned the paper because his "friend" thought that the present writer's views were too pessimistic, and that the latter would "feel better" after he had mingled more with "practical men." Inasmuch as the paper was directly based on conversations with many decidedly practical representative men of both races as well as upon several years' special field study of Southern conditions, the charge of pessimism due to academic seclusion cannot be taken very seriously.)

If the American negro becomes afflicted with racial mania, melancholia or paranoia, the fault will lie at the door of the white people of the United States. Listen to the voices that come to the freedman from books and pamphlets, newspapers and magazines! One says: "You are a great people in the making; you have qualities and powers that the world needs; your race is the youngest and most unspoiled; you have made in a few years an amount of progress that puts to shame the achievements of any other race during the same length of time; your vitality, your patience, your adaptability,

7

your sweet reasonableness, your childlikeness, your potentialities full of promise—these make you a Chosen
People. Only persevere and assert your powers, and
you will win a notable place among the peoples of the
earth." Another cries: "You are of all people the
most miserable! Your physical stock is deteriorating;
your fertility is rapidly decreasing; your bodies are
faster and faster becoming the prey of the race-destroy-
ing diseases; your progress, so far as you have made
any, is due to the help of the white civilization that has
coddled you and without which you would sink into the
savagery whence you recently came; you are not patient,
but dull and stupid and lacking in the self-assertion of
the people that have the law; your powers of imitation
are those of the jackdaw and not those of the Japanese.
You are childish, shallow, sensual and incoherent. Make
up your minds to the annihilation that is coming to your
race, and may your end be an euthanasia!"

And a third voice exclaims: "Industrial education!
Own your homes! Prove that you are needed! Thrift
and honesty and purity will save you!"

How sad the pathos of it all! As a rule, neither the
negro nor his friends nor his enemies has *studied* this
most difficult and complicated problem, except in a
scrappy and unsystematic way. "Studies" enough there
are, but little that satisfies even a tyro in any one of the
many sciences that have to do with the Study of Man.
Disputants seize on the same "facts" to prove theses
worlds apart. Prejudice against the negro race or in
favor of him has very often rendered the "facts" mis-
leading. Avowed men of science usually prefer to study
ethnological peculiarities in far-off peoples rather than
concern themselves with a question that is "in politics"
and is so full of snares to the wary as well as the un-

wary. A "favorable" study meets with the enthusiastic approval of one set of citizens, and an "unfavorable" study receives the praises of another set. And yet we are living in an age of organized science. Even such "political" questions as the tariff and trust regulation are receiving the careful attention of science and scientific experts. But where is the coöperative scientific group that is studying the negro question? How few are the first-class men that are making this most baffling, distressing and imminent of human problems the object of devoted and patient scientific investigation! Must we wait until all other pressing problems have been worked on before coming to this question of most immediate human concern?

Even the few who are doing worth-while work in this field are scarcely coöperating, and those who seem to be coöperating are seldom capable of doing scientific work. Meanwhile clamor fills the air; the gap between the whites and blacks is widening, at the North as well as at the South; money is being poured into educational and other philanthropic enterprises in behalf of the negro, while at the same time the dominant race, North and South, is instinctively reducing discrimination against the negro to a fine art.

Truth to tell, this whole subject seems to bristle with delusions and illusions. The negroes are talked about as if they were all alike. Even those who call attention to the immense individual differences among human beings in general and negroes in particular are all too apt to lose sight of this point when practical results are aimed at. Some of the negro's friends seem to hold the doctrine that a remnant always and everywhere can save a people. On the other hand, those who have no faith in negro possibilities explain away "exceptional" cases, and seem to aver that even if there were a remnant of good negroes these would leave no descendants, or if they did that the idea of ten men saving the city does not apply to the negro race. Indeed, both sides— all sides, for there are many more than two—seem to be concerning themselves with what the negro *may be* or *may have been,* rather than what he *is* and *has been.* Yet the man in the street knows that we cannot forecast the future except from the vantage ground of the past and the present. This notion is true in physical science, and needs must be applied to every case of the science of man, in spite of the unfortunate fact that the anthropological and social sciences have climbed only a little way up the ladder of scientific method and results, so that even the simplest questions of "races and peoples" are still in the region of conjecture and controversy. Bold, therefore, the men who, without long-continued scientific special study, would venture on prediction in a region where fog and mist obscure even the plainest landmarks.

Even if we admit for a moment that good work is being done in the study of negro character, for example, how many first-rate men are making a careful and conscientious study of the *Southern whites* and the *Northern whites* in their respective relations to the negro? Does it not seem a plain matter of common sense, for instance, that there should be a very painstaking investigation of "race prejudice" in the world generally, in the United States especially, and in the South most particularly? Even Southerners, to say nothing of Northerners, do not as a rule seem able to state their own views correctly as to what *is* race prejudice. Occasionally some writer makes a "try" at an explanation, but—well, nothing comes of the effort!

Finot quite correctly states that race antipathy is not primarily instinctive, but forgets to tell us anything definite about what it *is,* or to explain its causal efficacy. Other writers have made various and sundry remarks about the "former slave" factor and the economic competition that has something to do with certain forms of race prejudice. But most of the speculation on the subject is in the clouds.

One evident classification of race attitudes might serve as a point of departure for further study:* There is a race enmity to be found mainly among those who come into economic competition with the negroes; a race-pride which may be æsthetic and social and political; a race-conscience that is ethical and scientific and humanitarian. Only those belonging to the third class can lead successfully in the study of the negro question, and among them only individuals who have an intimate knowledge of the first two classes and a real sympathy for them, as well as an equally real sympathy for the subordinated race. To take an example, President Eliot belongs to the third class, and probably has some sympathetic knowledge of the second, but has had neither opportunity nor, possibly, desire to understand sympathetically the viewpoint of the first class. Some representatives of the humanitarian group feel it difficult to understand why an illiterate and even vicious white man should object to dining with a highly cultured negro gentleman. To them the attitude of the "low" white man seems essentially illogical and absurd; but it is not so to the man who knows the "low-grade" white man from the *inside.* The whole picture changes when one knows "what it is about." Social attitudes at bottom are concerned with marriage and all it stands for. Now,

* Compare paper on The Crux of the Question, p. 33.

race conscience may prevent the enlightened humanitarian from encouraging in any way the interbreeding
of the two races. Race-pride will deter the average man
who is willing to acknowledge the excellence of certain
individual negroes. But may it not require race enmity
to prevent the amalgamation of the "lower" grades of
the higher race with the higher grades of the lower
race?

Mind you, I am stating this simply as a matter that
deserves study. If it be true or possibly true that race
enmity serves the function above mentioned, will not
our position on the race question be radically altered if
we take this idea, even as a possibility, into consideration? I think so.

Practical men everywhere believe in the common-sense
principle of the adaptation of means to ends. But how
many investigators have pointed out the inexpugnable
truth that all our efforts directed toward the bettering
of the negro's life and the development of his character must be profoundly affected by the question, insistent and remorseless, What is going to become of the
negro; what are we going to do with him; where shall
he work out his own salvation in fear and trembling?
Some few stoutly declare that we must get rid of the
negro. Various schemes of deportation, colonization
and the like are suggested. But these hints of a radical
solution are generally so vague and have so little connection with accurate observation and reflection that
little heed is paid to them. It is the fashion to reply
somewhat impatiently to these radicals: Your suggestions are impracticable; the negro must stay with us.
Sometimes the additional claim is made that we cannot
get along without the Brother in Black, or that he cannot
get along without us.

Among the negro leaders themselves little favor is shown toward the colonization idea. The Booker T. Washington group and the W. E. B. DuBois group are one in rejecting the very thought of separation. Now is it possible that such able men as Washington and DuBois have failed to understand the temper of the white people of this country? Are they misled by the optimism of philanthropists? Have they failed to notice the growing *social* discrimination against the negro in the North and the increasing *economic* hatred of the negro in the South? And surely all men see that the old affection felt for the Southern negroes by the slave-holding class is rapidly passing away with the departure of the "old-time" Southern people from the stage of life. Nor can even a superficial observer miss the clear evidence that the old-fashioned "human rights" doctrine is no longer being embraced *con amore* in this country. The abolitionists have left few spiritual descendants, and the few have little or no power to carry out their views. The last introduction of a "political practice" Force Bill into the halls of Congress was only a perfunctory performance that was treated almost as a joke. Meanwhile, the Southern states continue to "keep the negro in his place"—without showing any popular intention of ever letting him climb higher. As Senator John Sharp Williams has truly said, the trouble lies in the "physical presence of the negro."

On the one hand, the conscience of the American people is not likely to deprive the worthy and qualified negroes of any of their civil and political rights; on the other hand, the Southern people show not the slightest disposition to encourage the negro in believing that "some of these days" he will be held the white man's equal in matters affecting the rights of citizenship. No statesman yet born has been able to disentangle the interwoven threads of domestic, social, religious, legal and political life. So long as the negro is debarred from the hope of being valued according to his character instead of his race, so long will the "problem" remain unsolved.

But am I wrong in believing—for I cannot now scientifically prove the assertion—that all forms of "equality" depend on social equality and that the latter depends on the right of intermarriage? My reading of history supports the contention. Fustel de Coulanges'* illuminating study, "The Ancient City" (to take one illustration), makes it plain that the Roman Plebeians never got their rights until intermarriage was allowed with the Patricians. Human life in society is one, and its basis is biological, with all the meaning of "natural selection" and "sexual selection," and with modes of "social selection" to boot. Willingness to "rear a dusky brood" is not impossible to the consciousness of most men; but race prejudice is driving the idea far afield in the United States of America and in the British possessions. As a rule, men *dare* not allow themselves, especially in the South, to think of such a thing.

However, without discussing the point, I am making the plea here, as elsewhere in this paper, that the race problem should be *studied,* and by competent, trained minds, and with all the methods known to the biological, psychological, anthropological and social sciences. It seems almost cruel to tell ten millions of people that there is "a good time coming" for them in this country, when the facts of increasing race feeling all point the other way. Even more cruel is it to inform them that they

* See Appendix: Ancient Rome and the Race Problem in the South.

are handicapped, hopelessly and finally, by Nature, and
cannot hope to develop as a race. "The white man
doesn't want the negro in his way—and, apparently, all
ways in this country are becoming the white man's way;
and nature does not want the negro anywhere!" Now,
the first part of this sentence, put into the mouth of the
pessimist, is probably true. This is becoming true in a
most sinister fashion as the years go by; but surely no
man that loves mankind can, without being morally and
scientifically sure of his ground, allow himself to accept
the doctrine of despair that condemns the negro to
ultimate destruction.

If the negro is to stay with us, we must help him to
develop himself to fit in with the present and probable
future civilization of the country. If he is to go abroad
on the earth, or to be segregated in American territory,
his training will have to take such a future into account.
Are we not wasting time and money in educating this
people in the dark? Shall we educate them to do economic battle with the white race, with the practical certainty in view that they will fail in their fight? Or can
we view with equanimity the thought of "high-grade"
negroes or mulattoes overcoming "low-grade" white
men? Doubtless some are doughty enough to say, Let
the white man go down if he cannot compete with the
negro. But it may happen that the negro's success, if
he achieves any, will be due to qualities not sought after
by the white race. The Japanese and other race "problems" will have to be solved before we can allow ourselves to harbor even the most pragmatic form of that
alluring doctrine: "The devil take the hindmost!"
After all, we cherish our own, whether high or low.
The Congress of the United States seems to have thought
so in their legislation with regard to Chinese immigra-

tion, and in other ways that need not be mentioned. Whatever we may say in print, we Americans have a "favored race" clause in that unwritten constitution of ours which is more "national" than our written documents. Even now the Anglo-American warcry, This is a White Man's Country, is sounding throughout the world, wherever whites constitute a fair percentage of the population. And politicians and statesmen are being compelled to pay heed to it. History should by this time have taught us the significance of race feeling as a compelling and often a controlling factor in the development of peoples. Our Bible is full of it. Our experience with the Indians has made us familiar with it, in spite of the romantic interest the red man inspired. Armenia, Austria-Hungary, the Balkan States, the treatment of Jew by Gentile—all these tell the tale; how is it that we have failed to learn our lesson with those object lessons before us? The Indians, whether "American" or Hindu, are interesting in a novel or a write-up, especially when we have no first-hand acquaintance with them; but woe to them or their ilk if they come into antagonistic relations with our social or our economic life! Though we marvel at the wonderful heroism and resourcefulness of the Japanese, many of us feel a sort of humiliation that a nation of white folk allowed themselves to be humbled by a nation of yellow people.

Is not feeling or impulse sometimes a more powerful historical force than ideas? Must not the noblest thought suffuse itself in feeling and get close to the primary impulses of the common people ere it acquire active and telling energy? The human instinct betokened by the saying "Birds of a feather flock together" is none the less true because man has grown more cosmopolitan and humanitarian in his feelings. We need a new Kant to arise who will give us a "Critique of Pure Instinct." When such a work is written and takes hold of the world's leaders, we shall have no more attempts to alter the eternal constitution of man's nature in favor of academic ideas however noble. When man's strongest acquired instincts or habits become suffused with his strongest feelings, as in the case of race attitude in America, let all of us pay due heed to the phenomenon and strive to guide rather than ignorantly to alter or suppress. I have already insisted that race enmity is not innate, but "consciousness of kind" is instinctive— and kind and "kin" at bottom mean pretty nearly the same thing to the average man. Nor is it singular that the Southern people especially take account of the "kin-ness" of things. Their whole history has shown their feeling for the kin, their fondness for local self-government, their powerful feelings about domesticity. A people cannot be altered by law and argument when the logic of blood and tradition speaks otherwise, and when history and social psychology give large significance to their point of view.

The practical psychology of the situation seems to indicate, on the whole, that the negro must find some more congenial field than the Southern states for the sphere of his development. While few Southern leaders make this admission, many would do so if a labor supply were at hand. And do the people of the North and West feel fundamentally different on this subject? I doubt it. In spite of all our manly talk about giving every man a "square deal," most of us are inclined to give the negro justice only on conditions that the giving does not harm the dominant race. And the very presence of a race in tutelage is a menace to the *character* of the ruling race, as James Bryce pointed out some years ago, even though the decline of the subordinate race may not carry the dominant race with it.

All men of good will and higher intelligence wish the negro well. But many are coming to wish him well *away*—as many miles removed as possible! And this wish is for the negro's welfare as well as for the white's. If we, the dominant race, after careful investigation, decide that it is best for both races that the whites and the negroes dwell in different lands, no amount of money is too great that will thus solve or "dissolve" the problem. Better spend treasure equivalent to many Panama Canals than keep up the direful tragedy now being enacted in a Christian nation.

If our American people have a "God-given destiny," surely we ought to begin its fulfilment by taking the beam out of our own eye in order that we may see well enough to take the mote from our brother's eye! The ten millions of defenseless negroes have a right to call on Heaven for vengeance on us if we fail in our duty to them. And surely the nation owes a duty to the "retarded South." For it needs no argument to prove that we white folk must do the best we can for the success and happiness of our own race. If investigation can help us to decide the fateful question, let us investigate. But we are only shallow mockers and hypocrites if we strive to educate these unfortunate negroes only to let them take into their mouths bitter Dead Sea ashes. If the negro is not to remain here, every acre he acquires complicates the problem; yet his advisers, North and South, are telling him to buy land. Already he finds that he cannot purchase city lots that are desirable, and the time may be coming, may be near at hand, when he will find it hard to buy good land anywhere in this country at any price. More and more, as the years roll by, is he being "ordered off the premises" in residence sections of the cities and in divers country communities, and even whole counties. If an owner of city lots is regarded as infamous if he sells his property to a decent negro, can we wonder if the lowest of the low among the poorer whites come to look upon the matter in the same light as that which illumines the "prejudice" of the dwellers in fine houses?

Summing up our thought, let us seriously ask ourselves the question, Are we preparing the negro to dwell in a Fools' Paradise? A small percentage of the negroes are doubtless getting a kind of training that will fit them for almost any emergency. Industrial schools are doing for the negro the sort of service he may need under almost any conditions. But even *their* work will be vastly more useful if directed toward a well-understood end, a carefully mapped out future for the students. How cheerfully would the people of the whole country give of their money and their service did they know that their means and their efforts would result in settling the negro problem. And how blithesomely would the better negroes work for the betterment of their race did they *know* that their people would have a fair chance somewhere, somehow, some time! At present many of the negro leaders have depression at the bottom of their hearts. How could it be otherwise, when facts are so insistent?

After years of silent observation and study, and careful reading on all aspects of the subject, after long residence in North and South, I am inclined to believe that we must find a home for the negro where he will have a fair chance, where he will be aided by us in every sane way, where he can prove himself to be a worthy race. If he fails, then we shall at least have done our

duty. If he succeeds, *we* shall enjoy the satisfaction of
having succeeded in the noblest deed that history records. Once we decide on such a course—and the negro
will help us to decide—it may take half a century of
time and many millions of money to prepare a place or
places for him and properly establish him therein. But
we are a people of large deeds, and our faith is such as
will remove mountains of difficulty. Let us not forget
that, while it is our pleasure to extend our markets and
facilitate our trade, we owe a solemn duty to these
people and to *our own people*. Not for one moment
would I be represented as saying that my tentative opinion as to the solution of the negro problem is necessarily the correct one. Much careful investigation is
needed before anyone can do more than hazard a well-
based judgment. If, however, what I have said helps
ever so little to direct the conscience of our people or
any one of our leaders toward the painstaking, intelligent, scientific, coöperative study of this vexed question, I shall feel that the weight of responsibility that
every honorable American must feel in this matter has
at least been a little eased from my own aching shoul-
ders. For of all things pitiable it is one of the most
trying and grief-inspiring to dwell in this sweet and
sunny South while the tragedy that is retarding two
peoples' development goes on around one! Praise or
blame for the people of the South are not important
matters. I doubt if a finer stock could be found anywhere than these Southern white folk, my own people.
But the situation is too much for us. We cry out strenu-
ously, Let us solve our own problem! But we are not
solving it; indeed, the complication of it is growing.
Nor can the Northern people solve it, for they are far
less equipped than Southerners in their knowledge of

the negroes and of Southern conditions. Our Macedonian cry must go out to all men who care for human beings, all men who have apostolic "charity" (*caritas*), and would not that a single man should be lost because he has not been understood.

So, while we need not cease talking and writing about the negro question, let us study it in the light of twentieth century science and Christianity! If we must finally reach the colonization solution, every year of delay adds immensely to the difficulty of the undertaking.

II. A BRIEF STATEMENT OF SOUTHERN HUMANITARIANISM

(Summary of commencement address to graduating class of University Training School, Oxford, Miss.)

1.   No person should expect to be listened to sympathetically in Mississippi or anywhere else in this country whose point of view in regard to the negro question is not substantially that of the American citizen and the Christian gentleman.

2.   The American citizen believes that all men have a right to "life, liberty, and the pursuit of happines," and that there should be "equal rights for all, special privileges for none."

3.   The Christian gentleman believes that God is the loving Father of all men, and that He "made every nation of men for to dwell on all the face of the earth, having determined their appointed seasons and the bounds of their habitation." (Acts: 17, 26.) And we further believe that Christ died for all men, of every race and nation; that we should love our neighbors as ourselves; that all men everywhere are our neighbors and brothers so far as rights and duties and spiritual life are concerned; that, finally, if we "love not our brother whom we have seen"—no matter if his appearance does not please our æsthetic sense—"how can we love God whom we have not seen"?

4.   The above view claims equality rights for all men. But equality of rights in the abstract does not

presuppose equality of exercise of those rights in the concrete. A young man of twenty may be an accomplished gentleman and a useful citizen, but he does not quarrel with the state for not giving him the franchise. Millions of noble and thoughtful women are not given the legal right to vote, even though thousands of their number are qualified to hold some of the highest offices in the land. Yet the insistent demand for woman suffrage is not as yet very general among women. Expediency and the general welfare must determine how far the exercise of rights must be held in abeyance; but to deprive human beings of their fundamental rights of life, liberty and the pursuit of happiness, except as a means for securing these rights for Society and Man in general, is un-American, inhuman, un-Christian. Nor has pride of race any justification in usurping for itself the rôle of Providence and deciding what shall or shall not ultimately be the destiny of any race, nation or people. The greatest good of the greatest number and the preservation of the highest civilization are principles that may justify the holding in tutelage of an alien race or people until in the process of time such race or people are fit to exercise their rights in a way useful to the general weal. But the pleasure or the convenience or the prejudice of the stronger race is not to be the arbiter of another people's fate for *all* time; rather let the enlightened thought of humanity decide as the years go by when and where every people may have their full and free development.

5. Just as the law insists that parents and guardians must show forth the character appropriate to their rights and duties in regard to the children under their charge, so the enlightened conscience of humanity insists with a mighty and compelling voice that a superior race has

rights over an inferior race only in so far as it has a
responsible conscience void of offense toward those
under its tutelage.   Unworthy exploitation of human
beings in any form is a spitting upon the image of God
and a dire insult to God Himself which He will most
surely avenge.

6.   The Christian gentleman or the ethical humanitarian is one who goes far beyond legal rights and duties
in his kindness toward those seemingly his inferiors.
He knows that his own superiority, if it exists, imposes
upon him the obligation of noble conduct toward his
inferiors—*noblesse oblige.*   And no more certain test of
true gentility can be found than real manliness and real
gentleness.   The bravest are the tenderest, and the brutal
are spiritual cowards.   The Christian gentleman is
scarcely distinguished by the cut of his coat or his gal-
lantry to ladies, but rather by the way he treats dumb
brutes and the human crawlers on life's hard roadway.
The Christian gentleman is a knight without fear and
without reproach, not a harsh and arrogant egotist; a
sayer of kind words, not a hurter of tender feelings; an
encourager of noble aspiration, not a scoffer at honest
effort.   And the Christian gentleman's words and deeds
apply equally to rich and poor, white and black.   His
heart responds to the tender words of South Carolina's
cherished Hampton, gallant soldier, upright servant of
the people, knightly Christian gentleman, who cried with
his dying breath: "God bless my people, white and black
—God bless them all."   And yet Hampton knew that his
"people" were really two peoples and that the whites
must rule.

7.   Thoughtful experience at the South is beginning
to admit not only that the "appointed season" of the
negro race has not arrived, but also that the bounds of

their habitation may not be set *here* for all time. The
negro will not be allowed to share the white man's
"season" through amalgamation. No sane leader of
thought and action desires such a "solution," which is
worse than the "problem." Shall the negro, then, remain
forever as a subordinate and an alien race, to be exploited in the supposed interests of the white man and
to have all hope of free development blasted in his
breast? Surely not! The present situation is bad
enough, but these "solutions" are worse. And do history
and experience show any other solutions to be possible?

8. Immediate and wholesale deportation is a futile
dream. But if the sovereign people of this rich and
powerful and God-fearing country decide that our black
brethren cannot in justice to them and ourselves remain
where they cannot hope to become a real part of our
national life, then we shall gradually, carefully, scientifically and thoroughly prepare the negro and ourselves
for an inevitable separation, and the brother-in-black,
"at sundry times and in divers manners," will find a
home for himself, and under his own vine and fig tree,
in his own country, "work out his own salvation." And,
if he works his own damnation, we at least shall not be
blameworthy, for we will prepare him during years for
his life apart, and all the world will help him *find* his
place, for God alone knows what each man's place is.

9. This is not a question to be settled altogether by
politicians and elections. The time will come when we
shall know what ought to be done with the negro. And
when that time comes let the statesmen and politicians
put into effect what the best research and the wisest
benevolence of the country sanction. In the meantime
let the negro "keep his place" and dream no idle dreams
of equality for which intermarriage alone could make

him eligible. Let him rather gird up his loins for brave effort to make himself worthy of a better fate and a fuller life. Let him wait in patience to be called up higher by God and good men, and then perhaps in his "ain countree" let him "make his calling and election sure."

10. Whatever his future, the negro must be educated for that future. Therefore, let us study him and the whole question, so as to educate him aright for his destiny and cause to cease the restless agitation and suspicion that are now a serious drawback to the development of the South.

III. CURING THE SOUTH: SALVE OR SURGERY?*

"It will but skin and film the ulcerous place,
Whiles rank corruption, mining all within,
Infects unseen."

Hard as it is to enter the holy of holies of a little child's mind, it is still harder to sympathize with the incongruities of an alienated personality; and hardest of all, especially for those brought up in another civilization or those who have lived all their lives in a peculiar environment, to practice the political-psychologic art on a whole people when that people's life is spiritually and materially abnormal, on account of an impossible situation.

To read the South's mind to-day is a much harder undertaking for either Nationalist or Southerner than was the case a quarter of a century ago. For the South has caught the commercial spirit, and the average solid citizen will say and do nothing that will "hurt business." On the contrary, he adopts an optimistic point of view, feeling that if outsiders are in a hopeful frame of mind on account of the belief that things are getting better in all respects, they are more likely to invest in the South and build up its waste places, or at least give it a good name as a section that invites the investment of capital with reasonable safety. These solid citizens do not intend to deceive others, but they deceive themselves. They

* Written for a prominent educator. •

27

shut off all communications from their widely appre-
hending social instincts, take counsel of their hopes, and
forthwith become optimists, without fully realizing that
their optimism is shallow if not dishonest, though not
consciously. Then, too, the exploiters! There are more
of them than one thinks, and they, too, are often unconscious or half-conscious in their seemingly altruistic desire to "get" all they can for the South. One cannot
gauge the feelings of the Japanese by their silken smiles
while in the presence of the "foreign devils"; nor can
one judge of the common people's attitude anywhere by
perusing the speeches and interviews of their leading
publicists. California withdrew her offensive legislation toward Orientals, but does anyone suppose that the
average Californian's feelings have changed in the least?
And is it surprising that the state's fixed feeling now
finds expression in the Alien Land Bill?

Inasmuch as instincts and habits and social subconsciousness are the real determining forces in national
life, one must not expect to get at the truth of things
Southern by a study of individuals' facile utterances,
especially to their guests. President Roosevelt was once
received at Charleston with open arms and the utmost
enthusiasm. When he was asked about the appointment
of Crum, a mulatto, to a Federal office in Charleston, he
thought he was told that the appointment would be acceptable. His hosts were in a good humor—for had
they not expanded their souls amid scenes of wining and
dining? "Let's not talk politics, but have a good time!
You'll do the right thing (that is, we hope you'll do
what we want you to)." No doubt President Roosevelt
thought that the Charlestonians were "disingenuous."
And doubtless some of them were, in a sense! Assertive

and social instincts do much of their influencing near
the margin and the threshold of consciousness.

But, replies an optimist, does it not argue well that
there should be an increasing number of liberal persons
who take a pride in pointing out the evidences of negro
progress, and who profess not to object to the exercise
of the right of suffrage by high-grade negroes—does not
the existence of such persons indicate a tendency toward
a better spirit toward the negroes?   In such an inquiry
many things have to be considered.   In North Carolina,
for instance, where our Northern brethren have met
such "liberal" persons, the negroes have been "squeezed"
politically for a number of years.   Since the Wilmington
riot the Republican party has been able to make no
progress, in spite of their alliance with the populists and
in spite of North Carolina's having a normally large
Republican vote.   We may also ask what evidences of
change of heart are these liberal souls able to report
among the people at large?   Have not the Southern
states continued to enact discriminatory suffrage laws,
Jim Crow laws, and the like?   Is not the South being
encouraged to treat the negroes *as aliens* by the growing
discrimination against the negro in the North, a discrimination that is social as well as economic?   Does
not the South perceive that all the fire has gone out
of the Northern philanthropic fight for the rights of
man?   *The North has surrendered!*   At least that is
coming to be the practical judgment of the commercial
and political South.   "They are going to let us alone;
we'll fix things to suit ourselves," is the underlying
feeling of many a Southern leader, even though the
Southern people generally may not be so optimistic.   Mr.
Alfred Holt Stone, in his recent illuminating book, represents the high-grade Southerner's attitude toward the

negro question when he seems to argue that the negroes should be treated as a "peasant class." Individual Southerners look with approbation and sympathy upon the economic improvement of certain negroes, always provided these negroes are "white men's negroes," and "know their place." As soon as these negroes begin to "put on style" and express their social *dignity*, even if this exhibition is confined strictly to their own race, mutterings and murmurings begin. Let these favored negroes take the mildest interest in politics or any decided personal stand against the dominant whites, then the trouble begins in good earnest. Furthermore, every prosperous negro who *shows his prosperity in a way to be seen by the whites* is a focus for hatred on the part of the "lower" whites, with whom the "higher" whites are vastly more sympathetic than they were thirty years ago. *White solidarity, ultimately dominated by the feelings of the majority, is the real danger to the negro.* So long as an individual negro's vote has no influence and is not the expression of a demand for citizenship (always, historically, *potential* social equality), there may be acquiescence on the part of many individual whites. But let the negro vote become conspicuous, or let the negro show a consciousness of equal citizenship, then the lower white and the higher at once feel that "this is a white man's country, and the negro hasn't any business voting."

The writer would be greatly pleased to have an opportunity to examine and cross-examine more of the liberal Southern optimists. Being himself an unswerving believer in human rights for all races and an uncompromising opponent of the "peasant class" idea, he nevertheless feels obliged to say that the low-grade Southerner's feelings on this subject have more reality and more validity than those of the occasional liberal optimist. And why? The caption of this paper and the quotation from Hamlet with which it begins point to the answer. If the negro will not be allowed to have a fully developed, self-conscious citizenship and spiritual freedom in the widest sense of the term, are we not treating the Southerner "case," with salves and lotions, when in reality a surgical operation is needed? During the last few years the number of well-balanced men holding to a belief in the ultimate separation of the races has apparently increased. Why? Because of the Southern man's underlying consciousness that the negro occupies space that could better be filled by the white man.

If right-minded men want nothing less for the negro than a full and free development of character and citizenship, ought they to be content with present tendencies, without making a thorough, coöperative scientific investigation of the situation, including a scientific attempt to understand the psychology of the white man's mind? We humanitarians are opposed to amalgamation, or peasantry, or perpetual friction and strife, as "solutions" of the negro problem. There are two other "solutions": One has been already hinted at—colonization (perhaps over a period of a hundred years); the other is a solution that the present writer advocated ten years ago to his classes and in public speeches—parallel civilization. Will it be feasible to have a parallel civilization for the colored folk? That, it seems to me, is a subject for long-continued scientific study. History shows no instance of such an arrangement. New Zealand's racial suffrage is the nearest approach to it; but the problem is already settled in this case, for the Maoris are dying out. Jamaica's "solution" is hardly one that the white people of the South would agree to, even if

conditions could be as good as in the District of Columbia! Besides, the American negroes are not Jamaicans
nor the Southern whites English. Further, Jamaican
civilization is hardly successful enough to be taken as a
model by progressive Americans. It may turn out, however, that a parallel civilization, with bi-racial suffrage
and the like, may be possible either as a permanent solution, or, what is more likely, as the best *temporary solution* until the negroes can be disposed of in a century-
long colonization and educational preparation therefor.
The writer is too old in years and experience to prophesy
rashly, but all successful prophecy is based on insight
into social and political conditions. More than that, it
sometimes happens that one can prove the existence of
instincts that will inevitably produce certain human results. Well, the present writer, believing that he had
acquired some insight on account of his special study
of the problems of character and on account of his long
resident study of racial matters, has tried the experiment
of mentioning to a few friends the thought underlying
Mr. Carnegie's kindly prophecy of personally owned
"sweet little homes" for the negroes of the South. The
reaction was extremely instructive, though it would have
been startling to the uninitiated to see the look of scorn
and contempt, or of smiling cynicism, that was to be
seen on the faces of prominent Southern educators, men
of culture and Christian nurture. On the other hand,
when it was suggested that it might be necessary some
of these days to start in the South the cry: "This is a
white man's country! Don't sell land to a negro. Buy
back the land for our children," the reaction was still
more interesting. *If something is not done within the
next few years the cry will be raised and the results of
it will tend to "settle" the negro question—*"in a way."

IV. THE CRUX OF THE QUESTION; ORGAN-IZING TO ANSWER IT

(Written at Conference for Education in the South, after conference with one of the great constructive educational leaders of the country.)

An honest man may be the noblest work of God; assuredly a well-balanced man is the rarest. For balance means not only equipoise in feeling, intellect and will, but sanity with salt enough in it, and ethical passion with just enough prejudice to be human. To be both interested and disinterested, intensive and extensive, idealistic and practical, cautious and hopeful—these are some of the seemingly opposite traits that must be held in solution in the character of one who studies the negro question. Nevertheless, questions must be answered in spite of the imperfections of the would-be answerer; nor will they consent to wait until some modern "angelical doctor" adequate to the task answers truthfully and yet *suaviter in modo*. Be it my office, therefore, in this brief paper, to prepare the way for a fuller statement to come when leisure allows, although this present writing must partake somewhat of the hurry and scurry incident to "writing on the wing."

THE SITUATION

Two peoples, representative of the two most widely differing races, inhabit the same territory, supposedly

share common institutions and a common religion, supposedly stand equal before the law touching political and
civil rights, supposedly come perforce into divers neigh-
borly relations; and yet the one race is regarded by the
other not only as inferior, but as destined for all time
to remain subordinate to that other. Time was when
such a statement would have raised a vigorous if not
indignant protest from the "friends of humanity" and
from chivalrous protectors of the weak. We should
have been told that in political, social and spiritual matters, as well as in rights pertaining to one's ownership
of his own body, a man's a man for a' that and a' that.
Is the old spirit of abolitionism clean gone, and is Southern chivalry become the memory of a valiant gentleman's past? God forbid that we free men's bodies only
to leave their souls bound by the shackles of ignorance
and vice and severed from that self-respect without
which there comes untowardly the early decline-and-
death of a people's aspirations.

And all the time men cry peace when there is no
peace. Though competent observers freely grant that
the races are drifting farther and farther from mutual
sympathy and helpfulness, nevertheless many a successful planter, or investor, or owner of Southern land and
industries asks us consientious fanatics of the faith
humanitarian and democratic to "let things be." Even
the voices crying in the wilderness and calling men to a
realization of their situation if not to repentance are
afraid to cry aloud and spare not, because of the feeling
fashions of the multitude. Though zealous for human
rights, and even the bondman's human feelings, they
fear lest they may fail to avoid the appearance of evil
exploitation or of sectional disloyalty, when they express agreement as to humanitarian principles with influ-

ential and benevolent gentlemen from the yonder side of the magic "line" that until recently used to part brethren from one another through sectional inertia and chronic misunderstanding. The mutual understanding of Northern and Southern idealists becomes an object of suspicion to the growing hatred felt for the negroes on the part of the masses of the people North and South.

The South is the most "democratic" portion of the Union, and yet appears to the world to suppress those whose erstwhile masters found for the principle that all human beings have certain inalienable rights and that taxation without representation is tyranny. Democracy has dressed herself in the arrogant habit of the aristocrat by the grace of God. Then, too, this same favored South is the most religious section of the country. And yet, by some strange and unheralded revelation made only to certain publicists and their kind, we are told that God intended the negro to be the servant of the whites— or to be "peasantry"—or to be everlastingly subordinated in vital ways. Conceive, if you can, of a God whose predestinating hand condemns a whole race of immortal spirits to the eternal punishment of spiritual slavery! If the negro is content to be thus disposed of by these very modern readers of the Almighty Mind, the prophet exclaims, "Said I not that he has no future; look how he behaves—like an unthinking beast, without that self-respect that makes a man a man." And if the negro asserts himself the soothsaying representative of Eternal Love cries out, "Back to your place, nigger! You are trying to get social equality and to destroy our civilization."

A study of the situation will show that comparatively few ordinary Southerners believe from the heart in negro education of any liberal sort or description what-

soever; while the few who really believe that all human
beings should be educated with one voice acclaim the
demand of Booker Washington for industrial education.   But no one has perceived any general eagerness
on the part of Southern communities to give the "only
kind of education that a nigger is fit for."   Truth to
say, much of this commendation of Washington's views
is based upon the thought that, if "what the negroes
need" is industrial education, then it follows that they
need no other kind, and will perhaps keep away from
the white man and his very delicate and sensitive "civilization."

The uncritical man reading the above might classify
the writer as a Northern man and a negrophilist!   And
yet, as a matter of fact, he is a Southerner of the Southerners, of the straitest sect of "white supremacy," and
in addition has observed for years the Northern feeling
of repulsion for any sort of physical proximity to the
negro.   Moreover, this same writer is deeply and intrinsically sympathetic with the Southern "orthodox" attitude, believes it to be rational at bottom, and would not
change the *status quo* in the South to-morrow if he
could do so with one wave of the magician's wand!
To your tents, O Israel!   The Chosen American must
rule!

Earnest and careful students of the negro question
who have occupied themselves with the ethical and
psychological aspects of the problems will have reached
the conclusion that nothing is contradictory or para-
doxical enough to be waved aside as unmeaning and not
worth investigation.   I plead guilty to the seeming speaking of foolishness and throw myself upon the mercy of
the court—the enlightened mind of the sincere student
of the most difficult, complex and dangerous of human

situations. In this paper I must attempt to show a real
reasonableness underlying this apparent blind contra-
dictoriness and strive at once to explain and to justify
my attitude.

THE SOUTHERN WHITE MAN'S MIND

The real problem is not the negro, but the white man's
attitude toward the negro.   Most observers find no
trouble in understanding, and even sympathetically, the
Southerner's prejudice against "social equality."   Whatever the ultimate explanation, one can with a show of
reasonableness postulate such a principle of explanation
as the *lack* of a larger human sympathy in trying to find
a basis for social discrimination against the negro; or
he may resort to the theory of caste, or that of æsthetic
dislike, or what not.   But, asks the dispassionate observer, what has "social equality" to do with the suffrage
and political rights in general?   Social privileges are
an affair of choice, custom, convention, fashion and the
like; then why should we pay any serious attention to
the man who seems to confound the social with the
political?
The whites used to contend that the ignorant negro
voter was the real menace.   Said they, we cannot afford
to allow an ignorant and often vicious horde to endanger our civilization.   Such a plea seemed reasonable
enough.   In fact, almost every thinker, North and South,
negro and white, assumes nowadays that the Southern
suffrage laws, so far as they disfranchise only the ignorant voter, irrespective of race, are wise and proper.
Some even go so far as to excuse or at least palliate the
offensiveness of a law that strives to save the privilege of

the suffrage for the ignorant white man, on the ground that though unlettered and even illiterate, he may have some degree of real political instinct and judgment in spite of his uneducated condition. And all Southern states do not have the "Grandfather Clause," perhaps caring more to shut out the negroes than to give privileges to the illiterate whites. The "understanding" clause, or the poll-tax provision, may be regarded as advisable psychological methods of discriminating against the negro. Waiving, for the sake of argument, the claims just made, I assert, without fear of being contradicted by competent observers, that the Southern whites in the mass do not want *any* negro to vote under *any* circumstances. Point out to them that the negro voter is no longer a menace to good government, and their reply is that "the negro has no use for the franchise, anyhow."

A good illustration of this was to be observed in Georgetown, S. C., some years ago. I found that the younger white voters were bent on causing trouble at the polls during a municipal election. I inquired whether they feared that the negroes might carry the election. The reply was in the negative. The "audacity" and "impertinence" of the negroes in "daring" or "presuming" to vote was the trouble. The spontaneous remarks of average citizens and the express utterances of influential leaders, such as Tillman and Hoke Smith, who are really representative of the tendencies of the Southern masses, point in the same direction. So I think that we may assume that the great majority of the Southern whites resent negro citizenship whenever expressed in a *quasi*-representative (racial) capacity. If it be true that the suffrage is the lineal descendant of the club and the fist, as defenders of the home, then we may connect together the following indications: The disfranchisement of the negro; the disbandment of colored militia in the South; the strong Southern feeling against the enlistment of negro soldiers in the United States army; Southern opposition to negro office-holding and jury duty.

Voting, whatever its origin, is the expression of the sovereign rights of the free citizen. When a man votes he practically says to every other man in the community, "I am as good as you are before the law." Now this is just what the average Southern white man wishes to *deny* in the case of the negro, so far as active citizenship is concerned. In effect he says, "You are not my equal as a citizen and you shan't pretend that you are. If you vaunt your equality at the ballot box there's no telling what other claims you will be making next. Efface yourself and keep in your place as a subordinate race."

But why does the white wish the negro to remain subordinate, in spite of the former's passionate belief in democracy and evangelical Christianity? Practically every white man will reject the explanation that he doesn't want a "race of former slaves" to enjoy political equality with himself. Such an explanation is sometimes made at the North and at the South, but not, ordinarily, by the average Southern whites in *spontaneous conversation*.

This passionate aversion to negro suffrage has grown in proportion as social class lines among the whites have become obliterated. For instance, the Tillman movement in South Carolina and the Vardaman movement in Mississippi carried with them the cry that the Democratic party is a "white man's party." Hence, under the influence of the "extremist" leaders, the rules of the

Democratic primaries in these two states read all negroes
—including negroes who have hitherto passed as "Democrats"—out of participation in the primaries.   In the
seventies negro Democrats were highly esteemed and
their votes were sought.   In proportion as the ranks of
the humbler whites achieved more and more success as
practical factors in politics, the negro—to use a term
made famous in Dr. Prince's "Dissociation of a Personality"—became "squeezed."   He is not even allowed
to become a sort of subconsciousness or penumbral "co-
consciousness."   He must relapse into complete political
unconsciousness, and is to be counted only to keep a
quorum.   *In fine, disfranchisement of the negroes has
been concomitant with the growth of political and social
solidarity among the whites.*   The more white men
recognize sharply their kinship with their fellow whites,
and the more democracy in every sense of the term
spreads among them, the more the negro is compelled
to "keep his place"—a place that is being gradually nar-
rowed in the North as well as in the South.

Thus it has come to pass that political privilege is
instinctively regarded as the legal expression of a *potential* social equality.   This feeling is especially keen in
the South because the people are social in their political
activities.   Picnics and barbecues are common and popular; social classes of all kinds freely mingle at times;
the "professional" politician is ordinarily more of a
"hero" and less of a grafter and exploiter than in the
large cities of the North; the identification of a party
with a race has become complete; the belief in that race
as the "chosen people of God" is practically an unwritten creed stronger than ecclesiastical dogma.   Indeed, at
the South, "white supremacy" is an integral part of the
religious consciousness, as much so as is racial faith

among the Jews or among the Boers. Now, recall the
Hebrew belief so often expressed by the biblical writers
that God punished the chosen people because they did
not exterminate the Canaanite tribes, and one has an
ancient picture on a large canvas of the at present less
virulent feeling of the Southerner, that the chosen
people must sustain their God-given supremacy, come
what will—"they the heirs of all the ages in the foremost files of time." George Washington was the father
of the white man's country, not the negro's country;
"my country" of the national hymn is not the negro's
"sweet land of liberty"; Jamestown and Plymouth Rock
were in no respects beginnings of a negro "native land."
Professor Burgess's definition of a "nation" is acceptable
to the South, for it stresses community of descent and
tradition. Even the "coon song" expresses comically the
tragic fact that "every nation has a flag but the coon."
The etymological meaning of "nation" (birth) is the
one to which the Southern people adhere. And shall
we say that they are historically and psychologically,
even biologically, unreasonable? The negroes, indeed,
are *aliens* to all intents and purposes, and aliens that
cannot be assimilated. In the body politic they are inor-
ganic substances that cannot be either digested or got
rid of, and tending to become virulent poisons! At heart
the white man's fear is not *objective* "social equality."
He does not believe that the negro race *can* ever be the
equal of the white race in any worth-while way. But
he shrinks from social *contact* except on a well-defined
basis of "white supremacy"; it is the negro's *assertion*,
present or possible, of his equal racial worth—this it
is that irritates the white man, for assertions tend to
become far-reaching acts.

Now, this principle of white supremacy is not a new

thing.   It is not only a result of white superiority, but
also of civic order and the public weal.   Even the declaration of the French revolutionists and the Virginia Bill
of Rights, while maintaining the doctrine of liberty,
equality and fraternity, distinctly state that the public
safety and the public weal must always determine the
realization and expression of human rights.   In the
family relations the wife and minor children do not
practice their "inalienable rights" in the same manner
that adult males do.   Rights are relative to public welfare.*

Historically, political and social relations have ever,
at least potentially, been closely connected. The plebeians
in ancient Rome got their political rights through the
assertion of social rights and in connection with intermarriage.   The first fruit of plebeian political rights
was the repeal of the anti-amalgamation laws.   And let
us remember that in Greece and Rome, as well as India,
it is probable that caste originated in racial differences.
In England, too, to take a more modern instance, from
the time of the Norman Conquest until the present, social and political relations have gone hand in hand, and
amalgamation has tended to solve all social-political
problems.   The average Southerner doesn't know much
about such history, but he has the instincts that have
made, are making and will make history.   For, say what
we will, may not all the equalities be ultimately based
on potential social equality, and that in turn on intermarriage?   Here we reach the real *crux* of the question.

If there were a blindly instinctive basis for racial dislike, not much could be urged in extenuation of the
anxiety felt by Southern racial orthodoxy.   But even

* See Ritchie, *Natural Rights,* and J. F. Stephen, *Liberty, Equality and Fraternity.*

the high-souled Tennyson, in "Locksley Hall," draws a picture of the reckless, disappointed youth who has an impulse to wed a dusky maiden and rear a dusky brood. It is just because primary race feeling is *not* deeply based in human instinct, whereas the mating instinct *is* so based, that a secondary racial feeling, race-pride, comes in from a more developed reflective consciousness to minimize the natural instinct for amalgamation.

Bad, even fiendish, as race prejudice may become, it may have its part to play in default of some higher force, in the conventional life of the soul among nations. And "secondary instincts" often perform an important function in nullifying or inhibiting primary instincts.*

* Southerners do not ordinarily have the biological and esthetic repulsion that is usually felt by Northerners toward the Negro. Familiarity, in biological matters at least, sometimes breeds complaisance or indifference rather than contempt. And the memory of ante-bellum concubinage and a tradition of animal satisfaction due to the average negro woman's highly developed animalism are factors still in operation. Not a few "respectable" white men have been heard to express physiological preference for negro women. If, therefore, animal appetite may become more powerful than race pride, it is not surprising that race hatred is superinduced in those who offend against race purity; for abnormal sexuality easily develops brutality. The race hatred of white offenders is an instinctive effort to neutralize the social effects of an impulse that would ordinarily tend toward the legitimation of amalgamation. Under the influence of race enmity, even concubinage tends to give place to impersonal and infertile forms of animal satisfaction. Thus the element of kindliness that often belongs to concubinage yields to a mere animal convenience that may be consistent with race enmity on the part of the white offender. Of course the increase of race hatred has the net result of decreasing the amount of interracial vice. Thus does the negro woman become more and more a cheap convenience of the occasional sort, and the purity of the white race is protected at the expense of the white man's appreciation of the negro woman's personality.

In this connection it will be useful to classify roughly
the various manifestations of race prejudice.*	(1)
Race enmity is largely based on economic competition
with those regarded as interlopers who do not belong to
the "caste of the kin" (as I am in the habit of calling
white solidarity).	Inasmuch as human relations are
organically connected, it usually happens that when unlike peoples come into industrial competition the feeling
of unlikeness—"I do not like thee, Dr. Fell; the reason
why I cannot tell"—becomes sharpened by the laws of
association and contrast, and economic hate easily be-
comes social hate.	For example, note the race feeling
against the Chinese, cured by exclusion of the Mongols
and followed by a similar outbreak against the Japanese.
In the latter case the "superiority" of the Japanese adds
fuel to the flames, just as the attempt to show forth the
wonderful performances of gifted negroes often seems
to accentuate the average Southerner's antagonism
toward the negroes as a race.	Consciousness of compe-
tition quite easily develops into the feeling that the
lowest white man is incomparably (withal representa-
tively) superior to the highest negro.	Here we have
federal racial solidarity with a vengeance!	(Compare
certain forms of the evangelical doctrine of the Atone-
ment.)	Sympathy with the lower whites, as it increases
with growing political and social solidarity, results in
contagious increase of race enmity among the higher
whites.	(Compare books on social psychology, chapters
on social suggestions, the "Mob Mind," etc.)	Personal
suffering due to negro criminality still further recruits
from the higher grades the ranks of this lowest and

* I apologize to the general reader for discussing this topic at
all, and to the student of the negro question for not discussing it
more fully.

therefore most dangerous level of race feeling, which nevertheless is possibly the only form that can success-fully prevent the animal passions of the morally less developed whites from tending toward social mingling with negroes and the ultimate effacement of the protec-tive "color line."

(2) *Race Pride.* Most members of the better class of citizenship in the South belong to this class, although here, as in all such classifications, there is much over-lapping. Not a few of the uneducated classes, especially those whose humanitarianism is genuine and practical, are by nature inclined toward race antipathy, but have a conscience culture developed toward a higher attitude. The resultant is a respectable form of race pride. On the other hand, some of the highest types of mind are drawn toward a view much lower than the highest on account of personal experience with race contact of the bitter sort. Race pride is social and æsthetic in its origin rather than economic, though at all times liable to drift toward race enmity on account of economic competition or the untoward personal experiences above referred to. Pride of race seems to be a form of racial self-respect and loyalty to traditions and institutions. However, it can seldom give a reason for the faith that is in it. Hence the "average solid citizen" is not able to account for his seeming inconsistency in his treat-ment of the finer types of the negro race. While he frankly admits the validity of enlightened moral prin-ciples, he fails to explain the subconscious relation of "equalities" to one another; nor does he clearly see the social-psychological principles that give some sort of validity to an extension of the biblical insight that no man liveth unto himself and none dieth unto himself. He easily becomes impatient or angry when his seeming

inconsistencies are pointed out, and not seldom contents himself with telling the Northern objector to "come South and live among the negroes for a while," or "take a few millions of the negroes up North."

(3) *Race Conscience.* This attitude is of course the highest and the only one that possesses real moral validity. But in order to be healthy it must have experimental and sympathetic knowledge of the lower attitudes. "First the natural man and then the spiritual man." The idealistic doctrinaire is not a real specimen of this type of attitude. "My people do not understand," can be said of him. Perceptive and empirical understanding must ever underlie logical and scientific thinking on *social* subjects, whatever may be true in other spheres of human thought.

Race conscience holds to the higher ethical utilitarianism, or "pragmatism," as the philosophical fashion now calls it. It sees clearly that biological assimilation is the basic principle of national solidarity; that science appears to corroborate the findings of common sense when it declares against mixture of extremely divergent racial types; it sees more or less clearly the correlation and interaction between political equality and social equality; it hesitates to oppose too vigorously even such a base passion as race enmity, to say nothing of race pride, because of the evident protective (teleological) function of race antipathy. If not *that, what,* then? it asks.

Evidently it must be the task of good men everywhere to help transmute race enmity into reasonable race pride, and the latter into spiritual and practical forms of race conscience. *How is this to be done?* To find out we must study long and hard. If it cannot be done, separation of the races would appear to be necessary.

Fear and Anger: "Preternatural Suspicion." Before

we can get to the bottom of the Southerner's mind we must notice—for that is all we can do in a rapid survey like. this—the feeling-tone that accompanies the prevailing attitudes above described. There are three fundamental emotions that have to do with social environment: anger, fear and love (corresponding to the three attitudes described above). Translating into the language of attitude and prevailing mood, we may call them hate, anxiety-obsession and benevolent kindliness. Now, little need be said of the third mode of feeling-reaction. Evidently it is the only one that ought to exist in a state of enlightened civilization. Nevertheless, it is felt uniformly by the very few only, and exerts an influence in special cases alone and in some degree of silent modification and amelioration of the other and stronger passions. Anxiety and a kind of vindictive dislike tend together to hold the field of race consciousness. Carlyle well describes the resultant of these fundamental feeling attitudes in his phrase *à propos* of the French Revolution—"preternatural suspicion." All observers coming South detect it in the very mental atmosphere. There is an ill-veiled "polite repulsion" toward the Northerner come South on observation bent, unless he has credentials from some Southern high priest of race orthodoxy. This last-named fact is suggestive. The combination of anxiety and antagonism that I have called *suspicion* is called forth not by the negro alone, not by the Northern "philanthropic" attitude alone, but by their combination in the historic past and by the possibilities of future force bills, cutting down of representation, political appointment of negroes, philanthropic efforts in behalf of negro ambitions and aspirations, and the like. Preternatural suspicion is due to a *racking uncertainty about the future,* a dread of ill-conceived interference from without, and a consciousness of apparent inconsistency along with a sense of being in the right nevertheless. Was ever people so beset? Some one ought to write a book on the Dissociation of a Sectional Personality.

Again the question, *What shall we do about it?* One thing, assuredly—we must study the phenomena and strive to understand them.

WHITHER?

Can progress and peace be hoped for as permanent facts of Southern development, granting that the above cursory account be accepted? Are we doing well to spend millions of dollars on negro education without having a reasonable hope that the developmental results will make for higher character and truer nationality? Shall we deepen the darkness of the situation by sharpening the intellect of white and black to the end that they may fight one another with a more subtle venom? Shall we leave the negro in spiritual slavery and the white in rancorous sectionalism and an alienated conscience? Shall we forsake the ideals of the New England "friends of human rights" and of Southern chivalrous gentlemanliness? Shall we leave a large and tragic human problem to "settle itself" when we have no reason to hope that it will settle itself aright? Shall we close the real "door of hope" in the black brother's face, the door of access to a fully developed manhood? Shall we permit our Southern youth of the dominant race to grow up arrogant and inhuman despisers of human rights and haters of practical democracy and large-souled humanitarianism?

On all hands it is admitted that nothing can be done

without the coöperation of Southern white men. *And these men will not coöperate until there is some answer to the question, Whither are we going?* The land, the institutions, the traditions are theirs. They claim their heritage and decline to share it with others unless they have reason to believe that such sharing will not endanger the material and spiritual weal of their children's children. "Solutions" of the negro problem have been put forward and are being put forward as theories; and yet we are further from a "solution" than at any time during the nation's history. Politicians, preachers, philanthropists, educators, historians, the man in the street (without considering these classes as mutually exclusive) have had their fling. Is it not time that a concerted organized, scientific, humanitarian attempt be made to study the whole question in all its bearings and through the coöperation of all the factors involved? Shall we to a great extent take tariff and finance and "conservation" and other national questions out of the hands of the man in the street, and yet leave a vastly more complex and more delicate question to be settled or unsettled according to the whims and prejudices, or at best the partial insights and halfway investigations, of untrained or ill-trained people?

As soon as the Southern people find that a wholehearted, unprejudiced attempt is being made to study the question in all its bearings and with their coöperation, they will be ready and willing to help. As soon as a tentative answer to the question, "Whither?" is proposed, and the Southern people see that what is worth while in their contentions is respected and that there will be no meddlesome nor doctrinaire interference from the outside, they will be willing to bend their energies in the direction that points toward peace and hope and safety;

they will be willing to educate the negroes for the part
the negroes are to play; they will be willing to revive
their Christian ethics as applied to the other race. Of
these results I feel sure from conference with all sorts
and conditions of men. These Southern people are normal Americans. They are reasonable and just. *But
they want to work toward some definite objective point,
and they wish for an open and above-board statement
of the designs and methods and bias of the persons
undertaking any investigation that may be made.*

HOW SHALL THE STUDY BEGIN?

This is not the place for an outline of the directions
wherein a scientific investigation should work. I shall
furnish later a full report on that subject, if such a
report be wanted. But it may not be unwise to suggest
here some method of getting the work organized and
started. I therefore submit, with much hesitation and
some perturbation, but sincerely and after a number of
years of close study of the negro question on the ground
and with first-hand data, a series of tentative suggestions—one of many plans that might be outlined.

1. Let some nation-wide group of leading Southerners and Northerners of all political and religious types
select some one man as director who by character, temperament, training and experience is best fitted to understand the question, the Southerners, whites and blacks,
the race question on the Pacific Coast, the Northern
situation, the national and historical perspective. Let
this man choose, with the advice and consent of the
group, a few well-qualified workers to assist him in the
work of a Steering Committee. This group should

probably form an association for the study of race problems.

2. Let this committee, after due conference, call a meeting of a selected and closely limited list of prominent Southerners and others who are well known in business (including farming), the professions, public life and academic circles, and have some first-hand knowledge of the subject. The larger number of those invited should come from the Southern and the Pacific states. They should represent all phases of attitude on the question, *including the most radical.* Let them be sounded personally before being invited officially.

3. Let the director of the work, as chairman of the steering committee, prepare, after conference with his colleagues and after the committee has made a tour of the Southern states and other parts of the country and foreign countries where race questions are pressing, a careful statement of the scope of the investigation. In that statement let him show the whites that they are sympathized with and let him show the colored people that their interests will be carefully considered.

4. When the conference has met, in some convenient Southern city, let the chairman read his statement and then call on the members alphabetically and by states to comment on the paper in a three to five minutes' speech. (A syllabus of the statement ought to be sent to the members of the conference a sufficient time beforehand.) Let each member of the conference, after he has spoken, leave with the secretary of the committee a MS. setting forth his views and opinions in full.

5. Let the committee carefully digest the proceedings and the paper and publish a report of the conference and also a smaller and popular syllabus of the larger report. Let the report be sent to leading men, libraries, etc., in

this country and elsewhere, and have the syllabus distributed very widely through the press and in every legitimate way, so as to reach especially the humbler classes of the white and the colored populations in this country.

6.   Let the committee appoint sub-committees to work through the ordinary channels of the association or institution or bureau, through universities in this country and elsewhere, through learned and professional societies, etc.   Let special investigators be put into the field under the direct supervision of the director of the work. Let some of the work be done through fellowships in universities, especially the better organized Southern universities.

7.   Let the investigators give frequently, at least once a quarter, a statement of work done, so that the central office can keep in close touch with the whole field. (Perhaps the central office might be in one of the border Southern cities, such as Memphis, Nashville, Louisville, Baltimore or Richmond, or, perhaps in the nation's capital.)

8.   Let the director, with the advice and consent of the committee or board, issue two bulletins of the work at convenient intervals—one a scientific statement of the progress of the work, the other a popular statement, both to be distributed in the manner described above in the case of the report of the conference and the syllabus respectively.   Let him also issue pamphlets, leaflets, cards, questionnaires, and organize correspondence scientifically.

9.   Some time after the conference of whites there ought to be held a conference for colored people only, inviting no whites to be present except the members of the committee, who should probably all be white, though

some of the coöperating workers should, of course, be colored men and women. Let a section of the bureau devote itself entirely to work done by negro investigators.

10. From time to time, at fit opportunities and during successive years, call conferences for reports of work done, for the reception of suggestions and criticisms, and the like.

CONCLUSION

If it were done, 'twere well 'twere done quickly. This statement is often as true for deeds of light as for deeds of darkness. The work itself may have to last many years; putting its results into execution, or coöperating with those who are getting the machinery of race adjustment into motion, may take a much longer period than the investigation. But we want to allay as soon as possible the *attitude* of suspicion, unrest, anxiety or exasperation. For a catastrophe may happen at any moment. There are sinister signs of this. Moreover, at any time something may arise in national or sectional politics that may make coöperation extremely difficult. As for the money needed—there will be no lack of it if our people learn to realize the vitalness of this investigation.*

* Is it rash to hope that the much-needed investigation of the negro question will begin during the administration of a Southern-born president aided by a Democratic congress? President Wilson has shown a high quality of courage and patriotism. Will he show forth his leadership by taking the initiative in ridding politics of the negro problem? Or will the present auspiciously begun Democratic régime timidly dodge this vital question because of its difficulty and its "intangibleness"? Will the Republicans continue to welcome to their national conventions the absurd Southern dele-

gations of negro politicians? Will the Progressives, with their voluminous program of "reform," remember that the existence of the negro problem is a challenge to the friends of human rights everywhere, and is the prime cause of the excessive Democratic solidarity of the South?

V. STUDY THE NEGRO QUESTION!

(Reprinted from Proceedings of the Department of Superintendence of the National Education Association, Indianapolis, Ind., March, 1910.—Topic: The Problem of Environment in Education— As the South Sees It.)

There is only one Southern problem, and it is that of environment. For Southern children are the truest of Americans by birth and tradition, and therefore, if they are being bred in the cult of caste, nurture due to conditions and not nature due to inheritance must be responsible for their apparent departure from the splendid type of American democracy.

But do not suppose that even by implication I am condemning my own dear people. Public peace and the safety of the state demand that the less-developed race (1)* be subordinate to the more developed, under conditions as they exist in the South to-day. The caste of the kin is the practice of the theory that blood is thicker than water; and the Sermon on the Mount cannot invalidate God's own law of the survival of the fittest. If these widely different races cannot blend their blood—and instinct and science say nay—the only real foundation for democracy, equality, actual or potential, does not exist and cannot be created. The principles of liberty, equality and fraternity are as abstractly true as Newton's Laws of Motion (2), but the resistance of race-consciousness brings about as real a friction as does the

* Numerals refer to appended comments.

resistance of the air in modifying the actions of bodies in motion.

The all-inclusive virtue, love itself, has a biological basis, and character values are conditioned by body facts (3). Thus it happens that the Southerner's loyalty to his race comes of his love of his kind, the kind he knows and values.

But *should* such conditions exist? Must Southern children of the dominant race grow up to scorn and despise, or else condescendingly to tolerate, their less fortunate fellow creatures? Or shall we legitimate lust and short-circuit the destiny of a chosen people? Southerners understand the apparent cruelty imputed to the God of Israel who is represented as commanding the extermination of non-assimilable peoples (4). But the more refined killing of to-day in the South is not the occasional taking of a negro's life, but the impassive and relentless murder of a people's hopes. But better this than worse that might be. Better twenty years of Europe than a cycle of Cathay. Better preternatural suspicion than rearing dusky broods. Sometimes we must be cruel would we be kind.

Only in the kingdom of heaven is there neither marriage nor giving in marriage. Now, the kingdom has not yet come in the South. Therefore, let him that would establish any kind of human equality on any basis other than that of a biologically based family life give us the recipe for life in a vacuum (5).

Again I ask, *Should* these things be? Must the Southern child be compelled to choose between the ideal and the real in a world where ideals must be realized in accordance with the laws of nature? Will sickly saintliness bring us salvation? Or must we seek safety in racial selfishness? God forbid the answer "Yes" to

either of these last two questions! Who shall deliver
us from the body of this death? (6)

I dare not hope to put this subject before you sharply
in a hasty minute or two. But I must make an appeal in
the name of the righteous God and of bewildered humanity. I ask that you leaders of education think on these
things in this wise: *Let us have this negro question
studied.* We are studying tariffs and the price of beef;
we become partisans about a pole, intangible and invisible;
our scientific expeditions scour land and sea for specimens of fauna and flora; we discriminate nicely the
uncertain tints of Mexican Indians; we explore the
heavens above, the earth beneath, and the waters under
the earth—all these we do, and much more, without the
waving of bloody shirts or the planting of party plat-
forms.

Let us take the negro question out of politics, out of
society, out of popular religious discussion, out of prize-
fighting—out of all wherein heat doth obtain rather
than light.

Let us put the negro question into science, and science
into the negro question. We have tried all else, and in
vain. Parties and churches and schools, and philan-
thropies of all kinds, have brought us not one whit
nearer a solution. The favorite prescription for a solution is education, especially industrial education. And
yet there are towns where negro artisans are not allowed
to work, and labor unions in plenty that negroes may not
enter. Education for *what?* Are the whites going to
neglect the training of *their* children's hands? When
the grandsons of the former slave-owners are dead, will
anyone prefer negro labor, skilled or unskilled, to
white? (7)

Can education abolish race-consciousness and repattern the convolutions of the brain? Aye, education may solve the race problem and all problems, but *when* and *where* and *how?*

Men and brethren, let us *study* the race problem. Let the study be national and international, for ours is not the only problem of race. Let the study be scientific and not sentimental; coöperative and not individualistic; continuous and not scrappy; professional and not *dilettante;* humanitarian and not partisan. (8)

Let us isolate the surd and square the whole equation —find a square deal. It is science, and science alone, star-eyed science, truth-loving science, spiritually intellectual science—it is the twentieth century's greatest power, the scientific research of to-day, that can prepare us for the doing of this nation's greatest duty, the solution of this problem, so as to free two unallied peoples and make the states of this Union *United States* indeed and in truth!

VI. COMMENT ON THE INDIANAPOLIS DISCUSSION

1.* "Less developed," not "lower." All admit the accuracy of the former term, without determining whether the negro's possibilities are limited. The term "lower" unfairly closes the question, at least in the popular mind, for it has acquired a static, fatalistic connotation.

Negro "equality" *in the South* depends on the feasibility of a parallel civilization:—racial representation in legislature and congress (as in New Zealand); negro industrial organization (as at Mound Bayou, Miss.); coöperatively managed places of amusement for the negroes (as in Memphis); negro libraries (as in Louisville); and the like. These things are needed whether the negro "goes" or "stays." This "equality" does not presuppose social intermingling with whites, but, rather, as complete as possible segregation of the negroes.

2. The average Northerner thinks that Southerners do not believe in the "rights of man." Southerners resent the imputation, but cannot explain the apparent anomaly of their actual conduct, and hence reply with a *tu quoque* or a charge of pharisaism. The trouble with radical Southerners is not their insistence on white supremacy, but their satisfaction at the prospect of permanent subordination of the negroes to the whites, without regard to the possibility of colonizing the negroes or of securing their segregation in some other way.

* Numerals refer to text of above speech.

3. The most exalted romantic and chivalrous love
can be completely inhibited by physical mutilation. Yet
love is not merely physical. Likewise humanitarianism
is not mere physical kinship, but nevertheless has a necessary, though often disavowed, biological basis.

4. New Testament morality is historically and practically meaningless without an Old Testament basis.
Under Old Testament conditions (largely existing in
the South), Old Testament morality is more or less
appropriate and inevitable.

Don't criticize human nature and its protective biological creed; but change the abnormal situation in such a
way as will respect natural law as well as moral law.
God still winks at the hardness of men's hearts, when
such hardness has a providential value. Matthew Arnold's "Might till right is ready" is the working creed
of the conscientious Southerner. But *when* and *how*
shall right be got ready? Interestingly enough, the
phrase "impassive and relentless murder of a people's
hopes" has not yet met with criticism from white Southerners. In their heart of hearts they know that the
expression is true, and this knowledge hurts their consciences. The present status is just the white Southerner's choice of evils. In the recesses of their hearts
Southern men are crying out: "Give us a better chance
to choose. Do not make the alternatives so cruel; we
choose the lesser evil, but we know that it is evil. Prove
to us that real citizenship is not based on the family
life, which in turn has a biological basis, show us that
the negro can be assimilated on a non-biological basis,
and we may ameliorate the negro's pains, even though
we can't cure them."

In the matter of the franchise, the South first des-
perately intimidated the negro; then systematically

cheated him without semblance of law; then cheated him legally; and now defrauds him of his political rights in a duly constitutional fashion with the consent if not the aid of the United States Supreme Court. What next? Well, self-sophistication may become even more refined. There is a movement on foot to educate negroes only with taxes that negroes pay. Southern legislatures would perhaps in some cases enact this scheme into law— indeed, Vardaman was elected governor of Mississippi on this platform. But the lawyers declare the plan to be unconstitutional. South Carolina has a "better" plan. When whites want an extra tax for a certain school district they vote the tax and specify the school for which the tax is to be voted. Now, in practice this generally means that the special taxes are voted for the white schools only. I give this illustration to show how an impossible situation leads fatally to the failure of "democracy" and to tinkering with conscience. Some white men seem to think that lunatics, imbeciles, children and negroes have rights as human beings but not as citizens. And they resent the very thought that "niggers" should get the same public benefits as fall to the share of "our own blue-eyed Anglo-Saxon children."

Does all this mean that Southerners are conscienceless? No; it simply means that healthy morality can function only under certain normal conditions. And these do not exist in the South.

Now, if some workable solution of the negro problem should come into view, various temporary adjustments, such as racial representation and the like, would most probably not be resented by the South. But the present suppression of the negro will continue so long as he is supposed to be infected with the microbe of social equality or any other "equality" that is associated with pos-

sible social equality—and which is not? No kind of
alleged equality is worth anything to a man if his children's children are to rank as social outcasts in the eyes
of the "desirable" people, the whites. Prominent negroes
say that they do not desire social equality. What they
mean is this: We do not ask for *social intermingling*
under present conditions. If negro leaders will assert
that they do not believe that social communion between
the races ought to be feasible in the remote future, I
for one shall not be able to respect them. These leaders probably believe that all the equalities, beginning
with unsuppressed suffrage, will "come in time," when
the negro has become rich and refined and educated.
The masses of the whites probably believe that such an
outcome is possible, and hence want the negro to remain
poor and coarse and uneducated—"a genuyne nigger,"
who "knows his place." Senator Tillman probably represents the opinion of many thousands when he says
that but for the anti-amalgamation laws not a few
whites would be glad to marry rich negresses. The
social taboo is largely conventional. Untrained children
do not recognize it, but soon "catch it" from their elders. I have seen white men evidently enjoying the
society of negroes, but becoming shamefaced when detected. There are other evidences that human sociality
on its lower and more animal side is not very discriminating. And these patent evidences are known to all men.*

5. As I have already indicated, the Southerner's instinctive feeling that sociality, actual or potential, is the
basis of all the equalities—this subconscious feeling, I
say, is the crux of the whole question.

* I regret that I must use the word "probably" so often. Such
caution, however, seems necessary if one desires to keep close to
facts and to eschew dogmatic prejudice.

Potential equality is of the essence of democracy. Extirpate "race prejudice" in a democracy and social communion and intermarriage are bound to follow. One of the reasons why Northerners fail to understand this is their æsthetic antipathy to the negro. Most Southerners like individual negroes that "keep their place"—and I daresay that the negroes, like all more or less primitive folk, are likable. The Northerner is protected from social communion and intermarriage by his feelings; the Southerner is protected by what he calls his principles—the superiority of the whites, and the like. I am speaking here only in a general way. Many Southerners—and their number is increasing—detest negroes; not a few Northerners like negroes. The present writer is consciously both Northern and Southern in his attitude. At times the Northern ingredient is strongest; at times the Southern. But both are usually swallowed up by the sense of pity—pity for both races put in such sorry plight. O the pity of it that "lesser breeds without the law" cannot take the kingdom of civilization by violence; but far greater pity if they could! Juridical and ethical abstractions hold absolutely only in a realm of pure bodiless spirits. Given humanity, as we find it—a sinful incarnation—we shall still find the Israelites tending to exterminate the Canaanites, or else to enslave them. Jefferson, De Tocqueville and Lincoln believed that the two races could not live together on terms of equality. Were they wrong? Has recent history made against their doctrines? Let patient research decide on the preponderance of probabilities. If the races can get along together, let us find out how the thing can be done without ultimate amalgamation, without unjust subordination for worthy negro individuals, and without keeping the South far in the rear of the world's best civilization.

6. The alternatives are here rather brutally presented. But I confess to an abhorrence of the idea of a Chosen People lagging behind the best that is simply out of pure altruism—saintly this, but sickly, yes, suicidal (with apologies for the spontaneous alliteration). Now, self-sacrifice that is demanded by developed conscience and God's providence is a sublime and perfect thing. But useless, foolish, quixotic self-sacrifice—call it what you please—is simply provocative of the laughter of demons. Jesus Christ begged that the cup might pass from Him. With great agony He drank it, because the drinking was *necessary* to God's plans and man's salvation. But He did not ask to be damned for His people's sake. On the contrary, He looked for a resurrection. There was a glorious end to be attained. But shall we say that Dr. Edgar Gardner Murphy's second-best civilization plan is the necessary, the only possible moral course? If so, let's adopt it. But let's make sure that it is necessary before we resign ourselves to the prospect of an extremely altruistic but hopelessly limping civilization.

On the other hand, how can a true man accept the maxim: Each one for himself and the devil take the hindmost? By all means let us help the Brother in Black—may God bless him, for he is a child of God! But shall we help him at the expense of our children and future generations? God forbid. Aye, He will forbid. Racial selfishness is perniciously bad; healthy racial egoism is sane and decidedly necessary. Altruism and egoism work together like the two hands. But be ye sure, O ye believers in abstractions, that the meek who shall inherit the earth are strong and sturdy meek whose self-respect is ultimately respect for God and whose love for neighbors is measured in terms of this heightened self-love.

7. "Education for what?" I speak of facts, real conditions, as they exist, say, in Mississippi and Tennessee. Education means soul expansion. How can a soul expand in prison walls? How can a dignified human soul acquiesce in any kind of ostracism? The negro who shows his manliness in protest gets himself hated. But to me DuBois is ideally truer than Washington—the latter is "wiser" than the former. Shall truth and wisdom tell different tales? Can any good come of it?

8. Better no attempt at systematic investigation than to start one that fails to be national and international, scientific, coöperative, etc.

VII. FUSE, FIGHT OR FAIL!

(This paper, which may be regarded as fanciful by some, was written shortly after the writer had held a conference with the white school principals of the Memphis schools on one day, and had then called the negro principals together on the following day. Neither meeting discussed the race question in any way. But the author knew the feelings and opinions of both sets of principals, felt strongly the tragedy of the situation, and was yet fully aware of the general apathy of the whole country with regard to a decisive settlement of the race question. It may be that the emotional form of the essay will have some value to some minds. Indeed, it may have a message even to the hard-headed practical man whose soul is big enough to receive it!)

I

"Their angels do always behold the face of the Father."

Angel of the negro race speaks:
"They say—do the Aryan followers of Jesus, the Semite—that the negro peoples are the child-race of the world. If their word be aught more than sound, let mine be listened to, for children grow up in the fulness of time, and I am the voice of the negro race speaking Caucasian language, the language of the adult races. Listen, then, O strong men of the earth, to the sacred voice of the Child!

"I have no history. I have no country. I use borrowed flags and borrowed languages and borrowed religions. My own languages and religions are the wails of infants crying in the night. Do I wish to make my needs articulately known, I must essay to use adult words of the great powers. Forgive me if my language seem only childish prattle.

"Some speak contemptuously and others pessimistically about my hope of growing up, because during the long ages of my existence I have not reached man's stature. Others believe that my blood enters somewhat into the make-up of that great Mediterranean race which conquered the world through culture and law and arms, and established western civilization. But I am making no speculative claims; howbeit I might be permitted to develop for a few centuries under favorable circumstances before final judgment is passed on my possibilities of adultship. The Teutons were quite childish two thousand years ago, and had to borrow religion, arts and almost everything else of cultural value from the Mediterranean peoples.

"This is an age when men talk greatly of evolution, of natural and artificial selection, of the imperceptibly slow processes of nature, of use and disuse of the brain, of the effects of environment on the speed of change, of the apparent arbitrariness of spontaneous variations. Give me time, without coddling and without intimidation. Then, if I fail to grow to man's estate, let me die the death of a child whose guardians have done the best they could for him. It may be that Nature has cruelly caused premature closing of my skull sutures, and that such a condition will always obtain. But men of science have not yet killed my hopes by fastening this accusation on Nature. It may be that what has not yet been done can never be done, and that my development is doomed to arrest because I have thus far failed to grow as fast as some other races. But philosophy has not yet declared that what has not yet been can never be.

Nor have European Teutons undergone their comparatively late development in the jungles of torrid Africa
as my people have.   Even my deficient brain weight
does not unduly distress me when I realize that my brain
is that of a man, not that of an ape, and that my association centers have hardly had sufficient opportunity for
growth.   Men of science tell me, indeed, that the brain
may yet prove itself to be the most plastic organ in the
body, as it is undoubtedly *the* educable organ.

"Remember, too, O Caucasian, that there is an education in social and political life; that there is education
in racial self-respect, in hope, in the encouragement of
one's fellowman.   Shall we not have such education
somehow, somewhere?   Do not quench the smoking
flax, most Christian Caucasians.   I have looked the
white man in the face and lived.   Give me credit for
ability to survive, and help me rather than discourage
me.   You are not afraid of my competition and you
can take no pleasure in depriving me of hope; therefore
give me a chance, give me a trial, give me time and
space, faith and hope, as my allies.

"My achievements under tutelage during slavery and
freedom have been exaggerated by some and underrated
by others.   So it is always with children's performances.
I am, however, hopeful, for my Heavenly Father's face
is still lovely to look upon.

"America, you have partially adopted an orphan child.
Will you educate it?   Will you give it a start in life,
or will you use it only as a drudge in your service?
Will you equip it well and send it to seek its fortunes,
or will you adopt it fully into your family?   *Will you
at least make up your mind what you are going to do
with this orphan, which is now old enough to take an
active interest in its own welfare?*

"*Don't* call me a child and yet expect from me the morality and mentality of a man. *Don't* say that I am a problem because I am a man, and then act as if you destined me to serve *your* interests rather than my own. *Don't* blame me for my backwardness and then begrudge any forward movement in my behalf. *Don't* leave me to be the prey of undiscriminating doctrinaires on the one hand and of self-deceiving exploiters on the other.

"Am I a human being? Then treat me as such. Are democratic and Christian doctrines true for all men? Then have them apply to me. Ought every child to be educated for its own sake and up to the limit of its powers? Then give me such an education.

"I do not ask that manhood's rights be given to me while in child's estate. But assure me, white friend, that my manhood *is to be* complete and free.

"You admit that I am not your property but your charge. Then help to free my mind from ignorance, my hand from sloth and awkwardness, my soul from superstition and cringing acquiescence in 'my fate.' Remember your own childhood. Forget not your Declaration of Independence. Be mindful of your Christ's commands. Those who are meek and patient enough to eat the crumbs that fall from the master's table ought some time, somehow, somewhere gain a child's portion. If I cannot be Isaac, let me at least be a better-cared-for Ishmael. If you send me away, let the protecting, self-sacrificing generosity of a mother spirit go with me.

"But why should I go? True, I am only a waif. But here was I born. This is all the native land that I have. Why am I an alien in this land of my birth? Why am I not part of the community? Why is it that in your heart of hearts you have solemnly sworn that I shall not be a complete citizen? Why do you begrudge

me an education, and are willing that some of your
children should remain uneducated rather than that I
should be compelled to go to school?

"May I be allowed to study the workings of the
white man's mind? May I try to understand why you
will not permit me to attain unto full-orbed manhood?
Let me confess that I desire nothing less than complete
personality and citizenship. I do not *seek* "social equality" if by that expression you mean social mingling with
the whites. I do not ask to exercise *all* of my rights
under the law of the land and the moral law, but
rather I want the assurance that all of manhood's rights
will come to me in time, as I prove myself worthy.

"To deny natural inequality would be false and futile.
But should human beings be treated as representatives
of a *race* rather than as free, self-respecting persons?
And should a child race be forbidden to grow up just
because it has had a retarded development, or because of
the exigencies of the white man's labor market?"

II

"It is not meet that the children's bread should be given
unto dogs."

The spirit of the white race answers:

"Brother in Black, your speech is reasonable from
your point of view, but I doubt whether you *can* understand the Southern white man's mind, seeing that his
Northern brother often fails to get into touch with it.
However, a child's questions should be heeded, and
answered as fully as possible, provided they be respectful and earnest, as yours undoubtedly are.

"First of all, as to social equality. You say that you do not seek it. By this you mean only that self-respect forbids your seeking to associate with those who do not want your company. But if your doctrine of the worth of *individuals* be true, you have a right to *potential* social equality at least. Of what avail is it for us to admit your abstract right when you can never exercise it in this white man's land?

"Two of your foremost men, Professor Kelly Miller and Dr. DuBois, see clearly that social equality is the basis of *all* equality. Indeed, the "pursuit of happiness" implies it, and with it the right to intermarriage. The Roman plebeians got no real rights, became citizens in no real sense, until they secured the right to intermarry with patricians. The Saxons became true citizens after the Norman conquest of England only through intermarriage. White foreigners in America become truly assimilated only through intermarriage. Your people instinctively feel that the suffrage in some sense constitutes citizenship, and citizenship means, and *must* mean, membership in the *nation*—those *born* of the same stock, or potentially able to be *grafted* into it. By psychological and historical association citizenship means national homogeneity. A nation ought to be made up of citizens only. We discourage your civic claims because they have no natural significance apart from their implications of social "rights," the exercise of which we cannot grant you.

"Some of your people have learned to think of the state as a product of 'contract'; however that may be, a *national* contract can obtain permanency only through national *status,* the actual or the potential status of kinship. People are fused into nationality. Jarring races do not constitute a real community. And yet you talk about 'individuals.' There are no isolated individuals. One's true personality is social to the core. Nations are made up of homes. Community of interest, without which a people cannot form a nation, is a phantasm of the imagination if it do not imply the intercommunion of homes. Indeed, politics, religion, art, business, education—all imply and presuppose sociality. Conscience itself is only secondarily individual and intellectual. It is primarily social. The church festival and the political celebration ought to teach you the essential sociality of all forms of national life. Because of her belief in the family as a sacred institution and her unwillingness to accept the mere 'contract' theory of nationality, the South is truer to nature, history and Holy Writ than are some other parts of the Union.

"We are emphatically 'members one of another.' Politics and religion of certain forms notoriously tend to 'run in families.' And with reason. Other things being equal, a man ought to vote and pray in spiritual union with his ancestors. The Jajauese understand this. Your people do also, and vote the Republican ticket— when they do vote—because their 'folks' do so and have always done so. Occasionally one finds a 'Democratic' negro *family* or a 'Republican' white *family* in the 'orthodox' South. Now, I do not claim that political equality *logically* presupposes potential social equality, but it *biologically* and *psychologically* presupposes it. Democrats do not always marry Democrats, nor do Baptists always marry Baptists—but they tend to do so, for biologically—and psychologically—based reasons.

"When you seek for *any* 'equality,' come out like a man and ask, not for present social communion but for potential social equality. Nothing less than this will bring your race to manhood's estate. And realize, please, that, while we do not deny your claim of abstract rights, we cannot allow the exercise of them in the midst of a white population.

"Leaving aside the Southern white man's apparently unconquerable distaste for racially mixed marriages, let us inquire whether such intermarriage is advisable, even were it allowable and feasible—and it is neither. If science could tell us that the amalgamation of the races would produce good results for this nation, and we should be willing to hearken unto her voice, in the course of a century 'prejudice' might be overcome and amalgamation might result. There is always such a biological tendency among the lowest classes of both races, and the doctrine of 'individuality' might in time bring it about in the upper classes. But science seems to advise against such an experiment. So we need not discuss the 'fusion' member of our three alternatives: Fusion, fight, or failure—even if our race feeling could be blotted out.

"Nor do conscientious Southerners want the negro race to fail. We wish you well, Brother in Black—*provided you keep in your place*. What *is* your *ultimate* place? That remains to be found out. Your place *now* is that of a subordinate race. Whether your 'place' will change in time, or in space, or in both, or in some other way, no one can tell. We only know that so long as the two races live together the whites will rule and negro individuals must accept the stigma of *representative* inferiority.

"You ought to have the fullest opportunity for development. You ought not to be exploited by the whites. There is no place for a peasantry in America. You should not be subjected to scorn and hate, nor even to condescending pity. To have you American negroes fail as a people would be a tragedy in this day of democratic and Christian enlightenment. It may be necessary to find you a land of your own and found for you a state that will give you full freedom.

"But enlightened Southerners do not want to deceive you or have you deceived by letting you remain in a fools' paradise. You don't belong to the *kin*. You cannot be assimilated. And unless you are assimilated you will constitute a *nidus* for disease in the body politic. Indeed, such is the case now. Your physical presence retards the growth and nationalization of the South. You are farther from assimilation to-day than you were in 1870. And yet as Christian democrats we would not have you fail as a people.

"If fusion is impossible and failure too painful to contemplate, how about the third alternative—fight?

"Now I would not have you suppose that I am urging you to contend with arms for your rights. By 'fight' I mean civilized, useful, rational warfare with the arms of the mind and the spirit.

"Fight! I say. And keep up the fight without ceasing. How? Not by agitating for your 'rights,' nor by alternately blessing and cursing a Roosevelt or a Taft, nor by waiting for the 'problem' to 'settle itself' by 'industrial education'—but by binding yourselves together, asking your Southern friends to help you, and insisting modestly but with steadfast determination that the race question in America be scientifically *investigated*. Think of the splendid scientific agencies in this country and wonder at the small amount of real study that has been given to a problem graver than war and pestilence! Race enmity is worse than the hookworm, for it stunts the generous soul of the chivalrous Southerner.

"Will the people of this country wait for more troubles from the Atlantas, the Wilmingtons and the

Springfields? Do they want to keep the South spiritually out of the Union, or to have the spirit of racial malignancy overshadow the Union? Are they going to desert you people, after opening to you various illusory doors of hope? Lincoln could as truly say to-day as he said fifty years ago that no nation can permanently remain half-slave and half-free. Your people are more or less free in body—free to wander and to drift—but their minds and souls are enslaved by the blighting 'check' of subordination; and the spirits of my people, a sacred nation, are enslaved by apprehension, enslaved by self-protective bourbonism, enslaved by *your* consciousness of political futility and stigmatised individuality.

"Why am I so insistent? Because I am the true spirit of the white man of the South, and I want you people to be free—for your own sake *and especially for the sake of my own people.*

"No man can predict what the end will be. But nowadays science does what she can to furnish the true prophets material wherewith to work. Let us no longer try merely to *patch up* the civic health of the South with educational and other tonics.

"Let us have more light and less heat. We cannot have peace until we have light.

"Lincoln, Jefferson and De Tocqueville are names great enough to arrest our tongues when we begin to cry 'absurd,' 'impossible,' whenever a radical settlement, colonization, is hinted at. Suppose such a settlement to be the only certain one. Would it not be the part of wisdom to get ready for it now? And if such a thoroughgoing settlement be shown to be unnecessary or impracticable, would it not be well to steer our policy in regard to this question, rather than to let it drift?

"If foresight is the characteristic of the civilized man and science the glory of our age, should we not call our science to help us secure foresight and end this present-day blind policy of drifting?"

VIII. THE HOME AND THE HABITATION

(Substance of lecture given at Mississippi College, Clinton, Miss.)

Thoreau says that sauntering means "Holy Land-ing," or else "without a land." Yesterday I got a new meaning for this suggestion of the great walking philosopher of the woods. I found that Mississippi is a sort of "holy land" for whites, and that the Mississippi negro is "without a land." I was storing up strength while the beautiful autumn lasted—strength of body and inspiration that nature, wild nature alone, can give. Avoiding the places where men do congregate, I joyfully sauntered, pursuing the trail that wobbled along miscellaneously with an occasional pretense of being a road. Breasting a little hill, I heard the sound of wailing, and soon perceived that a ten-year-old boy was "minding" his baby sister by teasing and bullying her. No adult person was near; the house seemed to be shut up. I need hardly tell you that the children were negroes and that the older members of the family were picking cotton in the field. The house was more or less a habitation, but could hardly be called a home. I do not think that a movement to provide care for that negro baby while its mother was away would prove popular. Was there not an older brother to tend baby? School age? Yes, but what of that—he is "only a nigger," and "nigger schools don't amount to anything anyhow—educating a nigger spoils a good field hand." This would be

77

said in spite of the fact that there was an industrial
school for negroes near by with a handful of pupils, the
scanty remnant of a flourishing school that has had
thirty years of devoted history, and the result of a
Christian white woman's sense of responsibility for doing something that would help to uplift the negro. The
school lacked pupils, and all around were pupils that
lacked a school. But why should the negro mother have
her ten-year-old boy go to school? Education equalizes,
and the whites won't have anything that appears to
equalize the races. After the cotton is picked, however,
that negro mother will send her boy to school, because
she believes that education will do something, she knows
not what, for him. Sometimes she may think that studying books will help to free him from excessive hard
labor such as she must perform; but for the most part
she has a dim feeling that human beings are to be educated, and that her child is a human being and hence
needs education. Even horses and dogs need training.
If she were told that training behind a plow was all that
her boy needed, she might reply that educated negroes
get along better, are less likely to be criminal, and are
more respected by their kind. Naturally, she wants her
child to have these advantages. If she is mistaken in
thinking that school will help her boy, it would be merci-
ful to tell her so; and if the average white man thinks
that education will "spoil" that boy, his allegation ought
to be investigated, for surely he does not regard a human
being simply as a domestic animal without a soul.

But let us suppose that the negro child is to be educated; then how much education does he get, and of
what kind? If he goes to the public school he *may*
reach the fourth grade. His teacher is unskilled and
unlettered. He has no money wherewith to buy the

school books he needs at first.   His six months of schooling during the year are divided into two periods with several months between them.   Is it surprising that the "literate" negroes that come from such schools are as likely to go to jail as are negroes that have not had these stupendous "advantages"?   If he should get an education that would teach him good habits as well as reading, writing and ciphering, and should become a skilled laborer, does he not cease to become a field hand, and thus complicate the labor problem, and at the same time enter into competition with the superior white race?

Granted that he will find work for some years to come, is there any indication that the white boys of the South are going to turn over the skilled trades to the negro?   And does the labor union situation at the North encourage the negro to hope for good things in that direction?   In a town to the south of this college town negroes are not allowed to work as carpenters and bricklayers.   In a community to the north all negroes have been driven out.   In a large town to the west all negroes not definitely at work are arrested because some one has shot at a street car conductor.   (This application of the "vagrancy law" would scarcely be tolerated if white visitors should be arrested as vagrants.)   To the east of this place a white man who mutilated a negro girl has escaped justice without any serious trouble in so doing.

Will education help such conditions?   Only on condition that the educated negroes have more white friends than the uneducated ones possess.   But the negro mother has a suspicion that perfectly illiterate negroes are more helpless than even partially educated ones.   If she is wrong it would be a pity not to tell her so.   If she is wrong we should be able to find out the truth, and then to ask ourselves the question, why should education be good for all other races but bad for the negro? And should we decide that the white man's temporary labor advantage ought to be the test of the advisability of educating the negro or else of leaving him in absolute intellectual darkness, so that he cannot even read his Bible or sign his name to a law paper? Knowing, as we do, if we know anything at all of the white people of this part of the country, that there are no people on earth more really religious and more tender-hearted and chivalrous, would it not be well to find out why good people seem to be so ruthless in "keeping the negro down"? But let us return to our sauntering walk.

The house on the right of the rambling road gives us painful thoughts, for it is not a home and hardly hopes to be one. How is it with the house on the other side of the road and a rod or two further on? It too seems to be poverty stricken. But it is a home. The mother is there. True, she is working harder than does the woman in the cotton patch. True, she herself works at cotton picking in a pinch. What, then, is her advantage? She is working for her children at home, and her children are attending a good school taught by competent teachers, and enjoying opportunities that promise illimitable possibilities. There is no bar to her children's hopes. Her boy may be president; her girl may be the wife of a senator, or something much better. Humble as her family may be, nothing stands in the way of their rising in the social scale through their own exertions by the grace of God. Her children will be vouchsafed all civil rights and due protection of laws. She and hers are the heirs of all the ages and need only to take their own. Not only do her children get education in school, but also in church, at home, and through participation in all the free institutions of a free and freedom-loving state and country.

Now comes the philanthropic friend of abstract human rights and tells us that these violent contrasts between the rights and opportunities of the two races should not exist. He asks the question: Do you believe it right or expedient to let the lazy and immoral white man believe himself to be better than the thrifty and moral negro? Do you think that the doctrine of a protective tariff should be extended to human rights, so that the negro is given a handicap and the white man a bounty?

Well, things human are never as simple as they seem. The mother of a weak and inefficient child might conceivably say to herself, "Why should I waste love and care on my weakling? Why not let the doctrine of natural selection and survival of the fittest obtain?" I need not say that she asks no such question and has no such thought. Just *because* her offspring is weak and inefficient, she lavishes on it all the wealth of mother-love, and stands like a lioness to defend the "unfit" child. Let the friends of abstract human rights use any argument they will at the South except that which would indicate a willingness to allow *any* negro to triumph over *any* white man! The solidarity of race is ours, is a part of our religion. We will do all we can to make our weaklings efficient; but we shall continue to love them and care for them and protect them even from their own foolishness. We are the people, even though we know that wisdom shall not die with us. Every white man is our brother in a sense whereof the negro can never know. The South fought for the principle that patriotism begins with the blood kin; nor could the arbitrament of arms change that principle in any respect. From the known to the unknown, from the concrete to the abstract, from the home to the nation, from the fact to the possibility—these are Southern slogans, and they ought to be rallying cries for all men who believe in the principle that, if we love not our brother whom we have seen, how can we love aliens that we cannot assimilate?

We are willing for the negro to come into his own, but not at the expense of white solidarity and white supremacy; nor even though the whole negro race were helped by the shaming of a few white individuals. Nature has selected us, God has made us a chosen people; we therefore take care of our own, and all of them. When philanthropists insist on lifting the negro up, we feel justified in saying that the white race must be lifted up correspondingly.

The abstract philanthropist, however, does not understand this position. He wants to know how it can happen that white solidarity or white supremacy can be injured by giving negroes the right of citizenship and a kind of courtesy that will not lead to social commingling of the races. Can we make the world understand our Southern position? For the civilized nations are asking the question put forth by the philanthropist. Our answer must ever be that democracy normally means equality; that every human institutional promise to pay must have a cash value in *social* opportunity, if these notes are to be aught more than the fiat money of philosophical abstractions.

Politics means social commingling. Aye, the wise saw, "politics makes strange bedfellows," is more than a figure of speech. Every barbecue, every political meeting, every "dollar dinner," every assertion regarding the Declaration of Independence and the Constitution—all these things and many more mean at least potential or

implicit social communion. We are willing to grant
the abstract dogma that every man's civic rights, and
hence his social rights, ought to be determined by his
intrinsic character and real, inner social availability; but
social equality in the abstract inevitably leads to the
assertion of the rights of social communion at some
time. Hence, although we Southerners appear to be
contending against the doctrine of abstract social equality, we are really fighting against anything that will lead
even *indirectly* to the *assertion* of the right to social
commingling between the races. History has shown us,
through patricians and plebeians, through Saxons and
Normans, that political and social rights are organically
connected in such wise that one inevitably tends to beget
the other. And De Tocqueville, in his great work on
Democracy in America, has pointed out once for all the
evident truth that, when all are equally citizens, all tend
to draw together in every way concerned with mutual
interests.

Citizenship is an empty name unless social communion
and intermarriage cause that necessary fusion of elements without which a democracy cannot persist. The
behavior of the negroes during reconstruction times is
still fresh in the minds of all Southerners. The negro
now "knows his place" tolerably well; and the South
will do or willingly allow nothing that will tend to make
the negro *think* that he is "as good as a white man."
Individually, and in the eternal vision of God, many
negroes may be far more valuable as souls than many
whites; but the blood, the tradition, the territory are
ours, and a strained and unnatural, halt and blind citizenship can do nothing for the negro but incite in him
ambitions that the white folk of the ·South are not
willing to tolerate. Show us, say the Southerners, that

there is no historical and no organic connection between the various equalities, but that human life is a set of arbitrary, disconnected "equalities," no one of which is necessarily connected with another; show us, too, if any assimilation other than that of intermarriage has ever welded together diverse peoples;—show us these things, and prove our instinct for solidarity to be but illusory moonshine, and we shall consider your arguments for the exhibition and functioning of abstract human rights on the part of the negro. We don't deny the rights; we insist only that they be held in abeyance because the public welfare demands it. And *we* are primarily the public, its welfare is primarily *our* welfare.

The negro has become segregated in church, lodge, and in all other institutional-social ways. It may be possible to segregate him in his political "rights." That is a matter for investigation. But he must be treated *as a race* politically as well as in every other social way. The very words, patriotism, fatherland, nation, ought to show us the social basis, yea, the *home* basis, of political institutions. To empty politics of the social feature would be to dehumanize it and render it even more dangerously machine-like than it often is to-day. Party leaders are treated as heroes. When men have heroes in common, and work for them, when men have ideals in common, and these are connected with their native land, how is it possible to allow the notion of mere "contract" government to displace entirely the idea of human *status* with its rich "fringe" of instinctive social relations?

The contract idea of the family has already caused untold mischief. True, marriage *is* a contract; but the home is also an institution of *status*. Reform and improve the status relations, if you please; let conjugal reciprocity in rights and privileges take the place of one-sided rights; but do nothing to injure the sacredness of a *status* that is founded on imperative instinct and hallowed by immemorial custom.   So with the state. We Democrats do not desire "paternal" government. But we do not wish for "machine" government, either. If government ever loses its human features and becomes simply a matter of bookkeeping and business, men will seek paternalism because it is at least human and founded on instinct.   Let the machine features of government be efficiently administered on a purely business basis, but forget not that the voter means vastly more than a numerical unit, and remember that contract can never destroy instinct and hero worship and the social values of politics.

Perhaps the South injects more sociality into its politics than the rest of the country does.   In the South conservative ideas of family life obtain, and the "old-fashioned religion" is more popular than elsewhere. Rural life and farming undoubtedly help men to associate politics with sociality.   Then, too, kinship and the call of the blood kin help to keep alive in the South the etymological meaning of the word *nature*.   At all events, even granting that the South is old-fashioned in viewing politics as connected with sociality, our making common cause against those who were concerned with negro domination during reconstruction times has resulted in a growing sense of race solidarity and a feeling that the Solid South idea has not only a political but also a racial and a social meaning.   If the South should become converted to the notion that some human institutions need not in any way be connected with social values, a change of attitude might occur with regard to giving the negro a chance at the ballot box.   Even if such a change should come, it would simply indicate that Southerners were willing that the negroes should have political representation as a *race,* and representation that would not interfere with normal political conditions.

On my way home from the walk above referred to I met a little negro child, a mere toddler. He smiled benignly and touched my coat in friendly fashion as I passed. Pretty soon he will "know better." My own child spoke of negro women as "black ladies" when he lived in California, where a negro was seldom seen and where it was unnecessary to discuss the negro question. A few months later the little two-year-old had learned to "discriminate," and had described a negro man at the front door as a "nigger," not a "gentleman." Nothing had been said to him by the adult members of the household; but he had become indoctrinated through the very atmosphere of South Carolina social life.

Both of the above incidents illustrate the evident fact that race feeling is not instinctive. If it were a deep-seated instinct, much of the Southern guarding of the "color line" would appear foolish; but the race feeling is a tradition and a part of religious culture at the South, and has hence become a sort of secondary instinct, a social custom and habit.

When I was a child no objection was made when a little white child caressed his colored nurse. Nowadays the thing is usually discouraged and oftentimes vigorously prevented. Even the children must not be allowed to "cross the color line," lest the negroes should in some way "presume." Much of the Northern man's reluctance to have the negro brought into intimate relationship with whites as a menial is now felt by many Southerners. Is all this simply a kind of cruelty, or is it the cruelty of real kindness? In most cases the latter,

I think.   Dear experience has taught the Southerner that the negro is best off when he keeps his place in every respect.   The old kindly relationships of slavery at its best are now impossible; the freedman does not wish the privileges of a Newfoundland dog, and the whites appreciate the patent fact that even the kindlier phenomena of slavery are now out of place, and that exhibitions of advanced democracy in social matters had better be reserved altogether for white people as their objects.

Granted, then, that the racial orthodoxy of the South has a measure of rational justification, should we exult in our position as a dominant race, continue for all time to make the negro acutely conscious on all occasions of his inferiority?   Shall we give full rein to arrogance and bourbonism?   Not so, if our civilization is really democratic and humanitarian—not to say Christian.   Let us regard the color line as one drawn by reason and conscience, and not by passion and prejudice.   If our rights and reasonable racial principles tend to be habitual and instinctive, no harm is done and much good, for we need habit and instinct for our everyday conduct.   But woe to us if we sell our birthright of democracy and humaneness for a mess of blind and passionate race enmity!   Holding fast to our dogmatic belief in our race and its rights, let us not forget God's child-races, and their rights, and our duties to them.   Let us not flaunt our supremacy in their faces.   Let us not tell them that we want them to exist simply for our own selfish purposes.   Let us hold out to them the hope of ultimate full development as a race, though never at our expense.   Although the white people of this country should never consent to have the South's development permanently retarded on account of a desire to "give the negro justice," there must be some way under high heaven whereby this conflict of duties can be ameliorated. Surely investigation will point out some method by which the negroes can get all that freemen should have, and yet without any crossing of the color line, without any holding out of vain hopes to the negroes that they may ultimately break down "race prejudice" among the whites.

I am a radical Southerner so far as the chief tenet of our distinctively Southern faith is concerned; but I have no sympathy with the kind of radicalism that forgets its humanity and revels in the thought of permanent spiritual slavery for the negroes. Much harm has been done to the negro's cause by worthy Northern and Southern champions who declaim against the extreme statement of "southernism"; for the Southern people have developed their "secondary instinct" of raciality so that it has become a fine instrument for detecting even the subconscious tendency on the part of the negro's special advocates to soften in some wise the sharpness of definition of the color line. Southern "prejudice" is not mere caste feeling, but is *race* feeling that can give a good reason for its existence. The negro is not simply a lower class in the community; he is a different race, with all grades of character and individual value. It is *not* expedient for us to treat individual negroes *as* individuals in any way that even indirectly suggests social recognition. An illiterate white may well be able to look the highest negro in the face and refuse him the slightest sign of social recognition such as he would accord a white man. Not that he need claim to be the negro's *personal* superior—in the sight of God. But the humblest white man is still a Caucasian, though the least of Caucasians; and the noblest negro is still an African though he be king of Africans. Only this attitude can prevent the gradual breaking down of racial distinctions. The true Southerner would prefer to put up even with hellish exhibitions of race ferocity than do anything to break down even the most remote outpost that guards the citadel of the elect people of this land.

Race pride in itself may be nothing worth while, but when it guards, however unreasonably in appearance, what Southerners believe the manifest will of God that the white race retain its leadership and make no pretense of ever sharing its heritage with any blood too alien for assimilation, race pride, yea, even race enmity, harsh and cruel as it may become, would appear to be the chastening rod of Jehovah that warns the two races to remain forever separate.

But—here is the problem: How to keep the races separate and yet retain the practice of American principles in their fulness in the same territory and under the same institutions, under conditions of daily contact! Young men, will you do your part in compelling the attention of our people to focus itself on the scientific investigation of this most human of practical problems?

Let us return now to our first illustrative example of home *vs.* habitation. A home is a state of congenial sociality wherein faith and hope and love do dwell. Has the negro faith in his past or hope for his future, or love for his present condition? The other day I heard a white man give the following synopsis of a lecture that he was going to deliver to a negro institute: The negro is an animal without a history, a man without a country, a citizen without the protection of law, a husband without loyalty, and a father without authority! Granted, gladly granted, that many a negro household proves this statement to be far from universally true. Nevertheless, what is home without hope? And how

can a people hope when there are no signs of ultimate
human freedom for them, freedom of complete spiritual
manhood and citizenship? A negro was recently asked
if certain negroes *lived* in such and such places. In each
case he said: "He *stays* there." A home ought to be
not simply a breeding place of bodies, but the nesting
place of free souls. Sooner or later the true home spirit
is lost when the children of the home may not look forward to complete living and full citizenship. For the
state and the church and all human institutions are rooted
and nurtured in the home. If children are bred to
believe themselves forever subordinate; if they feel themselves to be forever shut out from some of the legitimate aspirations of free humanity; if the very face of
Providence is veiled from them because of the accident
of race; if thrift and culture and good conduct count as
nothing in the life of the state and the pursuit of happiness; if, in a word, the future does not lure them on
to a day of the sunshine of sufficing human opportunity—how easily do the most sacred relationships
come to appear as dull limitations without promise of
perfection! How easily does faith shrivel and love pine
away when the buoyant presence of hope has departed!
Homes without hope? There may have been such in
the world's history, but they thrive but poorly when this
day and hour spell opportunity and freedom to the
favored nations of the favored races, and when every
normal individual of a favored race may become a complete individual.

The presence of the negro may be a black blight on
the South, but the really deadly blight is in our hearts
do we content ourselves in this Christian country of
opportunity with dull and stupid acquiescence in the

very existence of unfreedom in our land and at our doors!

"And now, men and women of America, is this a thing to be trifled with, apologized for, and passed over in silence?"

We white folk must rule in this white man's land, but how can we rule our own hearts through love to God and man when every circumstance of our daily lives encourages in us a temper of arrogant overlordship?

IX. RACE ORTHODOXY IN THE SOUTH

(From Neale's Monthly Magazine, November, 1913.)

The soulful brevity of wit and worth is something greatly to be desired in the discussion of the negro question. If one have no patent of nobility with regard to authoritativeness, he may show forth a virtue allied to it,—that of straightforward directness,—even if he may lack the larger wisdom and the wider wit. If the reader will kindly accede to the truth underlying the proposition just stated he will perhaps pardon a somewhat abbreviated presentation of a very large subject.

The race attitude of the Southern whites is not a code of cases but a creed of a people,—a part of their morality and of their religion. If this attitude seems not to square with the democratic and Christian ethics of the world, there is need that it take stock of itself. The cocksure arrogance that hugs its provincial self-sufficiency and casts sour looks at ethical world standards merits the name of foolish Bourbonism, if not a worse name. I, for one, hold that the South is compelled by the logic of events and the conscience of the world to explain her attitude to men of good will everywhere.

I

Here is the racial creed of the Southern people as expressed by a group of representative Southerners during the past few months:

1. "Blood will tell."
2. The white race must dominate.
3. The Teutonic peoples stand for race purity.
4. The negro is inferior and will remain so.
5. "This is a white man's country."
6. No social equality.
7. No political equality.
8. In matters of civil rights and legal adjustments give the white man, as opposed to the colored man, the benefit of the doubt; and under no circumstances interfere with the prestige of the white race.
9. In educational policy let the negro have the crumbs that fall from the white man's table.
10. Let there be such industrial education of the negro as will best fit him to serve the white man.
11. Only Southerners understand the negro question.
12. Let the South settle the negro question.
13. The status of peasantry is all the negro may hope for, if the races are to live together in peace.
14. Let the lowest white man count for more than the highest negro.
15. The above statements indicate the leadings of Providence.

This creedal statement is practically the *common opinion* of the South, or as near that opinion as I can set it down at the present writing. But is it a true orthodoxy, a *right* opinion? Not in its present shape, though much of its underlying meaning is right enough. Let us therefore attempt to restate, in the form of a commentary, the creed of "Southernism" in a more adequate form, in order that it may better give a reason for the faith that is in it, and better square itself with the recognized standards of American democracy and Christian ethics.

II

1. "Blood will tell." In this age of interest in
eugenics,—when men are coming to regard the forces
of heredity as the "capital" of the races, and the forces
of environment, including education, as racial "income,"
—we are not justified in neglecting the paramount importance of keeping up the physical stock of the higher
racial types, even if in so doing the less developed races
may not be favored to the extent of their desires. Judg-
ing the future by the past, as we must do, we have no
reason to believe that it will conduce to the ultimate
welfare of the world if we fail to give sufficient play
to the forces of selection, be they "natural" or "artificial," "biological" or "social." The popular concept
of the potency of blood and race has sufficient scientific
warrant for all the practical purposes of political insight
and foresight.

2. "The white race must dominate." History tells us
that the higher civilization of to-day has been wrought
out by the white race in its various branches. The rapid
rise in recent times of such a people as the Japanese,—
due as it undoubtedly is to the partial assimilation of
Caucasian culture by this Asiatic people,—gives us no
reason to believe that the dominant place in the world's
life and work will not continue to be held by the white
race that has made the rise of the Japanese possible.
Moreover, the Japanese are yet to prove that their recent
achievements in culture will stand the test of time and
that their powers of imitation are destined to lead to the
powers of initiative possessed by the white race. The
primacy of the white nations need not mean the unethical exploitation of other races; but it does mean that

the ethical stocks which now hold the supremacy are
not at all likely to yield it, should conflict arise.

If the white race holds its own there will be no opportunity for any other racial type to acquire such power
and prestige as that now enjoyed by the primary makers
of the world's civilization. Until another race shows
its ability to establish a religion, a code of ethics, social
institutions, forms of government, literature, art, and
so on, equal to those that have come into being through
the agency of the white nations, "the white race must
dominate." If the various races are kept apart geo-
graphically, there is no reason for supposing that any conflict need arise because of the superior world power possessed by the present leading nations of Europe and
America.

3. "The Teutonic peoples stand for race purity." It
is likely that the Teutonic stocks are the most dif-
ferentiated peoples of the white race, and that they possess to-day, partly through admixture with other white
stocks, a commanding position in all the continents,—a
position from which they are not likely to be dispos-
sessed. They are the great colonizers and empire build-
ers. Their influence among all nations is constantly
increasing. Hence their acute consciousness of race is
the strongest guarantee that the Caucasian stocks will
be kept comparatively pure from admixture with other
racial types, and that the Teutonic valuation of racial
pedigree will more and more extend to other peoples of
the dominant race. Indeed, there are indications that
the so-called Slavic and Keltic people are following the
lead of the Teutonic peoples in this matter. Until science advocates the intermixture of *primary* racial types
it is not likely that Teutonic ideals of racial purity will

be overborne.   And science shows no tendency to advise such inter-racial mixture.

4.   "The negro is inferior and will remain so."   It is generally admitted, even in the most conservative scientific circles, that the negro race, as a type, is at present inferior to the white race.   Although some scientific men see no reason for doubting the negro's ability to fit himself into the conditions of modern civilization in the future, no first-class man of science is rash enough to predict that the average of development of the negro race in the South will equal that of the white people of the South within any assignable period.   Nor should any "friend of humanity" wish to see the masses of the negro people lifted up at the expense of the white, either through the mixture of blood or through educational neglect of the whites in favor of the negroes. However promising the outlook may be for a small percentage of the negro people, the signs of promise for the poorest classes of whites are very much greater; and the Southern people can be trusted to see to it that their "submerged tenth" shall have greater opportunities for development than any that are likely to be offered to the submerged negro nine-tenths.   For the low-grade white man has the higher potency and promise in his blood, and furthermore there is a favored race understanding implied in the very conditions of the Southern situation, by the very nature of the case.

5.   "This is a white man's country," because the white man acquired it; made it what it is; contributes eight-ninths of the population; represents a much greater proportion of the intelligence, wealth, and civilization in general; formed a government and developed institutions for white men, and will not yield one jot or tittle of his present advantages.   Not only will enlightened

self-love compel him to hold that which is his, but the welfare of the world is better conserved by this country's remaining specifically the land of the white man.

Racial traits always color habits, customs, institutions, modes of thought, feeling, and action. But Afro-Americanism, no matter what its merits, will not be allowed to constitute any discernible part or aspect of the spirit of the people of this country. To grant to a nonassimilable people, with different *mores* or racial peculiarities, privileges that would stimulate them to seek for entrance into the psychological and social heritage of national temperament and disposition would be to love one's alien neighbor better than one's national self, —a counsel of perfection put forward neither by sound philosophy nor practical religion. To the white first— and also to the negro! If the whites prove themselves unheeding of the summons to go up higher, then it will be time to say, "To the white and the negro equally and at the same time." Let the sentimentalist that argues to the contrary of this position tell us wherein our view conflicts with the enlightened policy of the best peoples of the earth.

Nationality, like marriage, is something more than a contract; hence, until the constitution of nature is amended through triumphs of national self-sacrificing grace as yet undreamed of even by the saints, "this is a white man's country!" This doctrine by no means impugns the negro's rights to life, liberty, and the pursuit of happiness; nor does it condemn him to anything less than the freest and fullest spiritual life wherever he can assimilate himself to the conditions of his environment or can conquer for himself the right of racial ascendency. If he can unfurl his flag somewhere and truthfully say, "This is a colored man's country!" the

Southern white man will wish him success and help him to achieve it. But the white man of America wants and will have nothing less than white civilization, outside, inside, through and through, without in any wise casting aspersions on the yellow man's or the black man's merits, real or alleged. At bottom this is the white man's contention in this connection: This is a white man's country, because the requisite homogeneity in American civilization cannot be obtained except through intermarriage; all other attempts at assimilation are unnatural and unhistorical; the white man does not believe that the blood of the white and that of the negro ought to be mingled, for the product is advantageous neither to the white man nor to the welfare of the world. Hence all attempts to overcome the negro's inferiority, being intrinsically abnormal and unnatural, do not avail. Therefore the negro is unassimilable—and this land must remain a white man's country.

6. "No social equality." Since "social equality" can naturally and effectively mean nothing but amalgamation or "miscegenation" there must be no social intermingling of the races. Granting social privileges to negro individuals is an admission that sociality has nothing to do with race, but is a purely personal and private concern. But if the mayor of one of our cities should "keep the pig in the parlor," or have his servants sit at table with his guests, contrary to the wishes of the latter, the community would have the right to object. The "private" and the "personal" cannot separate themselves from *representativeness*. When a representative of a government serves grapejuice at his table he may be making history. No man can isolate his social conduct from the rest of his behavior. Public opinion has some rights even in the private sanctities of the home. The

people that put down patriarchal polygamy with an iron hand and sanction the attempt to prevent a citizen's pursuing his "happiness" through the use of alcoholic beverages will surely recognize the representativeness of race and the insidious danger of unrepresentative social example.

Since the world began so-called personal rights have had to yield to public expediency. Much as fair-minded men may regret the lumping together of all individuals of a race under a sort of social taboo, the vicarious sacrifice of such individuals is one of the sad but necessary incidents of the sacred solidarity of race. And if interracial social equality is to be guarded against, all approaches thereto must be prevented. The gentle trickling of water through a levee bank must be quickly and adequately stopped, lest the levee give way in time. The West Indian hurricane may begin its operations with little soft puffs of balmy breeze. For direction and the ulterior cause are the real forces, and not the trivial initial phenomena in themselves. In denying to *"Mister* Sammy Green," the estimable Afro-American gentleman, certain inoffensive social courtesies that are accorded to rough-and-tumble "Dago Macaroni," or "Dago Mac" for short, the white man is true to the principle of the representativeness of race. The *assertion* of the right of social equality by negroes is obnoxious to whites, because it indicates a disposition to unsettle the status of white supremacy. Conservative whites know that race friction cannot be avoided if individual negroes evince a disposition to have themselves treated as individuals apart from their race status in the white community.

When high-grade whites demand that certain negroes be treated as exceptional persons apart from race status they endanger the peace of the community, and therefore render themselves *persona non grata* to white people. Noble philanthropic views and a magnanimous sense of fair play should so discipline themselves as not to interfere with the best interests of both races. A situation that requires social rigidity toward any worthy person is by no means satisfactory; but so long as two diverse races live together one must remain subordinate if race friction is to be avoided; and individuals of the dominant race do a distinct disservice not only to their own race but also to the subordinate race when they espouse the cause of an *abstract* individualism that no longer has the sanction of the best thinkers.

Antagonism to racial coequality demands that the low-grade white who endangers racial purity, and who encourages thereby social assertiveness of any kind on the part of the subordinate race, needs to be disciplined by public opinion as well as by the vigorous and rigorous application of legal penalties. When whites begin to coerce unworthy individuals of their own race in the interests of racial morality, no longer will the world be able to point scornfully at a dominant race which allows its individuals to give by their conduct the lie to the anti-equality protestations of the dominant racial stock. Every young white man should be taught by his elders that the use of human beings as mere biological conveniences is bad enough, but that such conduct is peculiarly despicable when it leads to the virtual practice of inter-racial social equality of the gravest sort.

7. "No political equality." The right to vote is a conventional privilege of public order and not a natural right. If the public welfare is best served by denying the exercise of the franchise to any portion of the population, the state is justified in such denial. If, however,

the people of a state agree, even under sufferance, to a constitutional provision that prohibits the drawing of racial lines in the matter of the franchise, only temporary expediency justifies them in evading the constitutional provision through the indirection of state laws that are intended to operate against one race rather than against the other. Either the unsatisfactory Fifteenth Amendment should be repealed,—in which case the subordinate race would have to be allowed protection in another form,—or else some kind of racial representation might be provided,—perhaps municipal, legislative, and congressional delegates without votes.

No system of negro suffrage that would enable the negro to hold the balance of power in a political division between parties or factions of the white race should have the sanction of the state. The time has come for the whites of the South to cease pretending either that they are afraid of "negro domination" or that they are perfectly willing for "qualified" negroes to vote in appreciable numbers. The political elimination of the negro can be secured without depriving him of the democratic right of representation of some sort; and, sooner or later, the government of this nation will have to admit the natural fact of racial differences and the civil and political implications thereof. But to leave a subordinate people entirely at the mercy of any set of men,— no matter how well-intentioned and fair-minded they may be,—is to fly in the face of experience, especially where race feeling is the essential factor in a political situation. On the other hand, the frank admission of racial inequality under the conditions of local contact and the cultivation on the part of the ruling people of the spirit of *noblesse oblige,* as well as the practice of impartial justice to the "minor" or subordinate people,

will at least have the merit of arranging a peaceful
status pending the full and thorough investigation of
the race problem.

It appears probable that mankind values all rights
and privileges in terms of at least potential social equality.   All conventional rights are closely associated with
potential social status.   The social implications of political life are many and varied.   The suffrage is the democratic badge of complete citizenship.   Inasmuch as social
equality between the races is denied, and the negro is forbidden to expect or seek for that complete citizenship
which is at bottom secured only by means of facile intermarriage, the denial of political equality,—along with the
granting, however, of appropriate racial political activity,—would seem to be safeguards of white supremacy
and of the peaceful dwelling together of the races.   That
such a *situation* is *desirable* cannot be claimed by a
people that calls itself democratic and Christian.   However, criticism should be directed not toward those Southern whites who are free from race enmity and who
listen to the voice of race conscience, but rather toward
those who maintain that the present condition is *satisfactory,*—who look forward with equanimity to a *permanent* subordination of the negro people.

Though the prevailing race opinion of the whites in
the South may not articulately declare itself in favor of
the principles of democracy and Christianity in their
application to the negro people, I would call "race
orthodoxy" the opinion of those who are true to
American principles, yet hold to white supremacy and
all that it legitimately implies.   Were the masses of the
people able to appreciate fully the necessary ethical limitations of race attitude, they would undoubtedly express
themselves in terms similar to our present statement of

race *orthodoxy* in the South rather than in the crude, uncompromising, and seemingly unethical dogmas enunciated in our first statement of racial common opinion in the South.

Lack of faith in the common people's basal right feeling undermines the influence of many would-be leaders of ethical opinion in the Southern states. On the other side, subservience to mob spirit renders the utterance of some of the people's influential leaders void of ethical value in the eyes of the civilized peoples of the earth.

Those of us that see clearly the validity of race feeling, yet hold firmly to our heritage of democratic principles, should be sensible enough to oppose sentimental abstract philanthropy in the interest of the people's more deep-seated and ultimately reasonable instincts. At the same time we should brace ourselves firmly against all racial arrogance, brutality, and the cowardly use of the mob spirit to shut off free discussion and maim the influence of high-souled men that love not their people less because they love righteousness more. Nevertheless, after all has been said, we must hold to the dogma: No political equality for the negroes, but as much political privilege as will encourage and develop the civic consciousness of the negroes, help them develop a healthy race feeling, and leave them ground for hope that the white man will ultimately find for the "brother in black" a status freer than that which the subordinate race now occupies, without in any way giving up any of the racial principles that we have been setting forth in this statement of racial orthodoxy.

8. "In matters of civil rights and legal adjustments give the white man the benefit of the doubt; and under no circumstances interfere with the prestige of the white race." When the Supreme Court of the United States

declared the first and second sections of the second Civil
Rights Act unconstitutional the highest law tribunal of
the land showed that it was not racially color-blind, inasmuch as it practically recognized a condition rather
than a theory, no matter what its reasons for such a
decision. So far as tests have been made, the courts
have admitted the contention that the publication of a
newspaper statement that a white man is "colored" constitutes a libel. The ·states have been allowed, in the
exercise of their police power, to promulgate anti-amalgamation laws, thus negativing the merely abstract claim
of any two given individuals of different races osten-
sibly to pursue their individual happiness through the
establishment of the marriage relation.

Whatever, then, the reasoning of the courts may be,
the latent consciousness,—the subconsciousness,—of the
law recognizes the inferior status of the negro race. If
it is a good policy on the part of the state to recognize,
directly or indirectly, the negro's discounted status, it is
also good policy to buttress this conclusion by strength-
ening the prestige of the dominant race in cases where
probability and evidence are *equally balanced*. Where
doubt must be resolved in favor of a child on the one
hand or an adult on the other, law and public opinion
incline in favor of the child; for the law tends to protect
the weak. Where decision must be made in favor of
either a man or a woman the balance is inclined in
favor of the woman, for she is in greater need of protection; and chivalry is one of the characteristics of the
true American. But anything resembling a *racial* triumph for the negro individual is full of peril to the
peace of society.

Should not the negro, however, be protected just because of his weakness? Assuredly, but in a way that

will not endanger white supremacy or the negro's explicit recognition of it.   When an influential white patron attempts to see that justice is done a negro, that negro usually gets fair play.   The white man's sponsorship takes the question out of the category of race relations.   It may become necessary to establish special tribunals or special procedure that will take up cases involving *unfair* discrimination against the negro individual,—the attempt of might to establish itself as right. Nevertheless, when the evidence is approximately *equal* in a given case it appears inevitable that a white man's word should be accepted rather than a negro's, a white man's life protected rather than a negro's, a white man's rights in general respected rather than a negro's.   We must remember that Lincoln, the Liberator, said that in case of conflict he was "for the white man."   This principle in no respect militates against the vigorous prosecution of those who exploit the negro's weakness and ignorance.   The white man's representative pride in his race, however, is a racial and a national asset, and is the prime condition of the peaceful retention of the status of white supremacy.

If the unfortunate bi-racial situation involves something of the flavor of caste privilege, so much the worse for the situation; but, such as it is, we must make the best of it, or change it in some way that will benefit the common weal.   Important as justice is, order without justice is frequently safer for the state and more intrinsically equitable than justice without order.   Protect the negro, but let the guardianship be that of the superior race protecting the inferior, and not that of "the law" deciding the doubt in favor of the unfavored race.   If the machinery of the law can be got to educate the white man to despise the cruel exploiter of a defenseless negro,

it will be well.   Truly this is a consummation devoutly
to be wished.   On the other hand, let all the institutions
of this white man's country ever teach the lowest member of the dominant race that his representative superiority is the concern of all the people.   We cheerfully
admit that a condition wherein "benefit of clergy" must
to some degree be granted to one race rather than to
another is anomalous in view of the highest principles
of democratic institutions.   Curse the situation as much
as you please, O friends of humanity, but recognize the
preëminence of the white race everywhere and at all
times,—and teach the negroes to do so.

9.   "In education let the negro have the crumbs that
fall from the white man's table."   So long as there is
not enough money to educate white children aright, so
long as the dominant race feels unsure of the proximate
and the ultimate effect of educating an inferior race
that should continue to regard itself as inferior, so long
as the rather expensive industrial education evidently
needed by the negroes is also greatly needed among the
whites,—just so long will the ruling race provide *first*
for its own children and *then* for the children of the
alien race that happens to be living in a white man's
land.   It seems highly unfortunate that this must be so.
Education, however, means freedom, and the whites are
bound to give the greater freedom to their own children
who are destined to remain the favored people.   When a
practicable solution of the race problem comes in sight,
and when the requisites of a proper education are provided for white children, then the innate generosity of
the white people, freed from fear of the future and
realizing the pitful need of the black man, will show
itself as the quality of a brave and noble people.

The sensitiveness of the Southern conscience has been

somewhat blunted by the assumption of responsibility for negro education by the Northern friends of the negro. The whites expect the negroes to exert themselves in most self-sacrificing fashion to educate themselves. Believing that the handicap of the negro's presence is sufficiently severe, the Southern people would be more than human if they thought as much of the negro's needs as they do of their own children's. The whites do not fear general negro competition in any department of life; but they do dread the friction that will result from the negro's attempts to show his "equality," and they will never stand for the competitive overcoming of inferior or unfortunate white individuals by "superior" negroes. As a rule, the whites will conquer all along the line; but there is enough friction between capital and labor, enough striving among the classes of society, enough difficulty in having the people get their dues, without adding to our burdens and complicating our problems with a racial coëfficient prefixed to each item of our large economic problems. Hence, for some time at least, the negro will get what educational funds the white man feels he can reasonably spare—and no more. In this day when men are asking the question whether benevolence in general is worth as much as it costs in the long run, it ill becomes critics of the South to ask for "equal educational facilities" for whites and blacks. Let the negro prove some of the splendid qualities attributed to him by his friends by evincing a spirit of self-sacrifice such as the world has never before seen. He will need to do this in order to hold his own attention focused on the situation of his race,—desperate so far as spiritual freedom is concerned.

10. "Let there be such industrial education of the negro as will best fit him to serve the white man." To

say that the negro was "created" to work for the white man is to utter unmitigated nonsense. But the negro must remain a subordinate race so long as he lives in the same territory with the whites; hence he will continue for a long time,—unless complete local segregation shall come about with tremendous rapidity,—to fill the ranks of the simpler manual occupations. He may have his doctors and his lawyers and the like; but they must not be educated to claim professional equality with white practitioners. Professional life has many social associations and implications. If the industrial education of the negro is such as to make him a useful worker without bringing about competitive friction with whites, his industrial education will be a blessing to both races. If the negro continues to "know his place," no matter how much or how well he may be educated, even moderate competition with the whites, when not accompanied with "bumptiousness," may for a time be tolerated by the ruling race.

As long as education makes for freedom, latent if not patent opposition to negro education may be expected from the whites, just as in slavery times. This opposition will disappear as soon as the future of race relations is so forecast that the whites may be freed from the uncertainty of not knowing how soon the negroes will "claim that they are as good as white men." The evident fact that some negro individuals are better in character as measured by any known standard than certain whites in no way invalidates the principle of representativeness of race. Racial equality and individual worth are different things. And the imputation of representative racehood to the inferior white man is a process that cannot be expected to decrease, but rather to grow as the negroes become better educated.

It is a necessity of his position that the negro shall be a "suffering servant"; let us hope that he will be Jehovah's suffering servant as well as the white man's and his own race's.

11. "Only Southerners understand the negro question." But they do not. They undoubtedly understand the negro better than do any other people. They are not always able to state what they know of him, but they somehow manage on the whole to get along with him far better than could have been expected under the circumstances.

Whatever study of the negro question may be made, the Southern white man must be close to the center of it, in order that his experience, his intuition, his temperamental fitness to deal with the negro may be utilized in the interest of the interpretation of negro character and of race relations. For the Southern white man, however, to "go it alone" in the study of any human question would be simply preposterous. On the other hand, for technical scientific methods to expect to appreciate the *nuances* of racial and social relations of a peculiar kind is equally absurd. When Southerners are scientifically prepared and are free from more than a saving amount of provincialism, then they are doubtless the best fitted of all men to study the race problem. But the South is not as yet overstocked with such persons.

12. "Let the South settle the negro question." Yes, if the South can, and will, settle it in accordance with democratic and Christian principles. No human question can be regarded as permanently settled when one people remains subordinate to another simply on account of racial differences. Under present conditions the South's "solution" will vary with locality, percentage

of negro population, and so on. These local solutions are the very best under the circumstances, but a complacent satisfaction in them as permanent arrangements contradicts the humanitarian principles of civilization, and will sooner or later prove to be inimical not only to the world, the nation, the South, and the states concerned, but also most directly to the localities themselves. Nevertheless, whatever the "solution" shall be, it must take into account specifically the needs of particular localities and the mental attitude of the people concerned, both white and colored.

The South did not and could not settle the slavery question; it did not and could not settle the question of reconstruction. The actual method of emancipating the slaves was wasteful and injurious, and the coercive measures of reconstruction have in large measure proved themselves to be failures; but so long as the prevailing opinion in the South is in favor of reaching a settlement based upon the stigmatized subordination of all negroes for all time, the conscience of mankind will not approve. And surely the South has learned that no matter how honest it may be in its opinion it cannot expect to have its own way unless the enlightened sentiment of mankind is favorable thereto. The South is too close to the race problem to be competent to solve it aright; the rest of the world is too far away; the South, with the aid of the rest of the country and with the assistance of the best thought in the world, should take the leading part in the solution of the race question, provided the Southern people pronounce in favor of ultimately giving the negroes every opportunity of development of which they prove themselves capable. And nothing but experiment under favorable conditions can demonstrate what any given people can make of themselves. But as long as the two races live together under conditions substantially as at present, the negroes will remain a subordinate people.

13. "The status of peasantry is all the negro may hope for if the races are to live together in peace." Under present conditions, and admitting the continued subordination of the negro race so long as the two races live together, it would appear that some sort of caste civilization is necessary, wherein the lower race may develop its own individuals to the highest possible extent, but must rest content with a lower social, civic, and political status as compared with that of the ruling race. A sort of parallel bi-racial civilization, with a broad and rigid anti-racial caste line, may prove feasible. All historical analogy and the traits of the Southern white man, however, are against such a supposition. That the common opinion of the South, even of many of its highest representatives, should favor a "peasantry" solution is a clear indication that the South, unless prevailed upon to study the race problem in the light of the world of conscience, will make no attempt to solve a problem that it has already solved in its own mind, and is now trying to solve in practice by increasing the grip of the dominant race and fastening the stigma of inferiority on all negroes without regard to individual worth. Though this present racial discrimination is the best present arrangement,—especially when it is tempered, as it is almost everywhere, by the generous Christian attitude of a white minority and by the general good will of the masses of the people toward "negroes that know their place,"—the American people must radically revise their basal political principles and stultify their vaunted Christian faith if they rest content with the present arrangement, however necessary it may be

now and for the immediate future. If the results of investigation indicate that the present condition is a necessary evil, then all we can do is to temper the wind to the shorn lamb as much as we may without endangering complete white supremacy and ascendancy.

14. "Let the lowest white man count for more than the highest negro." If the statement "Let the lowest white man count for more than the highest negro" be a statement of race status under present conditions, it may be allowed to stand because of the principle of the representativeness of race as we have enunciated it; but if it means a final judgment of character value, and pretends to rank worth of soul and body simply in accordance with the accidents of race, it is pernicious moral heresy. If Jesus meant anything when he said that the harlots and sinners might go into the Kingdom of Heaven before the righteous, no human authority has the right to rank human souls at all, and least of all by superficial standards. To establish a caste of the kind in the interests of peace, race purity, and the public weal is one thing; to act as an arbitrary human providence in deciding on the personal worth of individuals according to racial characteristics is another, and a most inane proposition. But those who make the absolute statement regarding the worth of individuals do not mean what they seem to say. They all would practically admit the splendid worth of certain negro individuals if these individuals were living somewhere else than in America. The statement, then, is true of racial representativeness under the conditions of geographical racial contact, but is true in no other sense.

15. "The above statements indicate the leadings of Providence." The advocates of slavery said that the peculiar institution was the result of the "leadings of

Providence." Even so,—and so was the emancipation of the negro. In a sense it is always true that "whatever is is right." But we do not see the end wherein the full rightness doth appear. Even if we did, the end would not justify the means, except on the principle of self-preservation in the choice of the least of several evils. Let those who claim to read the Divine Mind at least have the goodness to show their credentials and admit science and the highest human morality to the counsels of the guild of latter-day prophets and interpreters of the Most High.

III

In our statement of what we have tried to put forth as an honest view of race orthodoxy in the South, as opposed to, but involving the truth of, a mere race common opinion, we may have unwittingly indulged in special pleading and other forms of unconscious disingenuousness; if so, our challenging statements may at least have the office of inviting a criticism as honest in intention as our statement has been. The trouble with most of us in this discussion of the race question is not our lack of fairness, frankness, candor, and ingenuousness, but our lack of "the incessant prevalence of detective discussion" of the scientific order. There has been little straight thinking on the subject. The emotionalists are of course cloudy; and the men of science are in many cases too disdainful of emotion to interpret its values. Psychological amateurism has been almost as common among men of science as among the general run of disputants; for the man who fails to see the overshadowing importance of race feeling, and who would settle the human problems without regard to the psychological and ethical interpretation of human prejudices, has missed the very essence of the problem; and his "scientific views" deserve as little consideration, so far as "solutions" go, as do the antagonistic or the benevolent vaporings of the emotionalist, or the deadly dull "common sense" of the merely "practical" man.

IV

Have we failed to learn the lesson of the slavery controversy and the Civil War and the evils of reconstruction? Shall we hide our heads in the sands of "compromise"? Shall we drift, drift, drift,—waiting on Providence, Who helps those who help themselves?

Whatever the answer to these questions, unless some one or ones can convince the South that her racial creed is unworthy and unpractical, she can be counted on to hold fast to it,—at least in its more conservative form, —with the consent, and with more and more of the active aid, of the masses of the white people throughout this country. If a division must come, the whites will assuredly stand together. The cleavage is now not between North and South, but between race and race. North and South are still somewhat apart on account of the inertia of the past; but the time is close at hand when the people of the whole country will either show the South a better racial creed (and I doubt their ability or their willingness to do so) or will adopt for themselves the creed of the South. Even now the solid Far West is joining hands with the South in racial matters; and the end is not yet in the growing solidarity of the white people of this country.

Shall the negro, therefore, be deserted or simply exploited by the whites? Not so! Very soon, let us hope, the common sense and the conscience of the country will be roused sufficiently to have this problem at least worked on systematically, seriously, in the fear of God, and in the love of man.

B. Reviews of Typical Views.

I. PHILOSOPHICAL

*Edgar Gardner Murphy: The Basis of Ascendancy
New York, 1909

Mr. Murphy is one of the choicest specimens of noble character that the South has produced. With love for his native section and appreciation of its excellencies, its difficult problems, and its brave attempts to meet them, he unites in his character sweet-spirited Christianity, broad humanitarianism and loyal national patriotism. He is in many ways a model for our young men and an inspiration to us all. He has scholarship, common sense, industry, keen powers of observation, a sense of humor, distinction of literary style, philosophic grasp, and many another attribute deserving of universal praise and admiration. His former book, "The Present South," received praise not a little from qualified men North and South. His work with the education boards and conferences merits the gratitude of our whole people. His pathetic struggle to help work out our Southern problems, in spite of his continued bad health, deserves and receives our warm sympathy. Hence it would seem that a critical but friendly commentary on certain phases of his recent book ought to have some value, if such work is done in the right spirit. The present writer hopes that he has that spirit, inasmuch as his temperament makes him warmly sympa-

*Review originally written for a distinguished Northern investigator.

116

thetic with Mr. Murphy, his experience has been national as well as Southern, and his political and ethical and religious principles are in substantial accord with our author.

The book exhibits a more or less conscious struggle between Northern and Southern points of view at their best.   Mr. Murphy realizes the validity of Southern race feeling in its broader and deeper aspects and Northern humanitarianism in its more rational forms.   He feels that the average Southerner is as much a humanitarian at heart as his Northern brother, and that the typical Northerner has at bottom as much race consciousness as the Southerner.   On the Southern side he sees the danger of even our best men's acquiescing in the idea of benevolent exploitation of the negro people; and he realizes the danger that is lurking in certain forms of Northern long-distance ultra-altruism.   He tries to hold the balance evenly in this book.   But, whether consciously or unconsciously, the first part of his book seems to be, in the main, pro-Southern and defensive of the South, while the latter part becomes largely pro-Northern and critical of the South.   Nor does he succeed in making a synthesis of the two points of view.

When speaking of the situation as it is and of the importance of race consciousness he seems to be almost a Southern partisan; but, when he comes to deal with the solution of the race question and the method of bringing it about, he apparently loses sight of the clear *implications* of race consciousness and race contact.   This criticism will, I think, appear justified in the course of the commentary on the book.   I emphasize this point at the outset because Mr. Murphy's ideals and reasoning are very attractive to the better spirits North and South and everywhere else.   In other words, to resume, Mr.

Murphy understands the ethics of the situation better than its psychology, the spiritual man better than the natural man, the ideal better than the actual. But surely it is of utmost importance in a vitally practical matter to "draw the thing" *as it is* "for the God of Things as they are." What ought to be can, in this matter, only be reached *through what is*. Doubtless Mr. Murphy would reply, I am drawing the thing as *I* see it; if so, my contention is that Mr. Murphy does not see it as it is. Vividly appreciating the tremendous importance and value of race feeling, he does not see its inner significance. There is no open way between his psychology and his ethics. Occasionally he drops a word that indicates a rather scornful attitude toward certain crude forms of race psychology, and this attitude careful men ought to share; but popular ethnic psychology, so called, is a very different thing from what our author himself calls the "moral psychology of the situation." Indeed, the whole race problem is found in the psychology of the white man's mind and not in the psychology of racial possibilities. Granted that the negro may attain unto a high degree of culture and strength of character, such a result will but deepen the problem if the white man declines to associate with the negro in any way that involves social contact—and all contact in civil life is at bottom social or closely connected with sociality.

Mr. Murphy seems to think that race consciousness can be evolved into something higher and finer. Perhaps; but we must know certainly that such a refining is possible, how it is to be brought about, and whether there are signs of such development in existence now. Useless and dangerous is it to advocate mere possibilities, which, as Hegel says, are really "nothing," in the face of actualities working the other way! Granting

that the negro ought to have a full and free development,
we are by no means sure that such development can
occur in the presence of the white race.   Nor is it by
any means a feasible assumption to claim that the white
man will or even ought to be willing that the South
should hold on to the negro in spite of Mr. Murphy's
admission that the negro's presence will render the South
economically less effective than other parts of the Union.
As a rule, economic inferiority carries with it some other
infirmities.   Character is "one body"; nationality is organic and biologically based.

But we are delaying the detailed treatment that will
make the above statements clear.   Be it noted, before
beginning our commentary, that the words Southern and
Northern are meant to stand for what is best in both
sections and that this best is largely common to North
and South, but that the sections cannot possibly, at
present, see the problem from the same angle, on account of differences of position and contact.

THE SOUTHERN VIEW AND TRADITION AS TO THE RACIAL SITUATION

1. *Its Uniqueness.*   "Has the South a field of experience peculiarly her own?" P. 217. . . . "The sympathy which the world has given, and has rightly given,
to the negro of these Southern states should not be permitted to obscure the situation of the stronger race."
121. . . . "No man can fully understand such a situation except the man who has been reared right in it." 39.
. . . "If the South had sinned against freedom in the
name of property, the North was now (during reconstruction) sinning against freedom in the name of government." 177.

Comment. The "uniqueness" is not simply a matter of history, geography, economics and the like, but essentially one of biology, psychology and social ethics and esthetics. Even the man reared "right in it"— "raised right in it," the average Southerner would say— is by no means qualified to understand it; but he has an immense advantage over those who live away from the Southern situation, when we ask ourselves what that situation means to human instinct. However, the Southerner's uncritical "raising" may be as destructive to the truth of his views as the Northerner's lack of vital experience in regard to Southern affairs.

Neither humanitarian generalities nor Southern "instinct" can tell us the whole truth, nor can both of these together; but, whatever the truth may be, the stronger race is the stronger factor and deserves the first consideration, the first place and the greater sympathy. And this on the principle of the higher utilitarianism as well as on the principle of the blood kin and race sympathy. More than this: the highest system of morality that the world has ever seen—Christian ethics—does not forget the biological basis of administrative and developmental ethics. For it says, and its saying is a law of nature, "To the Jew *first,* and *also* to the Greek."

Therefore, I should say that the psychology of the Southern white man's mind is the first thing of all to be considered in order that the first factor in causation, and the first factor in the solution, and the first factor in the final worths of civilization's resultants may be properly understood and evaluated. Such a study, of course, does not stand by itself, but is closely linked with the psychology of the negro's mind, with the psychology of historical causes, with the psychological results of environment—*à la mode* Buckle. But Mr. Murphy's modest insistence that the white man's side must not be "obscured" is putting the thing rather mildly. To the average man this is like saying: In considering the caretaking of flocks of sheep and goats, care must be taken not to let the sheep suffer too much from the lack of food! I do not say that Murphy means it that way, but I do think that his words would ordinarily be so interpreted in the South. After all, we are obliged to apply to this situation the words of Jesus addressed to the Syro-Phœnician woman. We dare not throw the children's bread to the dogs! And we ought not to let the crumbs that fall from the white man's tables be too scanty. If we can play the part or *a* part of Providence and prepare a table in the wilderness for the children of Ham, *that* may be better than feeding them on crumbs. We do not know what is best: let's study and find out!

We are *now* in danger of sinning against freedom in the name of both property and government. In order not to "interfere with property values" by disturbing the labor market—even twenty-five years hence and as a bare possibility—by talking about negro colonization, we run the risk of insisting that white planters at the South and white investors at the North must wax fat at the expense of Southern manhood and democracy and Christianity. And in the name of "government" we are in danger of asking that a system of race caste must be substituted for democracy, because "the safety of our institutions" demands it! I am here emphasizing Mr. Murphy's rebuke of the reconstruction policy; and at the same time pointing out a greater spiritual danger which Mr. Murphy does not deal with. On the other hand, I cannot agree with the song in another key in which Mr. Murphy seems to join: "When the negro race becomes strong enough it shall vote, for every

qualified citizen should vote!" This last is a chant of
the idealists who forget that the spiritual man cannot
come, and, if thrust forward, cannot thrive, except on
the firm basis of the normal "natural man," all of
whose equalities are offshoots of immanent social equality and the intermarriage that is its vital basis. The
caste of the kin is the last stand of "liberty enlightening
the world." [Even if we admit Mr. Murphy's contention
that "every qualified citizen should vote," it does not follow that the possession of education or money will "qual-
ify" a non-assimilable people.]

II. *Race Consciousness.* "The deepest thing about
any man—next to his humanity itself—is his race." 79.
Mr. Murphy tells us that Professor Giddings is right
in his assertion that "it is about the consciousness of
kind, as a principle, that all other motives organize themselves in the evolution of social choice, social volition,
or social policy." xix. And he also expresses the hope
that the South will never "minimize the significance of
race." xvi.

Comment. No Southerner could hope to have his
views on race consciousness expressed more forcibly than
Mr. Murphy here puts them. But what do his statements necessarily *imply?* I should say that he means,
that he *must* mean, if he means anything real and definite, that our humanity manifests itself in time and
space and motion in and through and with the "consciousness of kind," which is itself at bottom based on
biological kinship. We cannot afford to "minimize"
kinship as the prime material of all social structure, as
the prime motive of all social function. The natural
man is a racial man, who must reach spiritual development in and through and with the perennial sense of
kinship and the dependence of all social phenomena—

civic, political, economic, religious, esthetic, moral—upon
the sense of social solidarity biologically derived.   In
other words, we had better not forget the etymological
signification of the word *nation*.   Let us follow out a
common dictionary definition.   "A nation is an aggre-
gate of persons belonging to the same ethnological family, and speaking the same language."   Let us suppose
this meaning to be secondary and try another: "A
people inhabiting a certain district and united together
by common political institutions."   Here, obviously, we
need to find out what the word *people* means, though at
a glance we note the significance of the words, "united
together" (not discordant and jarring by nature).   Well,
a people is "the body (not bodies) of persons composing
(not discomposing!) a nation, community, tribe, or
race."   Eliminate the words nation, tribe and race, for
obvious reasons.   What is a "community"?   "The members of a body politic having equal rights and privileges,
civil and political, and united by common interests."
These definitions, taken from English sources, hint
pretty plainly at our chief difficulty in this negro problem.   We cannot frame a definition that does not imply
in some way equal rights and privileges and common
interests.   And, when conditions exist that keep these
equal rights and privileges in abeyance, we naturally fall
back on the rest of the definition of a community, "common interests."   *Interest* is "advantage, good, profit,
concern, utility; share, portion, participation in value."
Common is "general," which means either pertaining
to a *genus*, or *wide*, without narrow limitations.   Can
the secondary meaning, "wide" exist healthily without
the primary meaning, "pertaining to the same race"?
That is a most pertinent question, and not to be answered offhand.   I think we may safely assume that it

will be hard to get any "generality"—leaving aside glittering varieties—that has not a biologically generic tang to it. And when we find contrasting psychological-social "genera," or races widely differing in physical, mental and moral traits, and feeling no kinship with one another; and when we know, furthermore, that the one race esteems itself the "Chosen People" as compared with the other; and when the interests of the two races do *not* seem to fit in with one another unless one serves the other; and when we note that even in family life one person must be legally superior for the sake of security and authority; and when we see the "races" growing apart instead of together; and when the dominant race is bent on depriving the weaker race of all the distinctive marks of community and "generality," imputing to it fitness only for segregation or subordinated service—I say, when we find these things, dare we deny the native association between birth and nationality, and do we continue hoping to get a "community" out of a "natural" (birthly) *dis*-unity? Perhaps so, but surely not certainly so. The burden of proof is on those who hope to transform the natural man in such wise that he will substitute *contract* for *status* in race matters—a thing he never has done without intermarriage or the admission of substantial equality of races. Are we to assume that whereas we cannot get oil and water to mix we may nevertheless coax the oil to allow just a few *very* little drops of water to float with the oil on *top* without actually mixing with it? These questions, surely, cannot be answered dogmatically. If they can, is it not more scientific and historical and natural to answer them in the way the ordinary Southerner does? If his answer is wrong, show the wrongness to him in such a plain way that his common sense and his con-

science *must* approve if he is an honest man.   Now, I
think that the average white Southerner is honest.   And
I believe that these honest men generally control all that
can be controlled at the South.   Nor do I believe that
this last statement will be contradicted by any person
whose opinion is worth having—at least on this subject.

I can hardly believe that Mr. Murphy realizes the
implications of his strong statement about the ultimate-
ness and finality of race differences.   At any rate, if he
does appreciate fully these things, may it not be that he
overlooks to some extent the inevitable sociality that
is involved in equal civil and political rights?   The man
who will not sit with a negro in a hotel will not long be
willing to sit with him in a street car; the man who will
not sit with him in a street car will not long sit with
him on the jury bench.   If the negro's presence is unpleasant behind the counter of a department store, it
will soon become offensive in a post office.   How can
students of social nature overlook the simplest facts of
psychology, the law of association and the law of imitation?   Besides, can one draw a line in water and expect
it to remain fixed?   Can one actually tell us where social
communion ends and civic relations begin?   Can human
contact healthily exist on the compartment principle?
Does not a democracy believe that any child may live
to be president or to marry the president's daughter?
And can you strike out the natural, the vital, the poig-
nantly interesting, the eternally *human* aspects of democracy and leave anything else but a stupid lot of
paper "rights and privileges"?   Let believers in the
equalities *minus* their soul of social equality listen to
James Bryce, quoted by Mr. Murphy himself on p. 334
of his "Present South": "The social relations of two
races which cannot be fused raise problems even more

difficult (than the suffrage, etc.) because incapable of being regulated by law. Law may attempt to secure equal admission to public conveyances or public entertainments. But the look of scorn, the casual blow, the brutal oath thrown at one who dares not resent it—these are injuries that cannot be prevented where the sentiment of the dominant race allows them. Impunity corrupts the ordinary man; and even the better sort suffer from the consciousness of their own superiority, not merely in rank, but also in strength and volition. One must have lived among a weaker race in order to realize the kind of irritation which its defects produce in those who deal with it, and how temper and self-control are strained in resisting temptations to harsh or arbitrary action. It needs something more than the virtue of a philosopher—it needs the tenderness of a saint— to preserve the same courtesy and respect toward the members of a backward race as are naturally extended to equals."

III. *Negro Inferiority.* "Those with the capacity to govern will govern." 8. The negro's rights were "won for him, not by him." 9. Disfranchisement "bore in its origin only the slightest animus against the negro or his fortunes." 26. "Aggressive antipathies" have partly a "defensive basis" due to habits induced by Reconstruction and to fear of "a general encroachment upon the white man's 'blood.'" 123.

Comment. If those with the ability and capacity to govern *will* govern, and if the white folk are therefore the ones to govern, will they not govern primarily in the interests of their own people, the whites? Believing that the negroes are inferior people; that the individual negro cannot escape the fate of his race because of unusual qualities; that every negro *represents* his

race as such whether he wants to or not, because racial
lines as such are drawn and cannot be escaped; believing
with Mr. Murphy that rights won *for* a race instead of
by that race are really "rights" imposed by external and
perhaps hostile authority—is it surprising that the whites
should idealize every white man and discount every
negro? Is it surprising that the "democratizing of the
South" so well described on pp. 16 ff. of Mr. Murphy's
"Present South" should result in a strong belief that
the negro is not really a vital element of citizenship, and
therefore ought not to have the suffrage because he
cannot win a status that will show "sufficient evidence
of permanent common interest with, and attachment to,
the community"? (Virginia Declaration of Rights,
1776.) If "law is an expression of the will of the community . . . and civil distinctions can be founded . . .
only on public utility" (French National Assembly,
1789), is it not inevitable that the whites should regard
the negroes as bogus citizens and come to believe that the
real community would be injured, that "public utility"
would be outraged, if aliens, doomed to remain alien
biologically, were allowed to treat themselves as citizens
in a land where every contact of citizenship is closely
associated with social contact?

"As with the idea of equality in ethics and in religion,
equality before the law means the membership of a great
whole" (Ritchie: "Natural Rights," p. 255). If the
white man cannot get himself to look at the negro race
except as a race, and if he cannot regard negroes as
part of the "great whole" of the community, but as
aliens residing here on sufferance and because no one
knows what to do with them, what process of development will bring the white man to give the negro the
suffrage voluntarily? This point will come up farther

on, but it ought to be noted here, because of its connection with the apparent belief of Southern whites—a
belief too deep and instinctive for articulate expression
on the part of the average man—that *all the equalities
of actual life are based on actual or potential social
equality, and social equality in turn on biological kinship.* Cry "alas! that it should be so," if you will, but
the fact remains that *kindness* is *primarily kin-ness,* and
that a man sometimes cannot "love his neighbor as himself," unless he can manage to keep his neighbor on
the other side of the fence. The Jesus who told the
parable of the good Samaritan was also the Jesus who
explained to the Samaritan woman that the Jews had
no dealings with the Samaritans, and who soon Himself
departed from the country. Daily, hourly do Southern
white men show forth the qualities of the Good Samaritan. But the kindness shown is that of the *representative* of a superior race to a *representative* of an inferior
race. And the representative binds the race. Forced
and unnatural and ultra-altruistic morality of the "social
catholicity" order may have as deadly results as those
high-flown "affinities" that lead to adultery.

Conservative Southern whites have been brought up
on the Bible with its history of the Chosen People's sad
fate when they, supposedly, disobeyed God and let the
wives and children of the Canaanites stay *alive.* They
instinctively believe in the God of Battles and Vengeance, and in the God of Social Selection and Survival of
the Kin. They feel the subtile meaning of the social
solidarity of all *real* citizenship. To them the family
is very sacred as a condition of status out of which all
social contacts arise and in the form of which all civic
relations are seen. They vote for men as incarnations
of principles; they hold to principles largely because of

the men who have promulgated the principles and the
impressive and noble way in which these leaders have
taught the common folk who heard them gladly.   This
is idealizing?   Yes, that is one of the troubles—and one
of the permanent factors—not altogether to be frowned
upon by idealizers of present-day "national" leaders.
Carlyle may have failed in his task of teaching us the
overwhelming importance of hero-worship, but the way-
faring man may see if he will the vitality of the South's
belief in personality, kinship, family and blood.

Is the South wrong?   Is there any danger to "blood"
from inter-racial communion?   Is there any danger of
"social equality" from the practice of "political equality"?   Is the South believing in something unreal and
unpsychological when she practices the belief that all
forms of equality come at last to blood kinship actual
or possible?   Perhaps so.   But many an investigator in
other parts of the world than the South will warn us
not to deny the South's claim without careful study.
"Show us the futility of our over-great protective instinct; show us the unreason of our fears; show us what
will take the place of race-prejudice run out of a simple
man's mind; prove to us the sovereign power of high-
toned esthetic morality in preventing the mixture of the
races—show us some of these things," say the Southerners, "and we shall try to put our bogie fears to sleep."

IV. *Racial Contacts.* "The ultimate basis of intimate social affiliation is not individual (as is so frequently asserted), but social." 80. "The profoundest
need of every educated life is for another educated life.
The deepened instinct, the educative impulse, is assimilative, accumulative, social. It demands and creates an
environment." 99. "The individual man, in the world,
may escape almost every calamity or deliverance except

that which comes in the form of other men." 156 (cp. 136). "The stronger race must live, must find and equip and free itself, must rear its children—thronged, environed, influenced, profoundly determined by the weaker race" (cp. 241) 156. "There is nothing more perilous to the moral standard or social feeling than the presence of a large and distinctive class of a closely related population too ignorant and too weak to protect itself. It is easy to say that the case of such a population should appeal to the chivalry of the strong. And so it should. And so it does." 123. "The stronger becomes habituated to the conception of itself as identical with the state." 133.

Comment. Take the quotations of this section in connection with the extracts and comments of previous sections, and it will be seen how close is the connection between all acts of sociality among individuals and the races they represent. We shall also have to admit that the "educative impulse" tends to pull down barriers. The gentleman is welcome the world over, or tends to be, no matter what his nationality. Intrinsic nobility of soul distracts attention from color of skin. Now, reduce race prejudice, so called, to the minimum, and allow race contact to continue, is it not inevitable that the "assimilative" action of education will tend to break down barriers of blood? So say many Southerners. They seem to think that contact begets either coöperation or competition (race competition). They believe that coöperation is at bottom based on potential sociality. The festive board is usually an incident of all coöperative efforts, whether religious, philanthropic, political, esthetic, scientific or commercial. Desiring neither coöperation—except in a very external and therefore non-vital way—nor competition, which is likely to be decidedly anti-social, these Southerners naturally enough feel uncertain about giving the negroes an education that will make them the "equals" of the whites, or, worse still, make them *think* themselves equals when they are not.   But I must not elaborate, for this is not primarily a study of the negro question, but a study of Mr. Murphy's views of it.

V.   *Race Psychology.*   On p. 191 and elsewhere in the book Mr. Murphy hints at the importance of the "moral psychology" of the Southern situation.   Remembering this, note the implications of the following two quotations: (1) "We are not bound to assume equalities that do not exist, but we cannot arbitrarily fix the status of inequality from without." 197.   (2) "No true freedom can retard our freedom.   Every liberated capacity must contribute both its capacity and its liberty to ours."

Comment.   "Moral psychology" will help us to find out what equalities are natural and effective and safe and useful.   And it will show us that not every "liberated capacity" is really liberated.   "What will he do with it?"   How will it affect the other race?   How much revolution will it breed?   These are some of the questions brought out by a practical psychology of peoples.   True it is that liberated capacities of *our kind of folk,* folk with whom we can, sooner or later, associate on a basis of social and biological equality, will really enhance our freedom.   But how can there be *normal* liberated capacities in a race occupying an inferior social status and with no hope of raising it to terms of equality with a superior race?   Idealism cannot dare to dispense with biological and psychological reality.   The natural man must precede and condition the spiritual man.

VI.   *Existing Tendencies.*   On p. 32 our author makes

the usual statement that, if it is hard to convict a white man of murdering a negro, it will be hard to convict a white man of murdering one of his own color. In Mississippi, South Carolina and other Southern states there are clear indications of a growing regard for the lives of white men: for instance, notice the conviction of Smith, a wealthy man of Lowndes County, Mississippi, despite a decidedly good showing of insanity by the defendant. Note also the conviction of the Coopers in Tennessee for the killing of Senator Carmack. The tendency Mr. Murphy speaks of probably exists, but with the growing solidarity of the whites and the growing antagonism between the races, it is not impossible that the whites will evolve a high system of racial justice and morality that shall not apply at all closely to the negroes. There are examples in Greece and Rome of that sort of thing. At any rate, may not Mr. Murphy be assuming tendencies without sufficient regard to *all* the facts?*

On p. 105 our author assumes that the negroes are following their leaders better than they used to. This statement is by no means self-evidently true to the ordinary observer. There is a conspicuous loss of negro leadership in politics; negro leaders frequently show a good deal of jealousy of one another: the attitude of very many negroes with reference to Booker Washington is still uncertain. But I am not trying to disprove Mr. Murphy's statement. I only want to register a warning against accepting his opinion too readily.

*Of course I agree most heartily with Mr. Murphy in his high regard for the sacredness of every human life; but I am not prepared to argue that disregard of negro rights will inevitably lead to depreciation of the white men's rights. Logically, it ought; actually, it may not.

P. 188. "The South is at home within the land."—I
wish this *could* be assumed; but I should have to say
that the statement should be put thus: "The South is
as much at home within the land as could be expected
under existing circumstances, and as much so as any
other people would be under the same circumstances."

On p. 221 Mr. Murphy contends that democracy is
enforcing equality of rights everywhere. I wish he
would give instances. True, the *classes* are being compelled to free the *masses* in all homogeneous *nations*.
But we are holding Filipinos and Porto Ricans with a
pretty close rein, and tightening the reins on the latter.
"Might till right is ready" still seems to be good policy.
In South Africa the mother country is about to let the
white colonists manage the natives as seems best to the
dominant race. Democracy is gaining among *uniracial*
peoples, and showing a tendency to gain among people
who are overwhelmingly in the majority as compared
with their conquerers, and at the same time show some
capacity for self-government that will not seriously interfere with the weal of the dominant race (India).
Even in these last cases, we cannot argue as if they were
similar to the Southern problem, where the whites are
the "nation."

P. 228. Mr. Murphy holds that the disfranchisement
of all negroes is not the prevailing tendency.—How
about Mississippi and South Carolina, for example?
And in Mr. Murphy's own state of Alabama, does he
find that the common people, who settle "tendencies,"
want *any* negroes to vote?

On p. 231 we are told that the dilemma is this: Development or repression? Many of us put it thus:
Development somewhere else or a certain degree of
necessary repression here? Nowhere does it seem to

enter Mr. Murphy's mind that his rather contemptuous dismissal of all schemes of negro colonization is possibly a form of closing the door of hope in the negro's face.

VII. *Data Wanted.* On p. 61 we are told that the morality of the negro women has moved forward. This is probably true, if what is meant is this: there are more virtuous negro women in proportion to the population than there were twenty-five years ago. Very many Southerners do not believe this last statement; could they be convinced of its truth by an impartial investigation of conditions, the cause of the negro would be helped in the South. Many claim that prostitution has increased more than concubinage has decreased.

P. 64 note. We are warned against accepting census inferences to the effect that negroes are going out of the higher grade of manual arts. Mr. Murphy thinks that many, for example, who leave barber shops go to carpenter benches, etc. Then there ought to be more carpenters. The figures ought to show correlative compensation. Perhaps they do. It would be interesting to have, say, one hundred cases of the kind mentioned by our author. But the statement itself will be warmly questioned if it is to be put forward as a generalization.

P. 97. Blending with whites not so common.—Here again the facts are hard to gather and the interpretation very doubtful. Blending may be going on at a greater rate in the North, where people are less apt to detect negro blood in light mulattoes. It *is* true, without question, that dislike of negro blood is stronger than it used to be and that the whites are more careful in their observations of race mixture.

P. 97. The power of the negro race to "hold its own" is increasing.—Now this is one of the very points at issue, and one of the hardest to decide about. Is it wise to make such statements without giving the proof or pointing out the data?

V. *Doubtful Interpretation of Doubtful Facts.* (1) We ought all to admire the glow of Mr. Murphy's moral indignation. The present writer, for one, believes that the South is morally cursed on account of the presence of this negro problem. But we gain nothing by making doubtful statements about conditions and giving doubtful interpretations about these "facts." If the following statement were improperly used throughout the South it would do Mr. Murphy's cause a great deal of harm: "He" (the man accused of being "silly about the negro") "is struggling to save the ballot from degradation, the courts from paralysis, the schools from the touch of an ignorant and benumbing controversy, our industries from the destitution of crude warfare or depleting irritations, the law from injustices which will blight the wholesome progress of every class among us, our society itself from the reproach that its rights are partial and that its efficiencies, so far as they may be founded upon its evasions, are based upon the sands. If to fight against these things is to fight for the negro, then there are some of us who wish it to be known that we are fighting for the negro." 34 f.

Comment. Most Southerners would reply, and with much truth: The ballot is purer than it has ever been since the war, but is, of course, "degraded" in the estimation of people whom we won't allow to vote, because we believe that they can never be *real citizens;* the courts are *not* paralyzed, but becoming more efficient, and especially because negroes don't sit on juries—even negroes get better justice than they used to, though it is true that negroes will be discriminated against so far as they seem to endanger white supremacy or the interests of the whites as a race; the schools—for the whites—are very far from being in a "benumbed" condition, and white children are being brought to the schools without using compulsory law; our industries, our laws and other things of our civilization are rapidly developing. Yes, fighting against negro political disability *is* fighting "for the negro," and such fighting will be resented by the average Southerner. True, the better men of the South are sorry that the negroes must be discriminated against and deprecate *all* failure of justice in the courts. And the higher classes contain not a few men who believe such discrimination to be dangerous to morals and the whole spiritual life. But, says the average man, we are in an abnormal condition and must choose between evils. Convince us in a careful, scientific, not dogmatic way that the methods we have chosen are not conducive to *our* higher welfare, and we'll try to get better methods. *But don't tell us to help the negroes develop at our expense.* We are willing to develop him so that he will remain in the place we put him. If you leave him here we are going to be his Providence and do the best we can for him without endangering ourselves. And, in our judgment, we shall be endangering ourselves if we teach the negro that any one of his race, however highly developed, is a citizen in the sense that a native-born white man is, or a white foreigner whose children may at length be able to intermarry with our children. This plea of the Southerner may not be valid; but it has a closer relation to things as they are and as they are bound to be than the implications of the last quoted words of Mr. Murphy. Who is to judge between these divergent views of fact and interpretation? I should say, neither combatant, but those who have investigated

the phenomena in the dry light of science.   And who
are they?

(2) P. 89.   Mr. Murphy thinks that race sensitiveness
has increased because of the following factors: 1, community of interest; 2, community of suffering; 3, prejudice from without.—Perhaps so, but has he forgotten
what he said about "consciousness of kind"?   Is not *that*
becoming *spontaneously* more acute and more self-conscious?   And is not race consciousness—pan-teutonism,
pan-slavism and the like—growing the world over?   Do
not Caucasians talk about a "yellow peril"?   Does not
the world think far more of race differences than it did
when the French revolutionists were exhorting about the
"rights of man"?   A philosopher may not be blamed for
evolving a set of causes from his reflection upon *his*
ordinary experience; but what the situation needs is facts
scientifically gathered and scientifically interpreted.

(3)   "The South, in her soul, has no dream, nor notion, nor imagination, except of a democratic state." 187.
—Right, provided "democratic" means *white* democratic.

(4) On pp. 188-9 Mr. Murphy tells us about the *ingratitude* of the weaker race and the *brutality* of the
stronger.   Does he mean to imply that the weaker race
is ungrateful because it *is* weaker, and the stronger "brutal" because it *is* stronger?   May not the "ingratitude"
be negroid and not really what the white man means by
"ingratitude"; may not what he calls the "brutality" of
the whites be something very different, and may not
real "brutality" among the whites be so rare as to be
entirely untypical?   These questions are not asked in a
captious spirit, but because I, for one, need light on these
matters.

(5) On p. 238 our author has a passage, too long to

quote, about the sinister "education" the negro gets in
regard to his race from newspaper disparagement, popular unfairness and the like.   Now all this is due to the
radical belief in the negro's inferiority—all admit this.
And what we regard as inferior we finally come to dislike, as James Bryce so well pointed out in the words of
his quoted above. Will not the "solution" of the problem have to take this into account, and can we cure
esthetic and moral dislike by pointing out the fact that
it "hurts" the negro?   The saints are too few and the
sinners too many, and the handicap against increasing
the ranks of the saints is too much for the poor "natural
man" who may have aspirations in this direction.   The
negro is *persona non grata,* and thus he will remain to
the end of time: so says the Southern white man. Can
one say offhand that he is wrong?

IX.   *Dogmas.*   (1) In his preface (xvii) Mr. Murphy contrasts "spurious catholicity of race" with the belittling or denying of "individuality" in other races.—
Well, says the Southerner, that belittling and denying
will inevitably go on till the millennium *unless* we adopt
the opposing dogma of race catholicity in the only sense
of the word catholicity that has any hope for the lower
race—equal social recognition.

(2) P. 16 f.   Education by the ballot vs. public security.—Mr. Murphy believes that public security ought
not to be sacrificed to "education by the ballot" when it
is negroes that have to be so educated. But will the time
ever come when the whites are willing to call the negroes
real citizens?   They have never wanted to disenfran-
chise ignorant white men; will they ever want to welcome
the use of the ballot on the part of intelligent negroes in
considerable numbers?   They cannot well help allowing
a few of them to vote; but those few don't enjoy the

process overmuch!   The Southerners, not having force
enough, have invoked craft and the complaisance of the
United States Supreme Court to nullify in the spirit an
article of the Constitution of the United States.   An
overwhelming majority of the Southern masses would,
I believe, repeal the amendment to-morrow if they could,
though in my judgment the repeal would be inadvisable
unless accompanied by a new amendment giving the
negro some sort of racial representation in state and
federal legislation.   The Southern conception of "public security" will have to be profoundly modified by
stronger arguments than anything Mr. Murphy brings
forward if the negroes are to be allowed to vote.

(3) We now come to a dogma of Mr. Murphy's which
is, perhaps, his favorite, and which appears conspicuously in print for the first time, so far as I remember.
I shall give the substance of his contention as gleaned
from several references in this book: P. 56—So long
as the lower race is kept down, so long will fusion continue. . . . P. 74—Fusion occurs at the lowest levels.
. . . P. 76—The development of the negroes will not
increase intermarriage, "so far as one can now determine." . . . P. 94—Those who think that the educated
negro will turn from his race to the whites "know little
of the tendencies of the negroes and still less of the
tendencies of education."

Comment.   In the first place the fusion at the lower
levels is admittedly of an animal nature, a matter of
sexual convenience, but is by no means peculiar to "lower
whites."   It is probably decreasing more proportionately
with the lower whites than with better educated whites,
who *ought* to be morally better.   In some communities
it is not the lower whites who indulge in habitual concubinage, but supposedly substantial men, and sometimes

educated men.   As the prostitute's trade grows concubinage is said to decrease.   But, strange as the statement may seem to Northern and many Southern ears, not a few whites of supposed higher grades have expressed a sexual preference for negro or mulatto women, mostly the latter.   This preference would be much more widespread, as several persons have explained to me in talking about their own experiences, were it not for race prejudice, or conscientious scruples, or fear of being exposed.   What I have just said is based on investigation into the practices and opinions and preferences of definite individuals, and I hope these hints are sufficient to justify me in saying that Mr. Murphy's dogma is a tribute to his innocence.

Senator Tillman's belief that some so-called respectable whites would marry rich negro women but for the laws against miscegenation and fear of the community has, I believe, some basis in fact.   However that may be, I do not think that Mr. Murphy's view ought to be accepted without investigation.   I am glad that he guards himself by saying, "so far as one can now determine."

Readers of Kelly Miller and DuBois will find no trouble in reading the heart-views of these negro leaders about educated negroes "turning to the whites."   Of course these men would reprehend any turning to whites *as* whites, but they believe that a gentleman or a lady anywhere ought to have the right of the "pursuit of happiness" in getting a suitable spouse without reference to "race, color or previous condition of servitude." I may be mistaken, but such is the inference I have been compelled to draw.   *And why should they not think this?   Is it not natural and self-respecting?*   If some of us were negroes or mulattoes should not *we* hold the same view?   Almost every Southerner with whom I have conversed on this subject—and I have talked with hundreds of all classes and conditions of life—has said that in his judgment most of the educated negroes would like to have the *right* to intermarry with whites. This belief is probably exaggerated, but it is, in my judgment, nearer the truth than is Mr. Murphy's opinion. However, we know extremely little on this topic.

I may know little of racial feeling and less of education, but I find that the marriages between Jews and Gentiles of my acquaintance occur at the higher rather than at the lower levels. The cases are not altogether analogous, but, as Mr. Murphy brings the case of Jew into the discussion, I am privileged to use it in doubting the validity of his opinion.

(4) P. 166. Our author says that the declining race pulls the stronger down, etc. This may be true; but I fail to recall instances enough to warrant a ganeralization. It may be that our American kin in Hawaii are going down. It may be that we have all gone down with the American Indian. But some of us think that, no matter what happens to the negro, we Southern white people, with God's help, *are going up.* Doubtless the declining race will pull down the stronger if that stronger lets it take hold. And doubtless the drowning man sometimes drowns his would-be rescuer. But—what is the use in multiplying words? The question is one of fact. What are the facts of history and experience? Mr. Murphy's statement, in the absence of evidence, need not be taken to be more than a possible truth. If our author will limit the statement to different classes in the same nation, or to different races that intermarry, he will be at least uttering an opinion that I shall not quarrel with. But the white man has a marvelous ability to

get out of the way of a drowning race, whether it be Indian or negro!*

(5) On page 198 we are informed that society need have no relation to negro "rights." This idea is the most astonishing of all, especially since it comes from a Southerner. Here is the place where the battle wages. Has Mr. Murphy any right to end the fight and claim a victory without shivering a single lance? I have already touched on this point and cannot discuss it further now. The psychology of the white man's mind will show us some light some of these days. May those days soon come! I must insist, in closing this section, that man's life must be assumed to be connected in all the length and breadth and thickness of it. A happy and useful civic life of *con amore* coöperation is practically impossible when not based upon social intercourse, or at least the *hope* of it for one's children's children. So says the experience of ages. So the Southerner feels when he declines to hold open a "door of hope" to the negro that will usher him into ultimate hell fire of race strife. If there can be healthful political and civic equality without social equality, give us facts from history, and psychological and social science, and careful and candid observation, in order that we may believe; but do not expect us to accept without proof a doctrine that gives the lie to our Southern tendencies and our actual experiences. It may be that Southern people base too much on sociality and the family life; but we are hardly willing to renounce the peculiar genius of our people in

---

* I do not deny the *moral* danger that besets any race that holds another in tutelage. And I am unwilling to see any Southern folk exposed to this danger, if a way of escape can be provided. But it may be possible for the dominant race to rise—though perhaps not as high as it *might*—while the lower race is "going down."

associating *all* "rights" with social rights, just at a time when race consciousness is awakening the world over, and when men are calling for purer and more conservative family life.

THE NORTHERN VIEW AND TRADITION

I. *Democratic Idealism.* On page 9 we are told that our democracy insists that "class as class shall never rule." On p. 232 Mr. Murphy speaks of the negro as a "new class that may hold the balance of power." On page 235 occurs the expression: "Restrictions shall have no stigma of class." Pp. 240 and 241 speak of the training of the "people" in a sense that makes the word include the negro. Page 236 reminds one of the true, old-fashioned abolition fervor. If the negro's permanent acceptance of a low status be the condition of peace, "then we had better have something less than peace." The absence of "manhood" is more dangerous than racial disturbance.

Comment. Is the negro a "class"? And do the democratic arguments about class touch the subject in any way? Do Southerners show any disposition to injure "classes"? Our author (and the old but receding Northern sentiment) fails to see that the negro is not treated as a *class* at the South, but as a *race*—a very different thing. Orthodox statements about democracy refer to homogeneous or at least to uniracial situations; or, if they did not in the past, they are learning to do so to-day. No Southerner would deny Mr. Murphy's contentions about democracy *versus* aristocracy. Racial distinctions are very different things from superficial castes made by social or economic distinctions. The former have a bio-

logical basis.   If we agree that God made of one all
the nations to dwell upon the face of the earth, we
must also admit that he "set the bounds of their habi-
tations."   And if unassimilable types stray away or are
taken away, they introduce discord into the course of
nature.   This discord is not necessarily cured by talking
and acting as if the whites were a favored *class* of a
homogeneous population and the negroes *another* class!
Northerners generally have always tended to think of
negroes as individuals, and therefore cannot understand
the mass psychology of the South.   If I am not mistaken, modern social science is more and more taking the
Southern point of view, especially when dealing with
national life.

Referring to Mr. Murphy's last statement, which is
really founded on those immediately preceding it, I may
say that to the Southern negro it may be true that absence of manhood may be worse than racial disturbance;
but to the white Southerner it may be that absence of
manhood *among the negroes* is not so bad as racial disturbance!   At any rate, it is a peculiarity of the typical
Northern view that it has only two horns to its "lemma."
Now doubtless the true dilemma, as the word indicates,
has but two alternatives; so let us say that we may be
dealing with a trilemma or a polylemma.   The *either-or*
and *versus* attitude is hardly scientific in this connection.
Why should we have to choose between loss of manhood
and fear of racial disturbance?   The "solution" cham-
pioned by Jefferson and Lincoln (colonization of negroes) may prevent either of the fatal results that Mr.
Murphy deprecates.   And there may be other alternatives not yet mentioned.   Let's find them out!

II.   *"Out of Touch."*—Just a few references to show
that Mr. Murphy is sometimes out of touch with "his

people," as I suppose he would call most Southerners.
P. 58—"It soon seems to be incredible to us that anyone could have ever hoped to rebuild the South as a
permanent institutional exception to all that has been
known and proved of human nature and of human societies . . . promote the self-respect of one race by
weakening the self-respect of the other." Of whom does
Mr. Murphy speak? Most Southerners think that the
South, rather than the abstract advocates of "human
rights," had the "straight of it" as to practical knowledge
of human institutions. The South believed that the sudden freeing and enfranchisement of millions of slaves
of an alien race was an act contradictory of all human
experience and institutions. Mr. Murphy, in spite of
his lack of sympathy with the *sudden* enfranchisement
of the negroes, is still thinking of the negroes as a *class*
of citizens, whereas the South does not regard them as
true citizens at all! And the better men of the South
interfere with the negro's self-respect only in the spirit
of self-protection.

Southerners take "snapshot judgment" on the negro's
"inadequacies," says Mr. Murphy (p. 236). But does
Mr. Murphy help to eradicate that tendency by himself
pronouncing summary judgment on Southern leaders like
Tillman and Vardaman? I do not care for such leaders
in a *scientific* consideration of the negro question, but I
hope that I understand them better than Mr. Murphy
does, and I am anxious that they may have the credit
for some degree of sincerity and other qualities that I
believe them to possess. These Southern leaders could
not acquire so much power did they not represent the
people's views in large measure. In attributing their
hostility to negro suffrage only to snap judgment on the
negro's inadequacy, Mr. Murphy is condemning the de-

fensible opinion of perhaps a large majority of the common folk of the South.

We are informed on p. 237 that it is not right to disfranchise a people on the ground of their ignorance and then give them no schools.—Assuredly such a procedure would be pernicious. But who says that the negroes were disfranchised on the ground of their ignorance alone? Few Southerners wish to disfranchise illiterate or ignorant white men. Indeed, great ingenuity has been exercised in trying to retain the franchise for such men. *The negro is not a class, but a race.* The classes can be *assimilated* in the South; the races cannot. Here is the crux of the race question.

SOLUTIONS

I. *Methods and Processes.* I have not time to go further into the criticism of the book. Besides, I have already discussed its leading ideas and attitudes. For the rest I must content myself with giving a list of references under the above heading and the next, and then a few final hints that must take the place of comment.

References: xx, xxi, 48, 53, 79, 103, 111, 159 f, 165, 166, 170, 209, 213, 243.

II. *Results:* 11, 12, 113, 146, 218, 222, 241, 248.

On page 241, where Mr. Murphy admits that Southern industrial and commercial progress will never equal that of other sections if the negroes stay with us, he practically gives up the fight. Does he suppose that Southerners are going to rest content with a future less than the best that man can have? And does he think that commercial backwardness will not be accompanied with

other forms of maldevelopment?   Some may be willing
to be partially damned for their black brethren's sake.
Not so most of us.   If we cannot be great in the presence
of the negro, we will surely get rid of him, God helping
us, through the help of our country and the rest of the
civilized world.   The best white Southerners want the
negro to get all the development that he can get, but not
at their expense.   He shall not keep us down, they say.
We *will* not be a less-favored portion of this country.
We *must* come into our heritage, Africans to the contrary notwithstanding.   As things are now (as we have
already said) our finer spirits often want to get away
from it all, and our rougher spirits often want to make
the negro get out of it all.   When it comes to a "show-
down," if that should have to come, the plan of the
rougher ones will probably be the one adopted.   But shall
we rest supinely and wait for conflict, or for that second-
rate future that Mr. Murphy is self-sacrificing enough
to be willing for us to have?   There is a more excellent
way: Let us organize a nation-wide, a world-wide co-
operative and scientific study of this negro problem, and
get the masses of the white people and the black people
to help and to get themselves into trim for acquiescence
in the results that the best human wisdom may offer.

It is a sin against God and a crime against man to
leave this largest of human problems in the hands of
"people generally," without making a national scientific
effort to rid ourselves of this body of death in life that
so fearfully besets us.   What does it avail to have science and education when we fail to apply them to the
real problems of life that are close to the heart of a
people's safety and peace and development?

Finally let me say that, in spite of my earnest belief

that Mr. Murphy has not successfully seized some of the most fundamental psychological aspects of the race question, I trust that our people, North and South, will ever honor men of his splendid type of patriotism and Christianity and philosophic largeness of mind.

II. SOCIOLOGICAL

SOUTHERNISM AND "THE SOUTHERNER"

(From Neale's Monthly for August, 1913.)

I

Four years ago the publishers of "The Southerner" requested a number of Southern men, including myself, to give their opinion of the fitness of the book for distribution in the South.   This request was made because, it was said, a public-spirited gentleman wished to make the book more widely known in the Southern states, provided it were acceptable there.   The novel, which had already appeared as a serial in the *Atlantic Monthly,* had excited much favorable comment in sections other than Southern as a book of the times and of the South.

Having lived the greater part of ten years in the North, —although Southern born and bred, and consequently sympathetic toward both Southern sentiment and the new nationalism that was arising in the secession states,— and being a professed student of Southern questions, especially the negro problem, I went to the book with the expectation of finding something I could praise generously.   To my surprise, I found that Nicholas Worth, the ostensible author, felt intellectually at home only in the North, and especially in Boston; that he ridiculed the Confederate Veterans and the Daughters of the Confederacy; that he failed to see any sense in Southern sensitiveness with regard to the negro question, and that he seemed to mention religious life at the South only to sneer at it.

As I read Nicholas Worth's wholesale charges of insincerity and lack of frankness on the part of Southern political leaders, and noted the indications of his belief that the South was under the dominion of the "dead hand," I thought to myself: Even granting that the attitude and strictures of Nicholas Worth, schoolmaster, politician, and reformer, are well founded, his book is evidently not one to be read in the South, where reverence for the past and hero-worship now find no serious difficulty in aligning themselves with industrial progressiveness and religious and political independence.

I myself had spent several college years as an agnostic; I had bolted the Democratic nomination for governor of South Carolina, not having perceived the real meaning of Tillman's apparent violence and ruthless attacks on those whom I had been taught to revere; yet it had never occurred to me that the Confederate Veterans and the Daughters of the Confederacy,—though individuals among them sometimes had exhibited "amusing" yet understandable and pardonable exaggerations and excess of sentimentality,—were legitimate objects of ridicule, even to one like myself, whose life and training had given him perspective, and who was supposed to have some sense of humor.

Wishing to discourage the circulation of the book as a philanthropic free tonic for Southerners, I wrote the review for the publishers (in 1909), and summed up my criticism substantially as follows:

1. The author of "The Southerner" is not a Southerner of the spirit, whatever he may be of the flesh. There is something of North Carolina and something of

Massachusetts in his attitude, but none of that all-inclusive Americanism that alone is able to write about the South with sympathy of the heart yet with balanced critical discrimination.

2. When he compares North and South, as he often does, the South always gets the worst of it. He professes to appreciate evanescent Southern charm and romance; but in the background of his thoughts one feels sure of the ever-ready comparison between a Southern medieval barbarism on the one hand and the solid merit of an up-to-date Northern civilization on the other.

3. There seems to be lack of sympathy for the Southern temperament,—perhaps due to a proselyte's disgust felt for a forsaken cult. This possibly explains the author's talk about the "humor" of Southern traits and situations and his attitude as "business" *intellectuel,*—an attitude not uncommon in "New England-educated" Southerners living in New York.

4. Being out of sympathy with spiritual Southernism, he fails to do justice to the social and institutional life of the South.

5. His fundamental failure in part is due to a wrong view of the negro question. Neither the "business" view nor that of abstract humanitarianism, nor a combination of both, will ever enable anyone to understand the Southern white man's attitude toward the negro.

After sending my opinion of the book to the publishers I heard rumors to the effect that the real writer of the novel was a man who had the public ear to quite a degree. I could but regret the ostensible author's failure to understand both the plain people of the South and their old leaders, and still hope that, whoever he may be, the real author will yet disavow sympathy with the sad misunderstanding of the South on the part of "Nicholas Worth."

I shall not discuss the ethics of anonymity in this particular case. The reputed author, Mr. Walter Hines Page, has not disavowed his responsibility for the book. It therefore challenges attention on account of its alleged representativeness and because the author is generally supposed to be the American ambassador to Great Britain. The real author's conscious attitude may be entirely commendable: I assume it to be so. But my contention is with Nicholas Worth, who assumes to set forth the true inwardness of the Southern situation.

As a Southerner,—who is all the more an American because he is a Southerner,—I feel free to make this review count for the advancement of a large cause that all good men should wish to further, a proper understanding of the South and the negro question; hence, if for no other reason, I desire to keep clear of even the appearance of sectional rancor and self-conscious "smart" criticism. Moreover, personally I am unprogressive enough to hold fast to faith in the amenities of criticism and the courtesies of debate.

II

The story runs somewhat as follows:

Nicholas Worth III is ten years of age when the tide of civil war begins to be felt at Milworth, a little cotton-mill town in North Carolina. His father and his grandfather are Union men.

Nicholas recounts various experiences of his boyhood: the camp meeting, where the old "hymn-h'ister" is said to have "bawled along the corduroy tune," seeing "a vision of the wicked burning in Hell," whereat "he rejoiced, and he quickened his pace somewhat, for he had intimations of the ecstasy that was to overcome him an hour later"; and where the Reverend Mr. Babb selected as his text a "sulphurous sentence," after which he "preached and spat himself into a spasm," etc.; the Ku Klux Klan; the private school "for the flower of the South," wherein Nicholas fought a boy who insulted him because the father of Nicholas was not a colonel, and where he played "the game of Mathematics, Latin, and the Honour of a Gentleman—not a bad game for youth whether in that cloistered school or in the world." (p. 53.) One scene of these boyhood days pictures the frantic conduct of Confederate veterans as they ecstatically kiss a bust of Stonewall Jackson that had been unveiled. Later Worth undergoes "effervescence of spirit" when he enters a denominational college.

The next step is Harvard University, where our hero finds his true "intellectual home," unfavorably contrasts Adelaide Cooley, of "orderly mind" but guiltless of emotions, with his "slow" and "restful" Cousin Margaret, who figures as the typical Southern girl. Nicholas has fun with Northern misconceptions of Uncle Remus and the like; "exchanges confidences" with a colored student in regard to a lecturer's "Bostonian intonations"; gives a capital illustration of the fatuous lionizing of a negro student, and thinks he finds his religious doubts settled on a basis free from the Methodist-Baptist-Presbyterian-Episcopalian conservatism. After graduation he is offered a place as teacher in Harvard, but decides to go back to his "own" people, despite his intellectual preference for the frank and free North.

In Marlborough, his state's capital,—which he charac-

terizes as the "dullest settlement of English-speaking
people" on the face of the earth,—he meets Professor
"Billy" Bain, who is an advanced exponent of industrial
and home-making education.   They become great friends
right away on account of their mutual desire to vitalize
Southern education; but Cousin Margaret closes chapter
ten with her plaintive refrain, to be repeated in substance
at the end of several other chapters: "Dear Cousin, you
have lived away from us so long that you may forget
our own people.   You won't, will you?"

The school at "Energetic Edinboro" is given to
Nicholas.   He applies Professor Billy's practical principles (rather than Harvard's), and as superintendent
works for both the white and the negro schools.   Here
his troubles begin.   He gets a principal for the negro
school, "Professor" Marshall, from Hampton, after
vainly trying to obtain one from the negro college managed by the white Snodders,—Northerners that "grov-
eled in martyrdom," "neglected and tactless foreigners
in a strange land."

Worth's version of Southern life, as expressed by Captain Bob, the Republican boss, is characteristic of the
book: "We are born and baptized and grow up and live
and eat and think and vote and swear and drink and go
to hell—all by formulas.   You've got to keep to the right
formula."   But Nicholas tries to live up to the spirit of
his grandfather, who used to say to him, "Widen your
horizon."

Consequently Nicholas eschews narrow things, and
therefore declines to make a speech on Jefferson Davis.
He says to himself: That way lies ruinous limitation!
Indeed, seeing Margaret the center of wild Confederate
enthusiasm, he resolves to save her from the "shame."
(161.)   Margaret, however, alienates him still more by

saving some Confederate relics from the burning of St.
Peter's Church, barely escaping with her life. The lack
of "patriotic" sympathy between the young people becomes manifest. And,—though Margaret's soft remon-
strances are heard for a few times, and though she
praises him warmly for his educational activity,—she
drops out of the story, to give place to the English-
educated Louise Caldwell, who is "advanced" in her
views of patriotism, and keeps away from the "sentimental" Daughters of the Confederacy and the "beg-
garly" Confederate Veterans. (182.)

Election time grows near. Colonel Stringweather has
Thomas Carter Warren nominated. Warren is engaged
to Nicholas Worth's sister Barbara, but she breaks the
engagement when she sees that a little mulatto girl,
Lissa's child, is the living image of Tom Warren, and
finds corroborating evidence of Tom's—indiscretion.
Warren is said to be a poor candidate because he "does
not see the absurdities of the ludicrous life all about
him." (187.)

The Education Club founded by Bain and Worth, finding that the Democratic bosses will not champion the
club's projected educational reforms, decides to organize a bolt and to have their own man put up for state
superintendent of education in place of a "broken-down
Baptist minister," who had been nominated by the Democrats. Nicholas is chosen as Independent candidate, and
is "endorsed" by the Populist-Republican coalition.

At first he finds it hard to reach the people in his
canvass. Negroes form the greater part of his audience,
and Worth is belabored by the Democratic organ,—*The
White Man*. All sorts of charges,—social equality with
the negroes, sleeping in negro houses, etc.,—are urged
against him. It is insinuated that Lissa's daughter owes

paternity to him.   But at length Warren compels his
managers to drop their scurrilous tactics by avowing his
own responsibility for the mulatto child.

In his campaign Worth insists on fairness as to negro
suffrage, and tells the negro that the white man has "got
to" give him education, etc.   To his white associates he
insists that there is no negro problem, but that it is
simply a "social and industrial condition." (P. 52.)   His
canvass seems to be succeeding, when a catastrophe occurs in the killing of Colonel Stringweather by a negro.
This occurrence strengthens the prejudice against
Worth's "too much nigger" candidacy.

When election day is over Worth's friends believe that
he has been elected, but claim that the election has been
turned against him through intimidation and fraud, because men of the Democratic party feel justified in doing
anything to defeat a man who had sat at table with
negroes at Harvard, and who, they alleged, wished to
give negroes such treatment as would soon make them
think themselves on an equality with white people.
Writes Nicholas: "One paper published this inquiry addressed to me in 'sorrowful emphasis': 'Would you
marry your daughter to a nigger?' and it added: 'Until
the gentleman answers that test question we need not
pay more attention to what he says.'"   The death of
Stringweather and a race riot on election day had of
course been attributed to Worth's activity on behalf of
negro rights and privileges.

Having resigned his professorship because of his candidacy, Worth is at first inclined to consider the promise
of some of his friends the enemy to get a consulship in
Greece for him, but his brother Charles and his friend,
young Caldwell, persuade him that the Democrats are
simply trying to get him out of the country.   He there-

fore decides to remain, write the history of his common-
wealth, and become a "builder" of the society that is to
come.

Nicholas finds it hard to write history with his fond
mother near to interrupt him, and at times he has serious
doubts whether or not he can remain in a land where
there must be "silence on subjects of serious concern."
Nevertheless, his decision to stay remains unaltered.

Being invited to Boston, he delivers an address and
some conversational speeches in which he advocates
building Southern education on cotton; accuses Northerners of a certain type of "drawing the color line"; expresses his desire to escape the shadow "Southerner,"
and so on. After enlightening Northern audiences and
individuals in this way he goes South in haste to find
his sweetheart, Louise Caldwell, whose freedom from
sentimental Southern patriotism enables her easily to
take the place of "willing" Margaret in Worth's emancipated heart.

The last significant episode of the novel is the description of an interview between Nicholas and Lissa's daughter, who had been educated North by her father, had
passed for a white girl, had married a white captain of
industry at Pittsburgh, and had now come South to
visit the scenes of her childhood.

The book closes with indications that Nicholas Worth
IV is a chip of the old block and will devote himself to
the "uplift" of the people of his state.

III

The book is primarily a tract for the times, only
secondarily a novel. Hence we need spend no time on

literary criticism. The candid reviewer, however, will gladly admit that the author has given us some vivid touches of felicitous description and genial humor, despite the generally sarcastic sermons and rather forced and somber hopefulness of the story.

In trying to get at the "message" of the book we are helped by this peculiarity that marks it: the author evidently regards traditional Southernism as a sort of social disease. Since Nicholas Worth so interprets the Southern situation, I propose that we take up the case in detail, first considering the symptoms, and then passing on to diagnosis, causation, prognosis, and treatment.

First of all, let us notice the religious symptoms. Worth seems to hold that the close association of religion with education, the narrow and striving denominationalism, the over-great prayerfulness ("It seemed ill-bred not to pray."—p. 65), the tendency to suppress honest doubt, the Sabbatarianism ("no train ran . . . on the Sabbath,—not so long as the firm of Suggs and Babb did business for the Lord." p. 410), are symptoms of bad circulation of intellectual blood. However, his pictures of Southern religion are not typical, so far as my experience goes. Making "Christian character" the aim of education may be claimed as a Southern symptom; but *that* is not universally regarded by the world,—in England, for instance,—as in any sense a "retarded" piece of mentality.

During the 'seventies in South Carolina "sulphurous sermons" were so uncommon that we boys used to watch out for them with interest: we called them "H. and D. [Hell and Damnation] sermons." In our section religion was not characteristically terrifying; ministers were not hypocrites like Worth's spiritual guides, Babb and

Suggs. Granting that the South tried to conserve the "old
time religion," we may note that even German Biblical
criticism is becoming more conservative! The evangelical religious conservatism of the South, though in part
a sign of slow development, is partly temperamental; but
it may yet serve a useful purpose in slowing down the
speed of an overhasty liberalism that threatens to throw
out the baby with the bath water. Nor is it absolutely
necessary that Southern religion should follow exactly
the New England lines of development. Perhaps we prefer Old England lines with American improvements.

Next we look into the "patriotic" symptoms of Southernism. Surely Worth cannot tell us,—tell us, who
know,—that the scene of the kissing of Jackson's effigy
was a common thing in the South. But, suppose it had
been; should temperamental Southern emotionalism be
judged by Professor Worth's analytic intellectualism?
Besides, I have heard distinguished Northern visitors
say that they wished they could see the same enthusiasm
at reunions of Northern soldiers as they witness during
the gathering of Confederate veterans. Even though a
supposed student of social character may not be "intellectually at home" in the South as he is in Boston, I call
upon our author as one who would write for the world
not to paint Southern scenes as "symptoms" of disorder,
when they are really a part of that Southern "openness"
and "closeness to the soil" that he professes to admire.
Would he have Southern sentiment take on the dry rot
of intellectual aloofness?

The apparent political symptoms are more serious.
Worth seems to wish to give the impression that certain
tricks of the political trade are peculiar to the South.
Are all the repressions and suppressions Southern?

Have there been no "zones of silence" with regard to the true inwardness of the tariff, the trusts, the financial system and the like? Is our "Southerner" sure that even a small percentage of the "colonels" were hypocrites, and that they did not believe what they said with regard to "social equality," "negro competition," and so forth? The "colonels" were often leaders at the South because of their training in public affairs, their social position, and the like. If Worth claims that certain kinds of "politics" are a disease, I agree with him. But we Southerners have a right to our own peculiar form of the disease without having *our* leaders specially stigmatized as "insincere" and "hypocritical."

I pass over such alleged symptoms as the "oratorical habit." Fashions change in oratory as in other things. Southern college boys of to-day do not often "orate" in the set terms of their fathers. Southerners will always be orators, let us hope; that is one of their talents. The oratory of the political stump is not, I assert, half so bad as the hypocrisies of secret coteries and committees in high places remote from the public gaze. "Zones of silence" are to be deprecated in a democracy, but let us push publicity all along the line, and not waste so much time belaboring the "oratorical habit," which will doubtless become less blatant and more insidious as the "higher civilization" of which Nicholas Worth is a prophet permeates the South.

In describing Southern women Worth conveys the impression that they are characteristically languorous and helpless beings. If they were, that condition would be a transient symptom, due to historical and climatic causes, not a disease of character. Worth knows, of course, or should know, that helpless types have always

been exceptions, and that Southern women have risen to
every occasion that they have had to face.

When we come to the *racial* complex of symptoms the
pathologic taint appears. Indeed, whenever religion and
politics touch racial issues the one seems to forget the
universality of the gospel message and the other is silent
about the equal rights of man, "no taxation without representation," and the other democratic doctrines of the
fathers.

Although "Nicholas Worth" seems to look askance
on sentiment in love and patriotism, and shows esthetic
disgust at such terms as "beauty" and "chivalry" and all
rotund oratorical utterances, even he must agree with us
that race-hatred, the cry "This is a white man's country," the fear of "negro domination," the dread of the
assumption of "social equality" by the negroes, are the
real symptoms of a deep-lying trouble. Why all this
"præternatural suspicion" (as Carlyle would call it)?
Why this seeming anesthesia with regard to intellectual
and political freedom for all men and this hyperesthesia
with regard to anything that even remotely touches the
negro? I cannot agree with one of the characters in the
story that "nobody cares a damn about the nigger," because the whole mentality of the Southern whites,—consciousness, subconsciousness, and "superconsciousness,"
—necessarily is full of racial anxiety (*angst*). Here is
the "psychopathic complex" that disturbs Southern life.

Perhaps we should now attempt a diagnosis of such
"Southernism" as is held to be pathological, guided by
our knowledge of the crucial symptoms. "Professional"
Southernism is simply one type of attack. When a politician talks of the "maudlin craze for education" he is,
consciously or unconsciously, thinking of negro "higher"
education. All the apparent limitations of democracy

and of Christianity in the South are connected with the
"nigger" complex of symptoms one way or another.

I judge that Worth has attempted a partial diagnosis
from the following statements of his: ghosts of dead
commanders [hallucinations of the spiritual eye?]; rigid
orthodoxy of formulas [cataleptic condition?]; zones of
silence with regard to religion and politics, etc. [hysteric
zones of anesthesia?]; negro-in-America form of insanity [monomaniacal anxiety?]; all history a perversion
or a suppression [suppressed complexes of thought and
feeling that the patient is unwilling to face?]; fear on
one subject [anxiety complex?]; double life [a false,
"split-off" personality of hysteria?]; etc. Now, I think
that Worth on the whole is disposed to diagnosticate the
case as one of hysteria. Let us be careful, though. The
line between social health and social disease is hard to
draw, and social hysteria is an obscure, protean thing
that requires careful investigation. Some of the freakish conduct of the patient ("Professional" Southernism)
evidently makes our author suspect a guileful form of
professional hysteria. It is said that Charcot had some
patients of that kind in Paris.

On the whole, I am inclined to think that the case is
one of incipient hysteria. "Nicholas Worth" would admit that much, and would perhaps go much further. He
would agree, I hope, that there is nothing deeply wrong
with the patient's nervous system, but that the trouble is
one of stress and strain of life. Indeed, he calls it "defensive," and that term is one much associated with
hysteria by many savants of the day. A defensive reaction! Well, perhaps we had better now go on to study
the cause of the trouble,—the etiology of the case.

The author's list of causes: "error of slavery"; "crime
of secession" [Grandfather Worth]; "mediævalism";

"poverty"; "forced emigration" of "strong men" from the South; "killing" of the "working habits" by slavery; "rule of the dead"; the "old false position,"—all these would be but secondary causes if they all existed. Worth incidentally has mentioned the true causes,—"dormant race-hatred," "people fear what they do not know"; "three hundred tragedies" [mulattoes in an audience]; the mulatto woman who "passed as white." The South is suffering from the threat of a divided personality, a form of hysteria in which a diseased self,—accompanied by a group of symptoms that the patient will not or dares not face,—tends to usurp the place of the true personality. The abnormal, freakish self unconsciously disguises the real cause of its own appearance. So in the South the true self is democratic and Christian and humanitarian; but emotional race politics sometimes causes the onlooker to mistake the race-hatred simulacrum of the South for the real Southern personality.

A fear of "amalgamation" due to instinctive awareness of the terrible power of easily aroused and easily satisfied sex passion often masquerades as a belief in Anglo-Saxon civilization, or in some other "institution" that needs to be "preserved." But Southern men know, —and the mulatto tragedies testify to this knowledge,— that esthetic dislike of race-mixture has not defended race purity in the South; and they believe that race-prejudice,—aye, even race-hatred,—does tend to offer an adequate defense. Truly, some of the worst white offenders against racial purity are most savage against the negroes. Lust easily becomes transformed into hate. But most Southerners see the danger in the negro situation. They believe that legitimation of sexual relations between races would set free the flood of mongrelism; hence they guard all possible approaches toward any sort of social recognition of the negro. Mixed marriages

occur in the North. Light mulattoes "lose" themselves
in the white population from time to time. Most Northerners seem disinclined to recognize the representativeness of a race, but incline toward treating high-grade
negroes as individuals only. These are a few of the
aspects of the racial situation. Only a full study can
do them justice.

Southern women, too, know the danger threatening
white men and youths, as this story testifies. Refined,
upright Southern gentlemen may utterly disavow subconscious dread of "amalgamation" so far as they themselves are concerned; but they admit the danger for
growing youth and many adult men. When two races
are thrown together the *natural* consequence is either
race mixture or race antagonism. It is a general belief
in the South that increase of race antagonism has caused
decrease of race mixture.

I have said that the true self of the Southern white
man is democratic and humanitarian,—believing in the
rights of man and in the brotherhood of the spiritual life.
Yet, in spite of himself, feeling obscurely that all the
rights of man are as organically related as are the parts of
the body, the Southern white man instinctively strives to
keep the negro away from the assumption of any rights
and privileges that might ultimately imply social mingling and consequent racial mixture. He hopes at least to
insulate vice as much as possible. History shows that
race problems are solved by race mixture. Experience
suggests that all human rights are ultimately social, and
are based institutionally on the home. The white man
does not wish to disavow his Christianity and his democracy; but he feels that there are great instinctive forces
at work against the purity of his race; he realizes the
necessity of his apparent inconsistency; he cannot get

the world to understand; he ends by elevating "white supremacy" into a creed without being able to explain it even to himself.

Now, I do not pretend to say that I have explained the case. I am simply studying it, and this is not the place for a full treatment of the problem. But I do want to insist upon this: the real cause of any pathological "Southernism" is an abnormal situation, wherein a proud and highly endowed race finds itself on the same territory with an amiable, dependent, and, perhaps, promising people,—who nevertheless cannot be assimilated; for the simple reason that human beings have bodies as well as souls, and all true assimilation is ultimately based on intermarriage. Without biological mixture there is friction, antagonism, dominance of one race over the other. Science does not seem to advise the mingling of two such races. Even if it did, the Teutonic peoples do not believe in such mixture.

So there is unconscious conflict in the white man's attitude. He cannot square his racial orthodoxy with his democratic and Christian faith. Those of us who are sympathetically and yet scientifically studying the negro and ourselves hope to show the world the insistent need of relieving the white man from his burden of defensive inconsistency. Let him that doubts the marvelous and insidious power of sexual proximity, free from esthetic dislike and free from race prejudice,—let him, I say, study the recent development of sex psychology, and he will see the unnaturalness of putting two civilizations parallel to each other without expecting them to meet in fusion or in conflict. And Southerners know, from conversations with Northern leaders, that many of the latter fully expect the race problem to be ultimately settled by means of race mixture. Hence Southern opposition to

Northern efforts in behalf of the negro. Much of it
seems cruelly unfair. But anxiety studies neither logic
nor ethics.

What of the prognosis of this distressing social trouble? "Nicholas Worth" seems to think that the dying
out of the "colonels" will settle things. · Look around
and behold the successors of the "colonels." They make
a much defter use of the race problem than the "colonels" ever did. The veteran politicians of reconstruction
times had urgent need to free their section from misrule
and to keep it freed; the newer political leaders are
steadily intent on making the negro realize that he can
never be a real citizen. Nicholas Worth had better call
back the colonels!

The author of "The Southerner" assumes that the
races will always live together. If the cause of the
trouble is what Senator John Sharp Williams calls the
"physical presence of the negro," is not Mr. Worth taking a hopeless view of the future? Even now senators
are elected pledged to work for the striking out or the
profound modification of the fourteenth and fifteenth
amendments. The supreme court of the land gives no
promise to the negro. Discrimination against him,
legally, economically, and in every other way, proceeds
apace.

But Worth says that we must not expect too much,
and that we must take a far look ahead. Granted: but
we must study the forces in operation and ask whither
they are leading. The American ideal is invincible and
things must come out right. If the cause of the trouble,
however, is in the white man's mind, no prognosis of
this case will be satisfactory that does not deal with that
"symptom."

Worth assures us that he was silent toward his mother

with regard to matters that would pain her if they were
discussed.   Unless he will help us to remedy our real
trouble in some way that will reach the ultimate cause, it
would be better for him to refrain from setting forth
sarcasms as a basis for a brilliant "cotton" civilization
in the motherland that produced him.

The South sees no vision pointed out by a prophet
who does not love her from the heart.

My prognosis is this: So far as I can see, the future
holds no really permanent hope, no matter how much
educational and material advancement is made, unless
something can be done to remove the deep anxiety of the
Southern white man, which is due to the presence of a
"split-off" self, the defensive self of race prejudice.
Will Worth's treatment affect that?   Let us see.

Intellectual emancipation, religious toleration and lib-
erality, shaking off the fetters of provincialism, getting
rid of worn-out formulas and so on,—all these things
are coming to pass, even where the influence of Harvard
is not very evident.   The Southern whites are giving the
negro his dole and are allowing Northerners to spend
money on him.   The great agencies for the distribution
of money for education are learning to let the Southerners spend it in their own way.   These agencies are learning, too, to discriminate between the exploiting Southerners on the one hand, who coyly welcome all "Yankee"
money for the suffering South, and the elect Southerners,
on the other hand, who despise soft-soaping ways as
much as they abhor fire-eating.   In other words, the
South, like the rest of the world, is treating herself to
the newer education, and welcomes all help that is
straightforward and kindly, and neither grudging nor
condescending.

But does Nicholas Worth think that negroes are appreciably nearer equal rights, say the suffrage, than they were twenty years ago? Does he imagine that "rebellion" against the "generals" and the "colonels" is worth talking about? Does he find the youth of the South showing a disposition to treat whites and blacks as "a people" rather than as two races? Does he find that the ten thousand young white men who have been studying the race question under the guidance of Professor Weatherford are likely to advocate the negro's right to the suffrage, or that they realize that they have "got to [p. 243] do more for the negro"? Worth's recipe of education is all right. All social doctors are prescribing it.

But some of us do not wish to base all our education on cotton. We want Southern education, industrial and other, to continue to be as varied and as free as any other education on earth. We intend to stand not one pace behind the chiefest of states and peoples. We will hold our place in the world's work and in the world's progress.

And if the negro is in our way, and is the cause of all our trouble, we will relieve the situation as best we can; first, for our own sake (for even Reformer Worth must realize that the world knows that the white people are the more important part of the Southern population); and secondly, for the sake of the negro.

We need more wide-visioned, practical men down South, and we are growing them. In fact, the process has never stopped, though circumstances retarded us for a time. But Worth and his kind must not prescribe for us contempt for Confederate Veterans; for the "sentimental" South; for the Daughters of the Confederacy; for oratory; for Christian education; for noble women, and for chivalrous men. Such a prescription may not be too bitter (Professor Nicholas disclaims bitterness) ; but it is too sour!

Even a sour prescription may not be amiss at times for some persons; but the "sensitive" South declines to take corrosive acid. The proper tonic treatment of the South's ills is the scientific study of the negro question by men that are duly qualified and who are trusted by the Southern people. Perhaps the greatest danger in the treatment of Southern troubles is not the old slogans, but rather such deadly formulas as these: "There is no race question"; "The question will settle itself"; "We must leave it all to Providence"; "The American people are not ready to study the race question"; "The study will disturb economic conditions"; "You can't study race-prejudice scientifically"; "Things are getting better"; "Look at the progress of the South,—or the negro"; "Christianity will solve the race problem"; "Education will solve the race problem," and so forth. These are now the formulas that threaten our undoing. We advocate publicity and scientific study of all other questions; for how can we dissolve the "zones of silence" that surround the race question except by means of investigation that has the motive of humanitarianism and the method of science?

III. PHILANTHROPIC

"UNCLE TOM'S CABIN" SIXTY YEARS AFTER

The hundredth anniversary of Mrs. Stowe's birth occurred on June 14, 1912; the sixtieth anniversary of the publication of "Uncle Tom's Cabin" was in March, 1912. As a student of the negro problem for ten years I suddenly awoke to the fact that, though I had read all manner of treatises and some fiction connected with slavery and racial questions, I had not read "Uncle Tom's Cabin," a book often regarded as of epochal significance. And why? Because I had associated the book with controversy and fierce passions, and had been brought up to regard it as an exaggerated and unfair picture of Southern conditions before the war between the sections. It occurred to me, however, at this time, that I must no longer neglect what seemed clearly a duty in the case of one who was unwilling to pass over any significant contribution to a better historical understanding of the difficult problem that I had been studying so assiduously. So I overcame my repugnance to the book, a dislike not so much to what I knew of the book as to the unpleasant associations connected with it. I am therefore here setting down the results of my analysis of "Uncle Tom's Cabin" without expressing an opinion on its literary form or of its influence on the world at the time of its publication.

What value has the book for us *to-day,* and are the issues raised in it vital for us at the present moment?

I shall presuppose the reader's general acquaintance with the story, but shall nevertheless so express my analytical results that their bearing on the negro problem of to-day need not be prejudiced by the reader's lack of familiarity with the book. The page references are to the Everyman's Library edition.

In order to clear the way for an appreciation of the suggestive lessons of the book I shall begin with some aspects of it that seem most open to criticism. One is astonished to note how possible it is for an author to take true incidents, to write from a dispassionate and humanitarian point of view, and yet to produce an impression that produced enthusiastic praise from one side and fierce denunciation from the other. I think that we may assume that both the praise and the denunciation were sincere, that the authoress thought she was drawing the thing as she saw, and believed that she saw it as it was; and that the main message of her book may be as useful for us sixty years after as it was on its first publication to the opponents of slavery.

CRITICISM

We must be wary in our criticism of a book that has been translated into French, Italian, Spanish, Swedish, Dutch, Flemish, German, Polish, Magyar, Welsh, Armenian, Illyrian, Finnish, Modern Greek, and Portuguese. And when a million copies of a book were sold in a foreign country (England) in one year (1852), we may well be careful how we judge harshly something that has gained the suffrages of the human race. However, 1852 and 1912 are further apart in reality than the sixty years would seem to indicate, and we may hope that our criticism will be practically free from prejudice and emotional disturbance. Just because the book was so popular and had so much influence on the minds—and perhaps the muscles—of men, we must not shirk our duty of impartially estimating its significance.

1.   Untypical Incidents Treated as Typical.—This is, of course, the stock criticism. That the authoress herself meant the reader to regard even the extremest cases of cruelty as being typical of slavery in the ·South, and that she meant the darkest shadows in her picture to hold the center of the reader's attention, may be judged from the following quotation from her preface: "The object of these sketches is to awaken sympathy and feeling for the African race, as they exist among us; to show their wrongs and sorrows, under a system so necessarily cruel and unjust as to defeat and do away the good effects of all that can be attempted for them, by their best friends, under it.   In doing this the author can sincerely disclaim any invidious feeling toward those individuals who, often without any fault of their own, are involved in the trials and embarrassments of the legal relations of slavery.

"Experience has shown that some of the noblest of minds and hearts are often thus involved; and no one knows better than they do that what may be gathered of the evils of slavery from sketches like these is not the half that could be told of the unspeakable whole.

"In the Northern states these representations may, perhaps, be thought caricatures; in the Southern states are witnesses who know their fidelity.   What personal knowledge the author has had of the truth of incidents such as are here related will appear in due time." (xi.)

Thus the reader is led to feel that there is an "unspeakable whole" that even the dramatic powers of a novel cannot portray; although there are "individuals" that are "embarrassed" by the institution of slavery, the real "witnesses" of the atrocities are in the South. I am quite willing to believe that Mrs. Stowe believed everything she wrote in the above passage. Allow me, however, to contrast the impression she strives to give of the typicality of her gruesome stories of slavery with one of the true stories of my boyhood's traditions of things that happened "before the war."

Dr. —— hears a timid knocking at his office door. When he opens for the supposed patient he finds a cringing negro who asks for medical attention. The doctor says: "What is the matter with you?" The negro replies: "Ah's been w'ipped, mossa; Ah cain't tek off my coat." After removing the poor creature's clothes from his back the doctor finds the slave's back a mass of cicatricized lacerations, layer upon layer. He quickly ministers to the wretched creature, has him put in the negro quarters of the physician's own home, and calls a meeting of prominent slave-owners. The meeting appoints a committee to have the miscreant whipper arrested and prosecuted with all possible rigor. This man, however, finding out what degree of horror has been aroused in the community (in the "low country" of South Carolina), flees the country and is never heard of again. It is natural that thousands of Southerners who know little of cases of atrocity such as those perpetrated by Mrs. Stowe's Legree should feel that her picture of the times of slavery has not been drawn true to life. However, Mrs. Stowe wrote for the purpose of arousing sympathy, and might well have replied that those who painted pictures in the dim light of the pyramids of Egypt needed to make the colors bright and garish. And yet, even now, the world needs to know,

sooner or later, that "Southern atrocities" of the times
of slavery were no more typical than the burnings of
negroes at the stake to-day. We do not judge a civilization by its perverts, its exceptional criminals, its occasional orgies of maddened mobs, and the like.

Says our author (p. 433): "The separate incidents
that compose the narrative are to a very great extent
authentic, occurring, many of them, either under her own
observation or that of her personal friends." Even so;
but "separate incidents" may be very untypical, without
attention being called to the fact. In spite of this, however, it is true that slavery opened the door to all sorts
of atrocious possibilities, and surely Mrs. Stowe is to be
pardoned, especially when she is avowedly writing for
the purpose of arousing sympathy for the slaves, and
knows how hard it is to break through moral lethargy,
even if she had given samples of what *might* occur under
slavery as well as of what did occur. The analogous
remark might be made with regard to the status of the
negro in the South to-day. Even a very few lynchings
are symptomatic of a condition that ought not to be
allowed to obtain. Whatever the cause of savagery in
civilized communities, it ought to be investigated, and,
if possible, removed. It is not enough to hold up brutality and mob madness to reprehension, nor even to
make sure of convicting individual offenders: these
things are but symptoms of a trouble whose causes lie
deeper and the remedies for which may be correspondingly drastic. If one case of burning at the stake of
even the most demoniacal criminal occurred in England,
the whole British Empire would insist on something
more than the prosecution of the ring-leaders of a mob.
Hence the naïve suggestion by an English paper recently that President Wilson should put a stop to lynch-

ings. Mrs. Stowe knew that the deep inward injustice
of a system often showed itself best in exceptional cases,
and hence she took the artist's privilege of making her
picture as effective for her purpose as possible. When
she is told that slavery is mild in Kentucky (p. 16) and
yet finds terrible cruelties perpetrated occasionally she is
hardly to be blamed for believing that worse things may
happen on the great cotton plantations of Mississippi.
If she knows a case of a refined white lady herself
using the whip on a negro in the enlightened city of
New Orleans, what must she infer as to what might
happen in the out-of-the-way places of the South? If
the weapons of oppression or the incitements to the unchecked display of temper are put into the hands of
human beings, it is safe to say that such persons will be
dehumanized to some extent, and that the public opinion
of the higher minds will not be able to leaven the lump
altogether. Nor must we overlook the fact that Mrs.
Stowe opposes the thoughtful St. Clare type to the callous
Haley type, and that she depicts a humane Mrs. Shelby
as well as a weak and selfish Mrs. St. Clare. I think
that we are safe in saying that the book strives to point
out the terrible *possibilities* in slavery: and it succeeds
in doing that.

One mistake made by Mrs. Stowe needs mention because it is still current, namely, that of confounding racial
with social relationships. She compares the escaping
slave George with a Hungarian patriot (p. 201), and
(p. 148) she contrasts the refined little white girl, Eva,
with the hoodlumesque little negro girl, the celebrated
Topsy. It is entirely allowable to sympathize with the
escaping slave; but his case is decidedly not like that
of the escaping patriot. Nor is the difference between
Topsy and Eva a merely social difference. Had Topsy

been the refined child and Eva a little white savage, most
of the white people of earth would still prefer Eva. Indeed, just as a mother particularly cherishes her maimed
or otherwise afflicted child, so the average man of racial
conscience is inclined to stand up for his weak and worth-
less brother.   Racial *representativeness* is a very different thing from difference of social status.   No one
can come within shouting distance of the real negro
problem who does not appreciate this distinction.   Indeed, almost everything critical that can be alleged
against "Uncle Tom's Cabin" springs from the failure
of its humanitarian authoress to sympathize with race
consciousness as such.   To blame her for this failure
would be absurd.   Only now are the people of the
North, through contact with the negro, beginning to
understand that the caste of the kin in the South is not
simply a difference of social or other accidental status,
but is based on the ultimate meaning of biological kinship, with its presupposition of intermarriage among the
racially akin and its taboo of amalgamation.

2.   Offending Racial Sensibility.—The last remark
introduces us to another criticism of the story.   When
(p. 143) a white child is represented as throwing her
arms around a little mulatto boy and kissing him the
possibility of strong Southern sympathy for the book is
done away with, even now.   One such passage speaks
eloquently for what is execrated at the South as the
encouragement of interracial *"social equality,"* but
which, perhaps, had better be called the right of social
communion.   It is a manifest absurdity to assert that
every white man, no matter how low he is, has nevertheless an *intrinsic* value above that of every negro, no matter how high his character is.   But racial solidarity demands that the low white man should have a *represen-*

tative value quite apart from his intrinsic character; and every attempt so to portray the social communion between whites and blacks as to confound this distinction of representativeness is to alienate the Southern reader from the book and the noble-hearted writer of it. We are emphatically members one of another, and not the least so in racial matters. Even in halcyon apostolic days in the Christian church *minor* racial differences had to be considered in social life, and the apostolic concordat did not prevent the Christian church from dividing on national lines that were as nothing in comparison with the racial differences between whites and negroes.

When the little Southern girl, Eva, is represented as kissing her old black mammy (p. 168), Southerners know that there is no implication of "social equality" in the child's affection, if the representation be true to life. Eva would have kissed her kitten or hugged the Newfoundland dog with the same kind of "petting" affection. But the real little Evas of the South would not have tolerated any "equality" liberties on the part of black mammies.

On page 114, where the "rich dark eye" of the mulatto is spoken of, we have an instance of unintended affront to the sensibilities of the South. No one doubts the existence of beauty in races other than the white race. But the little touch reveals the tendency on Mrs. Stowe's part to adopt an abstract humanitarianism that instinct tells the Southern white man will sooner or later tend to break down all distinctions between the races. There are some truths not to be told, some appreciations of beauty that are out of place, some exhibitions of goodness, even, that are impertinent under certain circumstances. Fancy a mulatto reading about the "beauty" of a Caucasian-African mixture! Then, too, sad experience shows that there are types of white men and women that are strongly attracted by what is unusual in physical attractiveness; such expressions as that to which I have referred have a subtle influence that can lead to no good. If the mixed type occurs in Central Africa, there may be no harm in telling of its "beauty"—but so greatly do circumstances alter cases that what on the surface seems to be liberal æsthetic humanitarianism may be easily construed into racial disloyalty and a belief in amalgamation.

Some would say that these matters should not be discussed. I think, however, that overmuch reticence has already muddied the waters of the negro problem. Mrs. Stowe herself would probably have abhorred the idea of amalgamation: she evidently, as in "Uncle Tom's Cabin" itself (preface and elsewhere), hopes to see the negro colonized in Africa; nevertheless, in her abstract human charity, she fails to command the sympathy of those who would otherwise have appreciated such a noble plea as this: "To you, generous, noble-minded men and women of the South—you whose virtue and magnanimity and purity of character are the greater for the severer trial it has encountered—to you is her (the author's) appeal. Have you not, in your own secret souls, in your own private conversings, felt that there are woes and evils in this accursed system far beyond what are here shadowed, or can be shadowed? Can it be otherwise? Is *man* ever a creature to be trusted with wholly irresponsible power? And does not the slave system, by denying the slave all legal right of testimony, make every individual owner an irresponsible despot? Can anybody fail to make the inference what the practical result will be? If there is, as we admit, a public sentiment among you, men of honor, justice and humanity, is there not also another kind of public sentiment among the ruffian, the brutal and debased? And cannot the ruffian, the brutal, the debased, by slave law, own just as many slaves as the best and purest? Are the honorable, the just, the high-minded and compassionate the majority anywhere in this world?"

3. Idealization of the Negro.—Necessarily the book makes the most of the negro's supposedly more attractive traits. However much we may want to see justice done to human beings, our sympathies are hard to arouse unless the victims of a bad system have some heroic or some amiable characteristics. Nor would we for a moment assert that negroes now or during the times of slavery are to be regarded as destitute of such traits. But it is hard for us nowadays to think of the "gentle domestic heart" as a primary trait of the average negro (99). Their "instinctive affections" (101) may be strong, but one of the contemporary criticisms of the negro is the facility with which many of the race seem to neglect their own "flesh and blood" kinsfolk. It is hard to believe that so many negroes of roving disposition and feeble affection for home should be the descendants of a race whose love of family life was so "peculiarly strong" (101). Perhaps the degeneration of to-day may be due to powerful causes that did not operate under slavery, or did slavery rather suddenly succeed in suppressing the negro's evil tendencies? The same kind of criticism may be passed on the ascription to the negro (as a race) of love of beauty (183), talent for cooking (209), religious docility (391). Some of these supposed traits we shall discuss in another section: it is enough here to say that it is unlikely that Mrs. Stowe's knowledge of negro character was large enough to jus-

tify her characterization of the negroes in these respects. We must remember, however, with respect to
her tentative prophecy (183) that the negro will produce new arts, etc., she is careful to say "perhaps,"
and even then she locates this flowering of the negro
race in Africa, where "the negro race, no longer des-
pised and trodden down, will, perhaps, show forth some
of the latest and most magnificent revelations of human
life." Would Mrs. Stowe be able to write such words
to-day? I doubt it: I am inclined to think that her
optimistic glow would tone down into a prophecy nearer
akin to the Booker Washington industrial, money-mak-
ing kind of negro heaven.

But listen to this further prophecy, which now sounds
pathetic: "Certainly they will (succeed), in their gentleness, their lowly docility of heart, their aptitude to
repose on a superior mind and rest on a higher power,
their childlike simplicity of affection and facility of
forgiveness. In all these they will exhibit the highest
form of the peculiarly *Christian life,* and, perhaps, as
God chasteneth whom He loveth, He hath chosen poor
Africa in the furnace of affliction, to make her the highest and noblest in that kingdom which He will set up
when every other kingdom has been tried and failed:
for the first shall be last, and the last first." "Perhaps"
all this will happen in Africa, when the negroes have
come to their own: if there is the slightest chance for
such a development the lingering of the negro in this
land of the free and home of the brave seems to be a
direful tragedy, for I for one can see no sign of this
peculiarly Christian character developing in any considerable section of the Southern negroes. "Perhaps"
the American negroes will do better in Africa than they

are doing here, and much better than the "civilized" native African Christians.

One thing, however, about Mrs. Stowe's pathetic hopes we must sympathize with: her belief in the possibilities of human nature. Japan was regarded not very long ago as destined to take a rather humble rank among the nations, and no one dreamed even ten years ago that China would become a republic. Those cocksure individuals who condemn the negro race to perpetual servile spiritual tutelage are further from the truth, "perhaps," than the idealistic authoress of "Uncle Tom's Cabin." Let us, at any rate, rejoice in Mrs. Stowe's moral hopefulness, and realize that her idealization of the negro, her failure to understand racial solidarity, her wrong perspective with regard to the *actual* working of slavery in the South, were inevitable under the circumstances, as inevitable as was the resentment that her negrophilism kindled in the South. We shall never get far in any sort of study of the negro question until we realize that charity means clarity when its tolerance is discriminating rather than merely sentimental.

THE POINT OF VIEW

Northern vs. Southern.—Mrs. Stowe's notable effort to be fair, as seen in her portrayal of the attitudes of St. Clare, the Southern slave-owner, and Miss Ophelia, the Northern philanthropist, has not received the credit due it. And the gist of this contrast is in principle as true to-day as it was sixty years ago. Let us consider several instances of where the Southern attitude is contrasted with the Northern.

(1.) Miss Ophelia: "I think you slaveholders have an

awful responsibility upon you. I wouldn't have it for a thousand worlds. You ought to educate your slaves and treat them like reasonable creatures that you've got to stand before the bar of God with. That's my mind." St. Clare: "Oh, come, come! What do you know about us? . . . Well, now, cousin, you've given us a good talk, and done your duty; on the whole, I think the better of you for it. I make no manner of doubt that you threw a very diamond of truth at me, though you see it hit me so directly in the face that it wasn't exactly appreciated at first." (P. 180.)

Even so to-day, when Southerners wince because of being hit with "diamonds of truth," it is not surprising that the rankling pain prevents due appreciation of the diamond's beauty. When Northerners come South, enter fully into the difficulties of the situation, do nothing to encourage social communion between the races, sympathize with the white man's view of the representativeness of race, realize the danger of putting whites and blacks into competition with one another; but nevertheless treats the negroes as if they were reasonable souls and immortal creatures, and strives to have them educated in a way that will not unduly complicate an already intricate situation;—then the diamonds of truth will sparkle peacefully before the eyes of the South, and resentment on the part of the better classes, at least, will be conspicuously lacking. Whenever even the most radical Southerners can come to see that the "enlightened" treatment of the negroes will not have the effect of putting aside the Southern contention for the representative superiority in status of every white man over every negro, opposition to negro education and the more humane treatment of the colored race will cease. In my paper on Education and Equality and elsewhere I discuss some of the troublesome points in this connection.

(2) When Miss Ophelia discovers Eva perched on Uncle Tom's knee and hanging a garland of flowers around his neck, she exclaims in horror: "How can you let her? . . . it seems so dreadful!" St. Clare says: "You would think no harm in a child's caressing a large dog, even if he was black; but a creature that can think, and reason, and feel, and is immortal, you shudder at: confess it, cousin. I know the feeling among some of you Northerners well enough. Not that there is a particle of virtue in our not having it; but custom with us does what Christianity ought to do—obliterates the feeling of personal prejudice. I have often noticed, in my travels North, how much stronger this was with you than with us. You loathe them as you would a snake or a toad, yet you are indignant at their wrongs. You would not have them abused, but you don't want to have anything to do with them yourselves. You would send them to Africa, out of your sight and smell, and then send a missionary or two to do up all the self-denial of elevating them compendiously." (Pp. 181-2.)

Is this passage out of date now, has it lost its truth—and its sting? Can forced and unnatural righteousness in the abstract ever be appreciated by its—victims? And yet has not this very lack of loathing felt toward the negro's physical make-up caused dire consequences at the South? Add to the Southerner's lack of æsthetic prejudice against the negro a failure on the part of some to adhere rigidly to the caste of the kin and the creed of racial representativeness, what then would happen? Nowadays Southerners, having less to do with negroes and losing the old ties of domestic affection toward them, are more and more coming to feel the average Northerner's distaste toward the physical proximity of negroes.

On the other hand, Northern public opinion is saying more and more, "The negro problem is a matter for the South to settle: it is none of our business." Thus the negro is in danger of losing both his abstract Northern friends and his concrete Southern friends! As a prominent student of the negro question put it to me: "We are heartily tired of the negro question at the North." And Southerners are constantly confessing their growing æsthetic dislike of any sort of contact with the negro. All of which is a thing to be thought about very seriously.

(3) St. Clare: "What poor, mean trash this business of human virtue is! A mere matter, for the most part, of latitude and longitude and geographical position, acting with natural temperament. The greater part is nothing but an accident. Your father, for example, settles in Vermont, in a town where all are, in fact, free and equal; becomes a regular church member and deacon, and in due time joins an Abolitionist society and thinks us all little better than heathens. Yet he is, for all the world, in constitution and habit, a duplicate of my father. I can see it leaking out in fifty different ways—just that same strong, overbearing, dominant spirit. You know very well how impossible it is to persuade some of the folks in your village that Squire Sinclair does not feel above them. The fact is, though he has fallen on democratic times and embraced a democratic theory, he is to the heart an aristocrat, as much as my father, who ruled over five or six hundred slaves. . . . Now I know every word you are going to say. I do not say they *were* alike in fact. One fell into a condition where everything acted against the natural tendency, and the other where everything acted for it; and so one turned out a pretty wilful, stout, overbearing old democrat, and the other a

wilful, stout old despot. If both had owned plantations in Louisiana, they would have been as like as two
old bullets cast in the same mold!"

Even in the matter of just treatment of the negro
before the law, the country is beginning to find that in
spite of better facilities for protecting negroes at the
North, and in spite of the tradition for treating them
fairly, Northern officers of the law are sometimes unable
or unwilling to protect negroes from mob violence. And
Northern discrimination against negroes with regard to
public utilities and the like is showing a "Southern"
spirit; while labor union discrimination is far worse at
the North. Then, too, it is notorious how violent many
Northerners become in their feelings toward the negro
race when their residence in the South brings them into
contact with the race whose "rights" they have been
taught to respect. St. Clare himself brings out this idea
strongly (314-5). Southerners can *now* say to the
people of the North what St. Clare said to Miss Ophelia: "We are the more *obvious* oppressors of the negro;
but the unchristian prejudice of the North is an oppres-
sor almost equally severe." According to certain negro
leaders, the Northern "economic" oppression bears even
more heavily on the negro, especially when accompanied
with actual social "discrimination," than does the Southern drawing of the "color line," which is a matter of
principle at the South.

Mrs. Stowe knew that "the magic of the real presence
of distress, the imploring human eye, the frail, trembling
human hand, the despairing appeal of helpless agony,"
work as truly on Southern as on Northern hearts, and
that a system of things which repressed such natural
feelings is a monstrosity though the people living under
such a system are not only far from being monsters,

but at bottom may be better human beings than their more fortunately situated critics.

Think to-day of the growing callousness of feeling at the North with regard to the negro situation and realize that practically nothing has been done for the scientific *and* humanitarian *study* of the negro question; note that the country is drifting, with the eyes of the spirit closely shut, thinking only of present profits, without even striving to look ahead and ask itself what the outcome will be. Reflect that in the meanwhile there is practical spiritual slavery still in our land. When one thinks on these things, it is well to conclude this section with Mrs. Stowe's indictment of the North:

"Do you say that the people of the free states have nothing to do with it, and can do nothing? Would to God this were true! But it is not true. The people of the free states have defended, encouraged and participated; and are more guilty for it before God than the South, in that they have *not* the apology of education or custom. If the mothers of the free states had felt as they should in times past, the sons of the free states would not have been the holders, and proverbially the hardest masters, of slaves; the sons of the free states would not have connived at the extension of slavery in our national body; the sons of the free states would not, as they do, trade the souls and bodies of men as an equivalent of money in their mercantile dealings. There are multitudes of slaves temporarily owned and sold again by merchants in Northern cities; and shall the whole guilt or obloquy of slavery fall only on the South?"

Now slavery is gone from the land, and no one wants it back; but Northern "capital" is apparently not willing to help have the Southern situation studied for fear that conditions will be "unsettled," and talks as if the situation would "settle itself"—as if such questions ever did! When conscientious men are willing to allow a tragic moral problem to remain unstudied for fear that an economic status might conceivably be interfered with, they show forth the same sort of moral blindness as was evinced by the Northern merchants that Mrs. Stowe upbraided.

When Southerners complacently declare that the North has at last turned the negro question over to the South, they forget that the problem is national even if it were only Southern, and that the time has come for the South to ask the coöperation of the whole world in the study, at least, of what profoundly affects the fundamental principles of enlightened mankind. If the South is right in her view of the negro question, she should want the whole world to know it; if conditions should be changed in the interests of both whites and blacks, the South should aid all those who wish to put an end to whatever interferes with the economic, educational and moral deevlopment of the South.

THE SOUTHERN WHITE MAN'S POINT OF VIEW

It is doubtful whether anyone has ever classified concretely the differing viewpoints of the Southern whites with respect to the negro as well as Mrs. Stowe has done in "Uncle Tom's Cabin." I shall group into classes some of the representative views. Of course such classifications are only for the sake of convenience. The same person may change from one point of view to another, according to time, mood and occasion; besides this, all such classifications overlap to a considerable extent. But the important point is this: the main problem connected with the negro remains to-day, in spite of the absence of economic slavery; hence the views of the dominant race, being ultimately due to the presence of the negro, remain substantially what they were sixty years ago.

1.   "The negro is a wild beast and needs to be tamed so that he will show submissive docility in obeying man's will."—Such is the thesis of the "Legree" type, not a common one except when the mob spirit is aroused, or when some negro "atrocity" makes the higher classes of whites forget that the beast-spirit lurks in man *as* man everywhere, and that the white race has its full allowance of beastliness.   Legree's brutality seems to have been due largely to strong drink and an ignorant, badly balanced, superstitious mind.   He is practically the only real representative of his type in the book.

2.   "The negro is human, but is a species of man so different from the whites that he must not be treated as possessed of full human rights, for they mean nothing to him."—Haley and his friends represent this type. Here are some of its utterances, which one can hear to-day on all sides: "Honest as niggers go. . . ." (10.) "These critters ain't like white folks, you know; they gets over things, only manage right, etc. . . ." (13.) "Niggers, you know, that's fetched up properly, hain't no kind of 'spectations of no kind; so all these things comes easier. . . .   I treat niggers just as well as it's ever worth while to treat 'em." (15.)   "Put him to hoeing and digging, and see if he'd step about so smart." (20.)

3.   "Providence has designed the negro to be a servant of the white man, and servants cannot be expected to understand the higher life and motives of the higher social classes."—Mrs. St. Clare and, to some extent, Mr. Shelby illustrate this type.   This is how they talk: "We

can't reason from our feelings to those of this class of
persons. . . ." (127.) "I hold to being *kind* to servants—I always am; but you must make 'em *know their
place.*" (173.) "Mammie couldn't have the feelings
that I should." (178.) "It's a pity . . . that you have
burdened them with morality above their condition."
(256.)

With the growing solidarity of race-feeling this type
is rapidly becoming assimilated to class two, before-
mentioned, that regards the negro as specifically different
from the white race, and therefore not to be treated as
fully human.

4. "The negro is an inferior race, but is truly and
altogether human, and deserves to be treated humanely
under all circumstances and in every respect; even if the
negroes were only animals, it would be our duty and
privilege to be kind to them."

Let me give a few illustrations which are confined to
no particular social class: "Somehow I never could see
no kind o' critters a-strivin' and pantin' and trying to
cl'ar theirselves, with the dogs arter 'em, and go agin
'em. Besides, I don't see no kind of 'casion for me to
be hunter and catcher for other folks, neither." (67.)
(This "poor, heathenish Kentuckian" is shame-faced and
apologetic in his humaneness, but is typical, perhaps, of
the deeper heart of the South generally, when "politics"
and "social equality" are not concerned.) ". . . Treat
'em like dogs and you'll have dogs' works and dogs'
actions." (111.) "The Lord made 'em men, and it's a
hard squeeze getting 'em down into beasts. . . . Better
send orders up to the Lord to make you a set (of negroes) and leave out their souls entirely." (112.)

5. "The negro is something of a beast—a little more
evidently so than we are, something of a child—and

therefore needing correction: something of a savage—
and therefore needing civilization: but he is as truly
human as we are; we are responsible for him; and
something could be done to alleviate the situation if
public opinion were only solidified as to our evident
duty, and if we only saw a way out of our perplexi-
ties."

St. Clare is, of course, the representative of this class,
which includes those with race conscience who nevertheless understand the meaning of the race-enmity and the
mere race-pride of other types among the whites. St.
Clare holds that, although the negro is often what Mrs.
St. Clare declares him to be—"provoking, stupid, careless, unreasonable, childish, ungrateful"—in large measure "we have made them what they are, and ought to
bear with them" (177); "that if we were in their place
we should often, even with our 'superior' natures, do as
they do" (234); that more ought to be done for them,
"but one man can do nothing against the whole action
of a community" (272); that education is a dangerous
expedient, because "education frees," and people do not
submit to tutelage after they are full-grown.

I have put St. Clare's opinions in a form that will
make them apply to the negro problem of to-day, and I
doubt whether any dispassionate man is prepared to criticize St. Clare's views harshly. He saw the problem
clearly, and through him Mrs. Stowe shows her abiding
sympathy with the better Southern view of the negro
problem. But for her apparent approval of "social equality" in the case of the Quaker child's treatment of the
little mulatto, and a failure to see the full implications
of the representativeness of race and the far-reaching
possibilities of social communion, I think that much in
Mrs. Stowe's book might easily become an expression,

especially through the views of St. Clare, of the thinking South's conscientious bewilderment.

THE NEGRO'S POINT OF VIEW

Mrs. Stowe, naturally enough, does not represent the negro's attitude as fully as she does the various views of the whites. And it is to be expected that her portrayal of despairing pessimism among the colored folk, especially those of mixed blood, should be stressed more decidedly than any other aspect of the negro's feeling toward his status.

1. Racial Solidarity.—There are a few such expressions as the following, which are typical of the average black's attitude: "Him as tries to get one o' our people is as good as tryin' to get all, etc." (81.) "Don't want none o' your light-colored balls, cuttin' 'round, makin' b'lieve you's white folks. Arter all, you's niggers, much as I am." (219.)

The growing "get-together" of the white people has, of course, led to greater solidarity of feeling among all those who have any negro blood in their veins; yet, even now, one sees social lines drawn at times among the negroes apparently according to the degree of white blood among the lighter-colored folk.

2. The Pessimistic View.—"What's the use of living," etc. (23.)—"Ain't no use in niggers havin' nothin'." (102.) "What country have I but the grave?" (115.) "There is a God for you, but is there any for us?" (121.) The mulatto George is responsible for most of these expressions of untypical pessimism; but I am inclined to think—and I base my opinion on actual knowledge—that, though the higher orders of full-blooded ne-

groes are not as a rule pessimistic, many of them feel keenly at times the hopelessness of the outlook for their race, so far as fulness of life in the future is concerned. The average negro fails to appreciate the existence of a "problem," and does not bother himself with it, even if told that a problem exists: nevertheless, the close observer can occasionally catch the sound of a sigh or a sob. For example, one among a number: A certain full-blooded negro woman, educated, refined, the principal of a large negro school in the South, made this remark to one of my teacher friends who held the usual Southern views as to "social equality" and the like, but who was incapable of betraying confidence: "Mr. Blank, you see that girl of mine playing out there so light-heartedly. Well, I often wish that she had never been born, though she is a good child, into whose life no impurity has entered." Nor is this expression unique. Negroes are proverbially cautious and reticent with regard to racial secrets, but we must not conclude on that account that they cannot and do not enter into the spirit of Dr. DuBois' "Litany of Atlanta," which is one of the saddest plaints ever written.

With the development of a worthy minority of the negro race has come a hopeful outlook toward the future, especially because of the belief inculcated by Booker Washington that honest and trustworthy skilled industry will somehow ultimately give the negro all he needs, if not all he wants. All the same, not a few of these negro leaders are but whistling to keep their courage up.

NEGRO CHARACTER

In another paper I have given a slight psychological account—or sociological, if you prefer it—of divers characteristics imputed to the negro by the whites. In that short and inadequate study I tried to show that, according to average white opinion, the negro is prevailingly gregarious, appropriative and expressive, but is lacking in responsiveness (sympathy, gratitude, etc.), assertiveness (resentment, etc.) and perceptiveness (disinterested curiosity, power of observation, etc.). It will be interesting to see how far Mrs. Stowe agrees in her portrayal of negro character with the popular Caucasian view of the negro in the South.

NEGRO CHARACTERISTICS

1. Sociological.—(1) Appropriative.—There are no clear indications of this trait that I can find in the book. The nearest approach to it is to be noted in the character of the cunning Sam, who had a "strict lookout to his own personal wellbeing"; but as that trait is associated by Mrs. Stowe with white patriots in Washington (supposedly Congressmen), we are not justified, I suppose, in using this allusion as an illustration of appropriativeness! The cook, Dinah, is said to be "studious of her ease," but nothing is indicated with regard to a tendency "just to take things." I leave it to the experienced reader to determine whether the trait of appropriativeness is sufficiently conspicuous in the negro to deserve characterization in a book like "Uncle Tom's Cabin." Perhaps Mrs. Stowe was incautious when she states in her preface that negro character is "essentially unlike" that of the "hard, dominant Anglo-Saxon race."

(2) Gregariousness.—This trait is taken for granted in the book and occasionally specifically touched on: "And so much did his prayer (Uncle Tom's) always

work on the devotional feeling of his audience that there
seemed often a danger that it would be lost altogether
in the abundance of the responses which broke out everywhere around him." Perhaps the authoress knew of the
"carryings-on" at divers white camp-meetings, North and
South, and hesitated in consequence to portray excitable
gregariousness as characteristic of negroes.

(3) Expressiveness.—Our author here gives many illustrations, for her attention was of course struck with
the picturesqueness of the effusiveness shown by some
types of negroes. Apart from general references, the
following examples of expressiveness occur: Mandy's
"strutting" (47); Sam's "rolling up his eyes with a
volume of meaning" (52); the bumptious attempt to
use big words and the ridiculous misuse or mispronunci-
ation of them, "bobservation," p. 55; "collusetate," p.
82); "I'll speechify these niggers, now I've got a chance.
Lord, I'll reel it off to make 'em stare!" (80).

Fertility in excuse-making (210) perhaps belongs under this head, for it is usually the effusive negroes that
are facile in "explaining."

As to *perceptiveness, assertiveness* and *responsiveness,*
Mrs. Stowe gives us few data. In general terms she
tells us that negroes are responsive; but her portrayal
of this trait can nearly always be interpreted as expressiveness rather than sympathy. Of course she sets forth
Sam's cunning and the childish, hoodlumesque or savage
trickiness of other negroes; but we have little indication
that she regarded the negroes as observant, except in
their ability to note *social* facts—for instance, Mrs.
Shelby's influence over her household (50), and this
trait is rather the product of gregarious expressiveness
whereby negroes often "pool" their social observations
and get a sort of social generalization that they all fre-

quently act upon. The "passing of the word" and the "grapevine telegraph" are phenomena still decidedly in evidence.

As to assertiveness, there is no sign of negro revenge-fulness in the book except of the humorous kind. But no special attention is called to the negro's lack of resentfulness.

2. Psychological Traits.—Uncle Tom's observation (p. 33) that the negro children are "full of tickle" is most true to life. The organic sensations of the negro, including the sexual sensations, seem to be greatly developed. His imaginativeness, "sensual concretism," love of pleasure, eagerness for excitement, quick emotion, and so on, all seem connected with this inside "ticklishness." Apart from mentioning Dinah's inability to be helped by "systematic regulation" (211), a most significant lack and possibly one connected with weakness of development of the associative system in the brain, nothing further is given us of a definite nature with regard to the negro's psychological traits.

3. Moral Traits.—Apart from the character of Uncle Tom, whose morality is essentially religious, we have singularly little to show for negro morality. For the most part, Mrs. Stowe treats negro character as childish and non-moral rather than moral. It is interesting in this connection to quote the following paragraph that is true to-day, except that for the word "master" we need to soften the language and substitute the word "patron": "We hear often of the distress of the negro servants on the loss of a kind master, and with good reason; for no creature on God's earth is left more utterly unprotected and desolate than the slave in these circumstances." Much of the negro's attachment to white persons has a sort of utilitarian basis. Many of

them are adepts at making use of white people. And sore would be the fate of many, as the Atlanta riot and other events have shown, were it not that the negro's "best friend is the Southern white man." Of course the patron class among the whites is not large, and is probably rapidly decreasing; but we still hear of "Mr. Blank's nigger," etc.

II.   Servants' Traits.—Some of Mrs. Stowe's best touches in delineating negro character are to be found in the traits that characterize the servant class generally at certain stages of their development rather than negro servants in particular; nevertheless, there is a negroid tang about these servants' traits that is hard to analyze. Here are a few of the characteristics that are at least as much "servant" as negro: "Zealous and ready officiousness" (p. 62). "How easy white folks al'as does things" (p. 29). "*Our* folks" (referring to her owners, p. 30). "I can't do nothin' with ladies in the kitchen" (p. 32). "Mas'r can't be 'spected to be a-pryin' round everywhar, as I've done, a-keepin' up all the ends. The boys all mean well, but they's powerful car'less. That ar troubles me." (Note the non-moral weakness, p. 61.) As to the imitativeness, wrong use of big words, and the like, Shakespeare, or any other master of human nature knowledge, will assure us that the negro has no special claim to such peculiarities.

III.   Types: The Child, the Savage and the Hoodlum.—Mrs. Stowe of course makes no classifications of types and attempts no exhaustive treatment of negro character. Indeed, it is surprising to find out how much she has brought out with regard to typical negro traits when one considers her object in writing and her limited acquaintance with the negro. I·acquit her of all responsibility for the heading of this section. But I think that she has recognized and portrayed the three types, never-

theless—types which are still to be seen among the negroes, and without understanding of which the psychological, that is the fundamental, aspects of the negro
question cannot be well understood.

1. The Childish Type.—This may of course also be
hoodlum or savage. I must once more remind the
reader that such sociological types are not mutually exclusive.

The redoubtable Sam again furnishes us with an illustration of this type, for Sam's characteristics are "childlike and bland" rather than savage or hoodlum. Says
Sam, after he had been guilty of a characteristic piece
of childish cunning and mischief: "Yer oughter seen
how mad he looked when I brought the horse up. Lord,
he'd 'a' killed me, if he durs' to; and there I was a-stand-
in' as innercent and as humble." Most of the negro
characters are of the childish type.

2. The Savage Type.—Sambo and Quimbo (344 ff.)
are the principal illustrations of this type. Legree, the
cruel slave-driver, had found them well suited to his
purposes, callous enough for his training. Here is a
specimen of Sambo's savage humor: "Lord, de fun!
To see him stickin' in the mud, chasin' and tearin'
through de bushes, dogs a-holdin' on to him! Lord, I
laughed fit to split dat ar time we kotched Molly. I
thought they'd had her all stripped up afore I could get
'em off. She car's de marks o' dat ar' spree yet." (389.)

3. The Hoodlum Type.—The classical Topsy that
was not "made" but "grow'd" is the best type of hoodlum in the book. Though the typical hoodlum "grows"
in the town, and Topsy is supposedly a country product,
her traits are such as would have found a congenial
atmosphere in the slums of a great city. Many of us
have seen the type among the negroes: "The expression

of the face was an odd mixture of shrewdness and cunning, over which was oddly drawn, like a kind of veil, an expression of the most doleful gravity and solemnity." Her fantastic song-and-dance performance showed that curious combination of childishness, savagery and sophistication that we associate with the street gamin that will develop into a full-fledged hoodlum. Notice the bravado in her nonchalant complaining: " . . . 'She can't b'ar me, 'cause I'm a nigger! She'd 's soon have a toad touch her. There can't nobody love niggers, and niggers can't do nothin'. I don't care,' said Topsy, beginning to whistle." All three types produce criminals: the childishly ignorant and thoughtless, the savagely brutal and callous, the worldly-wise "professional" exploiter of the weak and the timid. Mrs. Stowe evidently believes that the childish type is commonest, and shows her belief in the entire humanness of the other types by describing a "conversion" of a representative of each. Isolation and ignorance in the country and the outcast life in the city are constantly tending to change childish negroes into the savage or the hoodlum types.

MESSAGES FOR TO-DAY

Of all the books written on the negro question, "Uncle Tom's Cabin" is still the one that most nearly touches the nerve of the problem. The South is still too sensitive to do the book justice and the North is becoming apologetic toward the South. Perhaps it is well that this should be so. Too long has the South been cruelly misunderstood. Too long has she had to bear reproach from the whole civilized world, which finds it so much easier to blame than to understand. In putting into a series of propositions what I regard as the main message of the book for this day I am not afraid to say that, if I do not misinterpret the book—and I give page references in order that my inferences should not stand unsupported—the mission of "Uncle Tom's Cabin" has not yet been fulfilled.

1.   Humane people do odd things (14), and economic motives prevent men from using their consciences in finding out and righting wrongs (40).   Such is the value of human souls, however, among exploiters and exploited, that sooner or later this nation will be ashamed of itself for allowing this negro question to remain unstudied in this age of science and humanitarianism.

2.   There is no use in calling people names, especially when the supposed wrongdoers are as likely to be conscientious as their critics are.   We may call a system barbarous without regarding its upholders as barbarians (236).   It is doubtful if the framework of society in New York City will stand scrutiny any better than it will in New Orleans (187).   Undemocratic withholding from a people of the full rights of manhood may sometimes be the less of two evils, but can never be right and should not be tolerated unless modern science and philanthropy, after due study, agree that conditions cannot safely be ameliorated.   But we must not conclude that because a system *as* system is bad that the actual conditions of those who suffer from it are as bad as the system seems to indicate on the surface.   Good men scorn to use their power to the full, and thousands of Southerners refuse to take any sort of advantage of the negro, but strive to protect him in his rights so far as regard for the public weal will allow (225 f.).   But whether a system of tutelage of a lower race be right or wrong, just or unjust, expedient or inexpedient, it is

hard to bring up children of the dominant race in a civilization where certain classes of human beings do not count as full men (281). It is humiliating for some of us to have negroes get clear off the sidewalk in order to give us a superfluity of room; and sad for us to see that our children seem to take this action as a matter of course, or even to demand it as a right. Although it is true that the "higher" exploit the "lower" the world over (216), it is peculiarly distressing to have the prime lesson of democracy and humanitarianism, to say nothing of Christianity, flouted by the most democratic people on earth, the masses of the Southern people. In order for a Southern man to train his children aright in the principles of democracy, must he try to keep them out of the way of temptation that besets them on all sides when a less developed race is held in practical subjection by a more developed one (223)? That is poor training; and yet none of us ought to have this temptation to arrogance, to impurity, to contempt for fellowmen, put in his children's path! When we see humane and noble men perfectly helpless when a mob desires to stab the state in its vitals by spurning the forms of its laws, and finds himself "compelled" to defend everything Southern because he feels that the wretched situation is itself to blame, and that effects cannot be prevented as long as their causes obtain; then it would seem high time to have something done that will relieve the situation instead of attempting to punish a few lawbreakers who imagine that they are "defending their homes," etc.

3. Kindness cannot take the place of justice (41). Sympathy at a distance (137) in this case benefits no one, but exasperates those who feel that they are doing wrong, but regard themselves as choosing a less evident evil—the complete subordination of the lower race, rather

than any possible assumption on the part of said race that it can ever have the rights of "the kin." Furthermore, two things are evident: First, that even kindness, at a distance or close by, that is accompanied by a feeling of repugnance toward its object, cannot do its real work; second, that unredressed wrongs, not only to a "lower" people, but to the cause of democracy itself, cannot be wiped out by an ocean of philanthropy. Finally when kindness has an unnatural tinge, and one side feels that it is suffering injustice and the other that it is, even though unwillingly "forced," doing injustice—unless there has been a special revelation from on high that democracy does not apply to all men or that negroes are not men—then it follows inevitably that a "hardening process" sets in on both sides (250), and the gulf between the races widens and widens. A glorious spectacle for the land of freedom and churches!

4. Religion is just what the negro needs; for it is a binding, relational force, and the negro needs relationizing, reciprocal sympathy, higher friendship, in his moral life. The best types of negroes are almost invariably honestly religious. Though the negro type of religion has suffered somewhat from emotionality and superficiality, the criminal classes are not usually recruited from the religious (149, etc.). While the negro's "docility" has its weak points, his social imitativeness is a fine foundation for character in a people that must undergo long training, and who need to be supported by a Higher Hope. One of the real wonders of the world has been certain types of Christian character among illiterate negroes. Industrial training for the negroes cannot save them without religion. Their faults are exactly those that will cause degeneration when their prosperity is merely materialistic and their morality utilitarian. They

must learn that a man should not be allowed to loaf, and that if he does not work neither shall he eat. They need to learn industrial efficiency. But their imaginativeness and predisposition toward sensuality—I speak generally —are just the kind of traits that need religion as a motive for moral conduct. And one of the fruits of the scientific-humanitarian study of the negro problem must be a decision as to what specific kinds of religious training the negro most needs. His present forms of protestantism may not be the best for him.

5.   The combination of industrial skill and conscience with religion should show itself in freeing the white people, especially the women, from a sort of bondage to negro servants (182). When all the white people that have to do with negroes are able to set them a good example of respect for labor, of industrial efficiency and of the reality of religion in everyday life, then the whites will be freed without needing to use the kind of severity that is generally practiced in order to get orderly and consecutive work from negro servants and laborers. When there is a Christian relation between employer and employed the one can dispense with unsympathetic severity, and the other will not take advantage of his employer's kindness (214). This statement may be denied by some, but careful study of the alliance of efficiency and religion in employer and employed will demonstrate the truth of this contention.

6.   How can we expect the negro to be honest and faithful when we give him no motive (215)? The economic motive is not enough for him. He frequently prefers time to money, and gifts to increase of wages. The personal touch of kindness, combined with firmness in requiring good results, will produce much better work

than does either rigid justice alone or a kindness that is not absolutely just or is merely soft and slouchy.

The ordinary negro does not so much want "social equality" as impartial justice along with some recognition that he is not simply a thing apart, but a human being that can be joked with and talked to without repugnance on the part of his employer. He is amenable to neither bare business nor mere mildness. Such statements as these of course need careful verification, but they are nevertheless based on experience.

7. Education frees (235). Hence the need of being able to forecast what the negro is going to do with his education, and whether it will simply have the ultimate effect of bringing him into sharper competition with the white man. If there is anything certain it is this: that the white men of the South will not allow the law of "natural selection" to help the negro triumph over his less efficient white competitor. Call this attitude unreasonable, if you will; but the principle of love is based on kinship, and no abstract humanitarianism will ever be able to supersede that which finds its exemplification in race-kinship.

Hence the study of the negro question that is demanded by the situation in this country—not only in the South—must find out how to free the negro by education without superseding the white man's religious regard for the weal of all who belong to the white race.

8. When men like Jefferson and Lincoln, not to mention others of note, believed that the negro must eventually have his own nationality (426), and when we see the ties of race becoming stronger in our day all over the world, it will no longer do to dismiss the idea of colonization of the negro with the usual remark that it is impracticable. We can call nothing impracticable

until adequate study has shown it to be so. Such a radical "solution" may take many years and many millions, but it is astonishing how many "impracticable" things become feasible when we set out to study how to meet an actual need. Wireless telegraphy, aviation, the Panama Canal, and many other achievements have been called impracticable. No big problem can be disposed of simply by an easy comparison of birth rate and shiploads. Let the sociological engineers pronounce judgment after proper study. If they find that colonization during a long period and costing a billion or so is advisable, they may be able to show how the thing can be done. If they cannot show the feasibility of the scheme, then the next best thing or things can be tried.

9. This is not a question to be trifled with (437). The dilettante has handled it long enough; let us give the expert a chance. To drift and wait "for something to turn up" is a process of cowardice due to a failure to face the facts. If those of us who regard this negro problem as the most serious one facing this country are wrong in our opinion, let a scientific study prove us to be in error. There are so many of us, North and South, that we deserve this much consideration. Some of us have yet to find the man who would declare, after a sufficient and serious discussion, that the negro problem does not exist, or that it will probably "settle itself" right.   .

10. The negro question is not simply a Southern problem. It is even more than a national question. The world must find out what to do with its backward races. If enlightened America, where the problem is most acute and where the people are so rich and so ingenious, cannot help in this matter, who can?

Whether or not Mrs. Stowe would agree to all these propositions in the form in which I have put them I know not. But she was a generous and godly soul, and I believe that her version of "Uncle Tom's Cabin" of to-day would be a plea for a complete study of the negro problem, in order that democracy and Christianity should not have to face the farcical condition in this country. We pretend to believe in special privileges to none and equal rights to all, and fight Spain in order to prove our sincerity; and yet refuse even to make a concerted and systematic attempt to rid ourselves of the spectacle of some millions of human beings in a state of spiritual slavery. We allow millions of children in a "dominant" race to be brought up to despise millions of their fellow-men, in defiance of their very school-book teaching and their training by the church. To all this the following reply is vouchsafed by a leading scientific light of this country: "The American people are not ready for a study of the negro question." In the meantime the leaders of thought and action in this country must not be surprised if the South at least, which is conscientiously striving to "hold the negro in his place," should complacently say to the world these words of Matthew Arnold: "Might till right is ready!"

IV. SCIENTIFIC

"THE MIND OF PRIMITIVE MAN"

By Franz Boas, 1912

(This study tries to give greater currency to the principal views of Professor Boas on the Negro Question, especially his earnest belief that the race problem should be scientifically studied; to show that the author's guarded admissions of negro inferiority are sufficient to establish a presumption against the advisability of racial intermixture; and to urge the inclusion of the psychological study of race feeling within the scope of any future scientific study of the race problem.)

This book is one of the latest (published September, 1911) that touches the negro question, and is of considerable importance not only on account of the scientific eminence of the author, but also because the book embodies a plea for the scientific study of race questions in general and of the negro problem in particular.

The first paper, on racial prejudices, was first printed in 1894 in the "Proceedings of the American Association for the Advancement of Science," and was subjected to extensive criticism by Professor W. B. Smith, in his "Color Line" (1905). Much of Professor Smith's criticism applies rather to the logical form and to turns of phrasing than to the general results of Professor Boas' reasoning. In the present book the author has revised his paper in such wise that the language of the just-mentioned paper is less open to criticism. One could have wished that the author had replied specifically to some of Professor Smith's criticisms, not because they threatened the validity of his main contentions, but rather because Professor Smith's book is a sort of *vade mecum* with many intelligent Southerners who will not see the author's fuller statement of his views in the book that we are now considering.   One is not, however, surprised that he does not see fit to answer a critic who uses phrases like the following: "Here the cards are conveniently shuffled and the terms changed from 'race' to 'people.' . . . The savant has deceived himself by conjuring with the words 'people' and 'race.' . . .   (Certain alleged facts) all cry out against this complacent assumption." Then, too, Professor Smith himself makes some statements that do not give us confidence in the entire justness of his insight: "Of Caucasians, the Aryan shines like the moon amid the stars."   One would naturally think that the people through whom came the Bible and Christianity had some claims to being regarded as at least a fairly well-lighted moon.   "We have often wondered whether the bee might not yet overtake the man." (Perhaps this is meant as a joke, for Professor Smith, of course, does not regard evolution as being in a straight line, and knows that the very highly specialized structure of the bee makes it impossible for the insect to develop in the human direction.)   When Professor Boas speaks of the fundamental difficulty for the rise of a primitive people being due to its being looked upon, in spite of its higher development, as "belonging to an inferior race," Professor Smith retorts: "Here again there is quietly assumed everything in dispute.   We deny outright that such is the 'fundamental difficulty.'   In a measure it has no existence at all, annulled by the prevalent doctrine of the equality of all men."   Now, whatever may be said with regard to the abstract belief of the people of this country in the "equality of all men," I had supposed it a matter of common observation that nowadays, even in the North, in practice the doctrine is not applied to the negro concretely—surely not in social matters; whereas in the South no pretense is made that the doctrine of the equality of all man is at all "prevalent" in practice, so far as the negro is concerned.

On the other hand, though Professor Smith has used in one or two places rather harsh expressions about the "learned savant" (Dr. Boas), he seems to us to make some amends for his perfectly inadvertent display of incautious terms of depreciation by the following generous tribute to Professor Boas' paper: "While, then, we greatly admire the testing, probing spirit of Dr. Boas, and thank him heartily for his broad-minded plea for the 'primitives,' we are unable to find in any of his pages anything but strong confirmation of the theses of our earlier chapters."

In effect, Dr. Boas seems to be writing on the principle that we have no just reasons for quenching the smoking flax; whereas Professor Smith seems to think that we should at least let it quench itself with its own smoke, and that we should do nothing to kindle it into flame. I think that disinterested men will sympathize with Dr. Boas' purpose, and will not refuse sympathy to Professor Smith's "Brief in Behalf of the Unborn." To Professor Smith all other important public matters, such as tariff and currency, sink into insignificance compared with the "vital matter of pure blood"; on Professor Boas the actual situation in the South cannot press very heavily, hence much of what is of deeply sincere, even though rhetorical, concern and anxiety in the South seems to him to be "emotional clamor."

II

In order to be fair to Professor Boas' thought, which is especially interesting because of its plea for the study

of the negro question by a man who has devoted his life
to the investigation of "primitives," let us put before us
a summary of his views, mainly in his own words. We
shall then be in a position to see the bearings of our
author's general positions, and can take up special points
in connection with Dr. Boas' main view.

"We must investigate in how far we are justified in
assuming that achievement is primarily due to exceptional aptitude, and in how far we are justified in assuming that the European type—or, taking the notion in its
extremest form, that the North European type—represents the highest development of mankind." (5)

Here is his summary of his answer to the first question as stated above:

"Several races have developed a civilization of a type
similar to the one from which our own had its origin.
A number of favorable conditions facilitated the rapid
spread of this civilization in Europe. Among these,
common physical appearance, contiguity of habitat, and
moderate differences in modes of manufacture were the
most potent. When, later on, civilization began to spread
over other continents, the races with which modern civilization came into contact were not equally favorably situated. Striking differences of racial types, the preceding
isolation which caused devastating epidemics in the newly
discovered countries, and the greater advance in civilization made assimilation much more difficult. The rapid
dissemination of Europeans over the whole world destroyed all promising beginnings which had arisen in
various regions. Thus no race except that of eastern
Asia was given a chance to develop an independent civilization. The spread of the European race cut short the
growth of the existing germs without regard to the
mental attitude of the people among whom it was de-

veloping. On the other hand, we have seen that no great weight can be attributed to the earlier rise of civilization in the Old World, which is satisfactorily explained as a chance. In short, historical events appear to have been much more potent in leading races to civilization than their faculty, and it follows that achievements of races do not warrant us in assuming that one race is more highly gifted than the other" (16 f.).

Here is a statement of some of the typical facts that lead Professor Boas to think that the Caucasian has not the monopoly of the "higher" anatomical characteristics:

"The European and the Mongol have the largest brains; the European has a small face and a high nose; all features farther removed from the probable animal ancestor of man than the corresponding features of other races. On the other hand, the European shares lower characteristics with the Australian, both retaining in the strongest degree the hairiness of the animal ancestor, while the specifically human development of the red lip is developed most markedly in the negro. The proportions of the limbs of the negro are also more markedly distinct from the corresponding proportions in the higher apes than are those of the European.

"When we interpret these data in the light of modern biological concepts, we may say that the specifically human features appear with varying intensity in various races, and that the divergence from the animal ancestor has developed in varying directions" (22).

Let us note also the summary of the results of the whole preliminary investigations:

"We have found that the unproved assumption of identity of cultural achievements and of mental ability is founded on an error of judgment; that the variations in cultural development can as well be explained by a consideration of the general course of historical events without recourse to the theory of material differences of mental faculty in different races. We have found, furthermore, that a similar error underlies the common assumption that the white race represents physically the highest type of man, but that anatomical and physiological considerations do not support these views" (29).

We may add to Professor Boas' summary of his first paper two of his significant statements, the first of which warns us not to judge a race by one trial only, and the other admits the preëminence of the white race in at least one important characteristic:

1. (Retardation in the development of a race) "would be significant only if it could be shown that it occurs independently over and over again in the same race, while in other races greater rapidity of development was found repeatedly in independent cases."

2. (The white race seems to show) "a remarkable power of assimilation which has not manifested itself to any equal degree in any other race" (10).

The second paper deals with the influence of environment, and is thus summarized (p. 75):

"We are thus led to the conclusion that environment has an important effect upon the anatomical structure and physiological functions of man; and that for this reason differences of type and action between primitive and civilized groups of the same race must be expected. It seems plausible that one of the most potent causes of these modifications must be looked for in the progressive domestication of man incident to the advance of civilization."

In the third paper, "Influence of Heredity Upon Human Types," occur two summary statements that contain what is essential for our purpose in reviewing the book:

P. 76—"Even granting the greatest possible amount of influence to environment, it is readily seen that all the essential traits of man are due primarily to heredity. The descendants of the negro will always be negroes; the descendants of the whites, whites; and we may even go considerably further, and may recognize that the essential detailed characteristics of a type will always be reproduced in the descendants, although they may be modified to a considerable extent by the influence of environment. I am inclined to believe that the influence of environment is of such a character that, although the same race may assume a different type when removed from one environment to another, it will revert to its old type when replaced in its old environment. This point has not been proved by actual anthropological evidence; but it seems reasonable to make this assumption by analogy with what we know of the behavior of plants and animals. It would, of course, be highly desirable to clear up this question by appropriate investigations."

P. 94—" . . . The differences between different types of man are, on the whole, small as compared to the range of variation in each type."

Here is the conclusion of the paper on "Mental Traits of Primitive Man":

". . . The average faculty of the white race is found to the same degree in a large proportion of individuals of all other races, and although it is probable that some of these races may not produce as large a proportion of great men as our own race, there is no reason to suppose that they are unable to reach the level of civilization represented by the bulk of our own people "(123).

Conclusion of chapter on Race and Language: ". . . Language does not furnish the much-looked-for means of discovering differences in the mental status of different races" (154).

We shall allow the following quotation to represent the main teaching (for our purpose) of the paper entitled "The Universality of Cultural Traits":

"There remains one question to be discussed; namely, whether some tribes represent a lower cultural stage when looked at from an evolutionary point of view.

Our previous discussion has shown that almost all attempts to characterize the mind of primitive man do not take into account racial affiliations, but only stages of culture, and the results of our efforts to determine characteristic racial differences have been of doubtful value. It appears, therefore, that modern anthropologists not only proceed on the assumption of the generic unity of the mind of man, but tacitly disregard quantitative differences which may very well occur. We may therefore base our further consideration on the theory of the similarity of mental function in all races.

Observation has shown, however, that not only emotions, intellect and will power of man are alike everywhere, but that much more detailed similarities in thought and action occur among the most diverse peoples. These similarities are apparently so detailed and far-reaching that Bastian was led to speak of the appalling monotony of the fundamental ideas of mankind all over the globe" (155 f.).

Summary of paper on "The Evolutionary Viewpoint":

"We are thus led to the conclusion that the assumption of a uniform development of culture among all the different races of man and among all tribal units is true in a limited sense only. We may recognize a certain modification of mental activities with modifications of forms of culture; but the assumption that the same forms must necessarily develop in every independent social unit can hardly be maintained. Thus the question with which we began our consideration—namely, whether the representatives of different races can be proved to have developed each independently, in such a way that the representatives of some races stand on low levels of culture, while others stand on high levels—may be answered in the negative. If we should make the attempt to arrange the different types of man in accordance with their industrial advancement, we should find representatives of the most diverse races—such as the Bushman of South Africa, the Veddah of Ceylon, the Australian, and the Indian of Terra del Fuego—on the same lowest level. We should also find representatives of different races on more advanced levels, like the negroes of Central Africa, the Indians of the southwestern puebloes, and the Polynesians; and in our present period we may find representatives of the most diverse races taking part in the highest types of civilization. Thus it will be seen that there is no close relation between race and culture" (195 f.).

Professor Boas' paper on "Some Traits of Primitive Culture" does not take racial affiliation into view, hence we need not summarize it; moreover, it does not add anything in principle to the views already summarized.

The tenth and last paper of the book deals with "Race Problems in the United States." Leaving aside that portion of the paper which discusses white American-European mixture, and so on, let us concentrate attention on what Professor Boas has to say with regard to the negro problem specifically. After saying that the information that we have with respect to the negro child is "practically without value" (p. 269), that most persons in the United States little realize what the African people have done and can do (270), our author expresses several opinions, the most important of which we shall quote, as they deal directly with the negro problem in the South.

"All the different kinds of activities that we consider valuable in the citizens of our country may be found in aboriginal Africa" (270). ". . . The traits of African culture as observed in the aboriginal home of the negro are those of a healthy primitive people, with a considerable degree of personal initiative, with a talent for organization, and with imaginative power, with technical skill and thrift. Neither is a warlike spirit absent in the race, as is proved by the mighty conquerors who overthrew states and founded new empires, and by the courage of the armies that follow the bidding of their leaders. There is nothing to prove that licentiousness, shiftless laziness, lack of initiative are fundamental characteristics of the race. Everything points out that these qualities are the result of social conditions rather than of hereditary traits" (271).

"We do not know of any demand made on the human body or mind in modern life that anatomical or ethnological evidence would prove to be beyond the powers of the negro" (271).

After stating that in his opinion the traits of the American negro are adequately explained by his history and social status, our author makes the following statement with respect to "race instinct": "Ultimately this phenomenon is a repetition of the old instinct and fear of the connubium of patricians and plebeians, of the European nobility and the common people, or of the castes of India. The emotions and reasonings concerned are the same in every respect. In our case they relate particularly to the necessity of maintaining a distinct social status in order to avoid race mixture. As in the other cases mentioned, the so-called instinct is not a physiological dislike. This is proved by the existence of our large mulatto population, as well as by the more ready amalgamation of the Latin peoples. It is rather an expression of social conditions that are so deeply ingrained in us that they assume a strong emotional value; and this, I presume, is meant when we call such feelings instinctive. The feeling certainly has nothing to do with the question of the vitality and ability of the mulatto.

"Still the questions of race-mixture and of the negro's adaptability to our environment represent a number of important problems.

"I think we have reason to be ashamed to confess that the scientific study of these questions has never received the support either of our government or of any of our great scientific institutions; and it is hard to understand why we are so indifferent toward a question which is of paramount importance to the welfare of our nation . . . (274). The importance of researches on this subject cannot be too strongly urged, since the desirability or undesirability of race-mixture should be known. Looking into a distant future, it seems reasonably certain that, with the increasing mobility of the negro, the number of full-bloods will rapidly decrease; and since there is no introduction of new negro blood, there cannot be the slightest doubt that the ultimate effect of the contact between the two races must necessarily be a continued increase of the amount of white blood in the negro community . . . (275).

"While the large body of the white population will always, at least for a very long time to come, be entirely remote from any possibility of intermixture with negroes,

I think that we may predict with a fair degree of certainty a condition in which the contrast between colored people and whites will be less marked than it is at the present time. Notwithstanding all the obstacles that may be laid in the way of intermixture, the conditions are such that the persistence of the pure negro type is practically impossible. Not even an excessively high mortality and lack of fertility among the mixed type, as compared with the pure types, could prevent this result. Since it is impossible to change these conditions, they should be faced squarely, and we ought to demand a careful and critical investigation of the whole problem (276). . . . The most important practical questions relating to the negro problem have reference to the mulattoes and other mixed bloods—to their physical types, their mental and moral qualities, and their vitality. When the bulky literature of the subject is carefully sifted, little remains that will endure serious criticism; and I do not believe that I claim too much when I say that the whole work on this subject remains to be done. The development of modern methods of research make it certain that by careful inquiry definite answers to our problems may be found. Is it not, then, our plain duty to inform ourselves that, so far as that can be done, deliberate consideration of observations may take the place of heated discussions of beliefs in matters that concern not only ourselves, but also the welfare of millions of negroes?" (277 f.).

III

NEGRO ABILITY AND CAPACITY

Desiring to be not only just but even generous with respect to our appreciation of the *possibilities* of negro character and achievement, let us, pending the investigation that Professor Boas does well to desiderate, accept our author's authority in this matter, and group together his most important suggestions with regard to negro capacity and ability.

(1) The historical fact of achievement does not of itself prove capacity and ability in a race. (This generalization cuts in two directions: While it frees the negro race from the imputation of infirmity because of its historical lack of development, it also debars us from insisting that the "wonderful achievements" of the American negro since emancipation show forth the negro's real powers of cultural assimilation and racial talent.)

(2) Specifically, "human" features are not a monopoly of the Caucasian race. (We should admit this contention simply on the assumption that Professor Boas' list of "human" features is the correct one. But I should think that ethnologists would admit the large speculative element in the statements that the negro's red lips, scantiness of hair, etc., are peculiarly human. May not some of the racial characteristics be due to adaptation to environment, so that a feature that would be more "human" in the tropics would be less "human" in the temperate regions? If we regard the temperate zones as more suitable for the evolution of a higher type of humanity, we naturally frame our concepts of humanness from the temperate zone point of view. However, I think that we should provisionally admit Professor Boas' contention as being at least the best that scientific speculation offers, inasmuch as we scarcely have the right to say that the higher type of man is necessarily produced in the temperate zone; nor should we allow æsthetic judgment to interfere with the best scientific speculation

as to what constitutes "human" features of body and mind.

(3) The retardation of the negro race proves nothing significant when we consider the immensely long age of mankind's life on earth, the highly probable concept of the unity of the human species, and the balancing of the negro's retardation during the ages with his apparently rapid advancement in a stimulating environment.

(We must bear in mind, however, this caution: Negro retardation has not been *proved* to be absolute, and may be only relative; but the raw material of Teutonic barbarians is by no means to be viewed as practically the same in *promise* as the barbarianism of Central Africa, to say nothing of Western Africa. Many unprejudiced observers of to-day would claim that an illiterate white man of the South has more political instinct than many educated negroes have; nor are facts lacking to sustain this contention. Nor has science disproved Professor W. B. Smith's representative suggestion that there may be *qualitative* differences of brain tissue, whereby white and negro brains of equal weight and apparent development would by no means be equal functionally. I think it would be fair to say that what we know of the relative bodily and mental values of the whites and negroes would compel us in all fairness to say that, though Professor Boas' careful statements with regard to negro retardation should be accepted, the presumption still remains against the probability that negroes and whites are intrinsically equal in capacity and ability. True, the presumption is *only* a presumption; but if we should find any positive evidence in favor of the probable inferiority of the negro, especially when such evidence is furnished by those who claim all they can for primitives, the "prejudice" against negro capacity and ability becomes a probability that must be taken into practical account.)

(4) The range of variations in each type is greater than the differences in type. (We should expect this in varieties of the same species. The important thing, perhaps, may be the kind and the direction of the variations, rather than the mere degree of variation. The mere fact of there being more large and heavy brains among whites, for instance, may not be a very significant fact in favor of Caucasian superiority. If along with these racial differences, however, go others that indicate Caucasian superiority, we have a right to say that the presumption against the negro's equal endowment is decidedly increased by any general indication of Caucasian superiority in size and weight of brain.)

(5) General and detailed similarities of thought and culture occur among most diverse peoples. All races show representatives among peoples and individuals of highest and of lowest levels.

(Here, again, we should expect such phenomena among varieties of a single species. But the *potentialities* of a primitive Greek myth or a Norwegian saga, for example, may be very different from those of an African folk tale. "What will he do with it?" is the question that must inevitably be asked. Are there any signs of a great epic in the African civilizations? Is their folklore wisdom anywise comparable to the beginnings of Greek philosophy or Hebrew prophecy? An underlying "concept" has little significance in human culture compared with the *potentialities of development*. I sometimes read a book of adventure that has been enjoyed by my children, and discuss it with them on seemingly equal terms. But I am not warranted on that account in supposing that my children will necessarily become interested in the psychological, social and philosophical ideas that interest me. Nor can I conclude that because my children show equal interest in adventure they will hereafter develop equally in other directions of interest and thought. An African tribe may develop practical wisdom superior to that of the early Greeks, and yet fail to make any æsthetic or scientific or philosophical use of its concepts. Some of the shrewdest observations on life that I have ever heard have come from illiterate negroes who have shown a singular incapacity for abstract thought.)

(6) Language does not furnish us with a standard for comparing the capacity of a race for culture.

(Admitting this generalization, are we therefore justified in saying that noble literature and high philosophy *can* be expressed in African dialects? No doubt the African languages express all that an African needs to express, and that they can be so developed as to set forth some of the higher concepts of civilization; but is it at all likely that they ever can become the plastic instruments of thought in a way at all comparable to Greek and English? If the ethnologists and language experts will tell me that I am mistaken in thinking that the *presumption* is against the cultural possibilities of African dialects, I am perfectly willing to change my views on the subject. Indeed, I hope that I am mistaken, and that every human dialect has within it possibilities of limitless culture in all human directions.)

(7) All the essentially valuable activities are to be found in aboriginal Africa.

The American negro is equal to all the demands likely to be made on him, whether physical or mental.

Shiftlessness, licentiousness and lack of initiative in the American negro are probably due to social causes.

(Let us hope that these statements are true. All our generous feelings, all our chivalry, all our humaneness should be aroused on behalf of this unfortunate negro people.   We must, however, note carefully whether Professor Boas himself is altogether hopeful with regard to the negro's capacity and ability.

The problem that interests us in America is not so much the negro's ability to prove himself equal to the demands likely to be made on him, but whether he is able to meet all the important sorts of demands that *Caucasians* have shown themselves able to meet. Granting that negro licentiousness, lack of initiative, etc., are probably due to social causes, we must ask ourselves two further questions: 1. Is it possible to remedy the negro's social disabilities in this country, except through mixture with the whites and ultimate obliteration of the color line? 2. If the negro should be separated altogether from the white race, will he be able to stand alone? If we must give a negative answer to these questions, our judgment with regard to the promise of aboriginal African traits will avail *nothing*.)

RACE MIXTURE

(1) Through a process of domestication the primitive races become assimilated to the civilized races.

(2) The desirability or undesirability of race mixture between negroes and Caucasians should be known, for the differences between the races will very probably tend to disappear, and in time the negro race as such will disappear in America.

COMMENT ON (1) AND (2)

If Professor Boas is correct in thinking that domestication of the negro will ultimately break down the

color line and lead to the "solution" of the negro problem through fusion of the races, he and other investigators will find that the investigation cannot content
itself with a study of the "desirability or undesirability"
of racial intermixture. It will have to face another
problem: How can the whites, whose feeling of prejudice against the negro is rapidly *growing,* be got to take
a cool, scientific view of the probable potency of negro
blood? Granted, for the sake of argument only, that
the negro is intrinsically, though as yet only potentially,
the equal of the white, can the white race be got to found
its attitude toward the negro race on a utilitarian-ethical
basis only, or will economic, æsthetic and historical reasons continue to operate against the full recognition of
the negro's probable worth? Will present historical and
social and æsthetic prejudice against the negro be allayed
in any way when even ethnologists who are favorably
disposed toward primitives seem to admit the *present*
substantial inferiority of the negro race?

Even if it could be scientifically proved that an infusion of negro blood would help the white race, the prejudice against a really great branch of the white race like
the Jews is sufficient warning to us not to confine our
discussion of race problems to the question of equality
or inequality of physical and mental endowment.

NEGRO INFERIORITY

(1) The detailed characteristics of a race will be reproduced in its descendants.

(2) Race-mixture and the negro's adaptability to our
environment are problematic matters.

(3) The negro's powers of assimilation of culture are
apparently less than those of the white race.

(4) The negroes would probably revert in large measure to their primitive status if left unsupported by the white race.

(5) The negroes will probably show for all time a smaller proportion of great men than the white race shows and has shown.

COMMENT

These "five points" give us anything but a promising outlook for the "desirability" of race-mixture. If the negroes as a race are probably inferior to the whites with regard to the powers of assimilation, the production of great men, and the permanent stability of their cultural acquirements, and if their adaptability to our culture is a problematic matter; and, finally, if the negroid characteristics tend to persist, is it not the part of wisdom for the white race to assume that there is enough intrinsic inferiority in the negro race to justify the whites in asking that science *prove* the actual desirability of race-mixture before the *slightest* encouragement is given to the process of "amalgamation"?

Professor W. B. Smith may be incorrect in his statement that Professor Boas' first paper contains nothing to justify a change of Southern attitude with regard to its belief in negro inferiority, but I think we should admit in all candor that the burden of proof is thrown on those who believe that there is no substantial inferiority in the negro race.

RACE PREJUDICE

(1) Race "feeling has certainly nothing to do with the question of the vitality and ability of the negro."

(But belief in the negro's physical, mental and moral inferiority may have something to do with race feeling. Apparently one author's guarded admissions with regard to negro disability are scarcely reassuring even to those who are willing to view the idea of racial mixture from a dispassionately scientific point of view.)

(2) One of the primary causes of race mixture is the "increasing mobility of the negro."

(The proportion of mulattoes to negroes seems to be much larger in the North and the border states than in the South. The few instances of intermarriage of white and colored occur at the North with the sanction of law. However, the indications do not point toward the lessening of race feeling at the North, but rather in the contrary direction. Have we then any right to prophesy that the social discrimination against the negro will ultimately die out? And can we view with equanimity the idea that very light-colored mulattoes will increasingly "lose themselves" in the white race, because of the failure of the whites to distinguish superficial negroid traits? If a slight infusion of negro blood will cause no deterioration in the white race, racial feeling *may* ultimately become a negligible quantity. But until the people of this country believe that even the slightest degree of mixture is innocuous, they will view with alarm any tendency toward the diffusion of negro blood in the white race, and probably race prejudice will more and more tend to become race enmity.)

(3) Race "instinct" is not a "physiological dislike," as is "proved by the existence of our large mulatto population."

(But is not "physiological dislike" increasing? Besides, are our experiments in civilization to be based on the indiscriminateness of the sexual instinct? At the best, brute passion *tends* toward perversion and lustful orgies. Do we want our problem settled by allowing lust to have its way? Of course, our author will answer with us in the negative.)

(4) "Fear of the connubium" is at the basis of race-feeling.

(This is undoubtedly true, and there is a clear parallel between Roman life and our own in this respect. [See Appendix: notes on Coulanges' Ancient City]).

(5) "Emotions and reasonings are the same in every respect," *i.e.,* in present race-attitude in this country as compared with that of ancient times.

(This statement may be correct, but I doubt it. Fear of intermarriage and "corruption" of the blood is certainly a feeling common to present and ancient times. But surely the race-feeling of the twentieth century is a phenomenon not really paralleled in ancient times. It would be hard, perhaps, to state the differences in the "emotions and reasonings"; but I doubt if we can reasonably assume that the racial self-consciousness of to-day makes no difference in the attitude of the "higher" races toward those that are less developed. "Races" are not to be treated as "social classes." Indeed, one of the most important features of the investigation of the negro problem that ought to be made is just this complex race-consciousness of "Teutonic" peoples.)

(6) The peculiarity of the race-attitude of to-day consists in the whites' "retaining a distinct social status in order to avoid race-mixture."

(Even so: and our author might go further and insist on a careful study of the relations of social "rights" to political and civic rights, because, in the South, at least, it seems to be assumed that all the "equalities" are at bottom based on potential social equality.

If a careful scientific observer like Professor Boas should study the race-feeling of the Southern whites, I think he would find that belief in the racial inferiority of the negroes is common to practically all whites of the South. Scientific investigation must give unequivocal *proofs* of the negro's practical equality with the whites with respect to body and mind before the "prejudice" features of the fear of racial intermixture can be at all reasonably attacked.

Under the circumstances *should* we attempt to weaken the "color line" in any respect? That is the real race question. If mixture of the races can be proved to have no deleterious effect; if it can be shown that the absorption of the negro population by the whites would not lower the potency of white blood, then there would at least be *room* for argument. But, *with a reasonable presumption against negro "equality," nothing should be done that even squints at the ultimate obliteration of Southern race-consciousness.* Here we stand squarely with Professor W. B. Smith and others that agree with him.)

STUDY OF THE RACE PROBLEM

(1) We should be ashamed that our government and our great institutions of scientific research have not studied the negro question.

(2) Practically the whole work of investigation of race-mixture needs to be done.

COMMENT

Professor Boas' plea for the study of the race question is the most notable thing in his book. The race question *is* a problem, as he clearly sees. Even if the study of race-mixture be by no means the only important item to be investigated, a judicial, scientific pronouncement on that matter alone would be of incalculable advantage. It would sharpen the whole issue, as well as give us some practical data to work with. So long as "race-prejudice" is largely based on belief in negro inferiority—and Professor Boas could hardly claim to have deprived that belief of all validity—we should be very cautious in attempting to modify a race feeling that probably has a rational basis.

The real strength of race-feeling in the South does not, of course, reside in race-enmity, nor even in race-pride, but rather in the conscientious belief that underlies Professor W. B. Smith's "plea for the unborn."

Nor must we underrate the significance of strong feeling, even when it leads to excess of rhetoric and "emotional clamor." Feeling affects votes and policies; and so long as it cannot be shown that feeling has no probable validity, sympathy for "primitives" and abstract beliefs in the equality of human "rights" have no sort of chance for victory as opposed to race "prejudice."

I daresay that Professor Boas and other prominent men of science are quite ready to admit that the psychology of race-attitude is a very important phase of the race question and needs careful scientific study. Hence, in the division of labor that must obtain when a systematic scientific, coöperative research is organized, we may safely assume, I think, that all thoughtful scientific men will welcome the inclusion of psychological and sociological study in the scope of the investigation.

Should science show, in spite of the reasonable presumption to the contrary, that the absorption of the negroes within the white population could produce no serious consequences, it may be, nevertheless, that impartial science will come to see the inadvisability of having race-friction continue for a long period of years because of a tenacious race-consciousness based on æsthetic distaste, economic competition, growing "physiological dislike," and perhaps other factors that may be pointed out by an investigation. The agitation in California against the Japanese is itself of sufficient diagnostic and prognostic importance to demand immediate scientific study.

Pending the organization of scientific investigation of the negro problem, it is to be hoped that we shall have more books like that of Professor Boas, the temper of which is so admirable and its statements so authoritative and judicial, even though their speculative element must necessarily be large.

C. Views in a Club.

I. CLUB FOR THE STUDY OF THE NEGRO QUESTION

(Nov., 1911. Read before a club.)

Nowadays, to the making of clubs there is no end. Many of them have no sufficient reason for existence. When, therefore, several very busy men undertake to establish a new club they ought, in the interest of their reputation for sane common sense, to give a clear-cut reason for their action. Having been requested by the original promoter of the club to give some sort of apology for the club's desire to live, I propose to put forward several questions that would seem to be pertinent, and attempt to give definite and rational answers that may prove suggestive to the members.

I. Is a club for the study of the negro question an undertaking that is worth while in itself?

Yes: because the negro question is intensely human and hence interesting; connected with the welfare of the club members and their families, community, state and nation, and hence practically important; obscured by clouds of passion and prejudice and vapors of sentimentality and cynicism, and therefore needing the genial and stimulating light of moral and intellectual tolerance and open-mindedness.

On account of the national importance of our study, in case we attempt it seriously, Vicksburg is a peculiarly appropriate place for the projected club. The Vicksburg National Military Park threads its way between city and county domain, between private property and church property, and its outlook tower, hard by a school for Christian education, is a symbol that our club might well adopt as expressive of our desire to look calmly over the situation from a standpoint that includes within its horizon city and county, state and section, and our nation upon which the stars look down so peacefully to-day, but whose peace and higher prosperity have often been endangered and may yet again be threatened by the situation that President Taft speaks of as "the most serious facing the American people."

II. What can we expect to gain from such a study?

Besides the considerations already adduced, we may expect to bring about one or all of the following results: The better understanding of study material close to hand; the production of a typical club that may stimulate the formation of others like unto it; the demonstration that typical callings like medicine, business, the ministry and teaching can work successfully together on a problem that affects our entire civilization. Who knows that this club may not be the beginning of a scientific, practical and Christian study of the negro problem by the qualified people of this whole country?

III. Why should we study the negro question just at this time?

Because it is the dominant question in the economic, social, political and religious life of our state and the South, and perhaps the most serious problem that confronts the nation, the church and humanity. Furthermore, a presidential election is coming on and promises to result in the election of a man of fearless and independent, truth-loving spirit.* With an occupant of the presidential chair who is at once a scholar, a patriot and

* Governor Woodrow Wilson.

a practical man of affairs, and at the same time one who has a Christian spirit and a humanitarian outlook, we may expect a thoroughgoing attempt to have our national problems studied disinterestedly and scientifically. Furthermore, this question will likely engage the attention of the Triennial Convention of the Protestant Episcopal Church, a church that seems determined to claim its responsibility toward the negro race, and which is in close touch with the national church of England, whose leaders are also facing a great question of race in South Africa.

IV.   What shall be the scope of our study?

We should use the typical material that Vicksburg locally commands—hill and delta; city and country; river traffic and railroad lines; Mississippi and Louisiana. Then, too, we should use the special interests and talents of our members, who are unusually representative of the various points of view from which the question may be studied.   One can reach material of the economic and legal kind; another, material medical and anthropological; another, facts pertaining to religious, moral and ecclesiastical matters; the fourth, psychological and educational data.

V.   What shall be our method?

As in the preceding question, so in this and others that follow, the club itself will have to determine what it wants to do.   The suggestions here given are simply tentative and suggestive.   I would suggest, in order to start the discussion in definite fashion, that the following phases be considered in our planning: 1. That the members take turns in leading the discussion, preferably through papers, and that each be furnished with a copy of the paper that is read. 2. That the papers be based on observations, conversations, letters, readings, as well

as on well-ascertained first-hand facts when they can be
got. 3. That a record be kept of the discussions. 4.
That a schedule for eight meetings be arranged, consist-
ing of one paper from each member of the club as at
present constituted, followed by a paper or discussion
based on the members' papers, by some invited guest
who is well qualified to add something to the discussion.
5. That whenever the club is unanimously of the opinion
that a visitor would be of service in the discussion of
the topic, efforts be made to have such a person attend.
6. That our proceedings and the record thereof be so
conducted that it will be possible to prepare our results,
or some portion of them, for publication, without undue
expenditure of time and effort.

VI.   How can we secure among ourselves a fair, impartial and disinterested attitude with regard to the question before us?

By cultivating a mental attitude formed by something
like the following processes: Full, frank and explicit
statement of views; sincere self-criticism and patient
submission to the incisive criticism of others; sifting and
verifying all alleged facts; questioning all generaliza-
tions; willingness to doubt views not sustained by veri-
fied facts; eschewing right heartily the vice of infalli-
bility with regard to our own feelings, impressions, views
and habitual attitudes.

VII.   With whom shall we coöperate?

With those who can probably be got to favor and promote a scientific and a Christian study of the question.
Professional philanthropy and dilettante juggling with
statistics should be no more to our taste than partisan
politics and effervescent emotionalism. Careful workers
like Hoffman, Boas, DuBois and Odum, even though
they may have their personal views that we need not

accept, can help us because of their sincerity and their fitness to do investigational work. Some of the prominent church leaders hold balanced and statesmanlike positions and can aid us in our study of the relation of Christianity to our problem. Occasionally we may find one who is not a professed student of the problem, but who is nevertheless well qualified by temperament and experience and native insight to further our study. It should be a part of our task to get into touch with representatives of the classes just mentioned, and to help them as well as try to be helped by them.

VIII. Shall we set forth the basal assumptions on which we proceed? If so, what are they?

Yes, we should be clearly conscious of what we regard as necessary fundamental assumptions, if we would avoid cross-purposes and the generation of heat rather than light.

What these assumptions are must be determined later. Just now I shall venture to state two that I regard as all-important: 1. We should hold to the general principles of organic, psychical and social evolution as indicated in the celebrated phrases, Natural Selection and The Survival of the Fittest. We must regard ourselves as a chosen people, and therefore with no right to lower the standard of our race and nation. 2. We should firmly hold to the broad principles of Christianity and Democracy,.and the sane principles of liberty, equality and fraternity which spring from Christian and democratic principles.

I think that we dare not deny either the naturalistic or the idealistic basis of modern thought. If these two general assumptions do not seem to square with each other, it behooves us to reconcile them as well as we may, but on no account give up either of them. Nature and spirit cannot ultimately be at war. If we are merely naturalistic, we shall assuredly be lacking in appreciation of the spiritual values without which our civilization is vain. If we take the spiritual point of view only, we are in danger of leaving the truths of science out of account, and these truths must come from the same Author who is the Source of spiritual power.

There is a third assumption that is a necessary implication of what has just been said, and which must be held if we do not wish to indulge merely in more or less pleasing intellectual exercise,—namely, that the so-called negro question is a real problem, but *one which can be solved.*

IX. Having in our club representatives of the business, clerical, medical and psychological attitudes, shall we call in representatives of the legal, literary and other viewpoints?

Yes, if our own little group, after assimilating one another, believes that it can assimilate others sufficiently like-minded with ourselves. Hence it is advisable for us to understand one another pretty thoroughly before attempting to introduce others who may waste our time or who may have temperaments or attitudes that cannot be got to work harmoniously with our own. We have no monopoly of the negro question, and others are perfectly free to discuss the question and form clubs in any way they may wish. Hence, under the heading of "organization," I shall advocate plans that will tend to keep our club from dissipating its energies and yet at the same time keep itself in touch with the very best thought on the subject in which we are interested.

X. What shall be our organization?

Again I give a few suggestions merely for the purpose of starting the discussion, for the club itself ought to determine its own organization, after each member has been heard fully.

1.   Meetings every fortnight, on a definite night of the week.

2.   Meetings held in rotation at the members' homes.

3.   Definite time-limit for adjournment.

4.   Host to notify members and guests on the day of the meeting, and to act as chairman.

5.   Agreement as to nature and time of refreshments (evening meal?).

6.   No new members without unanimous consent.

7.   No new member to be elected until he has visited the club at least three times, and has agreed to the plans and procedure of the club.

8.   Invitations to guests only by unanimous consent.

9.   No publicity to proceedings except by unanimous consent.*

10.   No dues, except payment of the expenses of visitors and special dues by unanimous consent.

If the club wishes it I shall present orally a list of subjects, with suggestions as to the points needing investigation; also a list of speakers and topics for the next eight meetings, alternating members and visitors in such wise that there will be two discussions on each topic, one led by a member and another by a visitor.

I am also prepared to give a list of books that are accessible, most of which I have worked over quite carefully.   If each member can procure a book or two, we shall easily be able to get access to the chief works on the subject that are worth while.

* Acting in the spirit of this paper, I secured the consent of each member of the club before making public use of club material. I thank these gentlemen for giving their cordial consent.

I may also state that I have written a number of papers on our subject and shall be glad to have the members make use of them. They may not have much value, but will at least prove suggestive, coming as they do from one who has made a somewhat special study of the question during the last eight years.

II. PROCEEDINGS OF THE WATCHTOWER CLUB

(Dec. 1, 1911, to Jan. 12, 1912)

(These notes are given simply as a "sample." I wish to thank the members of the club for permission to publish these "minutes.")

The club began its existence in this wise: A certain clergyman was very much interested in the discussion in the Episcopal church relative to the negro, and found himself anxious to know more about the whole subject. Finding that a certain psychologist and educator whom he had come to know well had been working on the negro question for eight years, said clergyman proposed one evening that an informal club be organized, to consist of four members: the clergyman, the educator, a prominent physician, and a prominent business man—all native Southerners (a Virginian, a South Carolinian, and two Mississippians), all Democrats and all Episcopalians. The proposer further suggested that meetings be held every fortnight after the evening meal; that each member entertain in turn; that no publicity be given to the meetings; that no more members be added until the four charter members had assimilated one another's views; that the educator formulate a plan for the first meeting. The clergyman agreed to speak to the others mentioned for membership.

Here follow brief notes of the meetings; the papers read; the discussions held; and other matters more or less pertinent to the club and its purpose. Roman figures refer to meetings, Arabic figures to remarks made by individuals.

I. (Dec. 1, 1911)

One absent; one tired; one the host; the fourth, reader of the outline plan.

The following paper was read by the psychologist-educator: (See paper by T. P. B. Title—Club for the Study of the Negro Question.)

DISCUSSION

Paper and its plan approved. Some talk about books mentioned by the writer of the paper. Desultory discussion. Net result: Recommendations of paper adopted; supper voted successful; tired man got a little livelier after digestion got a headway; amicable adjournment.

II. (Dec. 16, 1911)

All members present. Prominent ecclesiastic of the Episcopal church also present as invited guest. Chairman explains object of club to guest.

REMARKS OF THE GUEST

I am especially, and naturally, interested in the spiritual side of this question, for it is fundamental, in all deep human questions, and especially in this one wherein the interests of civilization and Christianity are at stake.

Trying to make a hopeful start in the discussion, I want to say that I think the negro is gaining industrially and morally through industrial education. (Here the guest mentioned several towns in his state where negro farming is improving on account of the work of negro industrial schools.) It is interesting and important to note that white people who have been opposed to the negro industrial schools in these communities are now among their warmest friends.

The only apparently valid objections that I have heard urged against these schools is that their graduates do not become better laborers and cooks and nurses working for the whites in the community, but go out into "higher class" occupations. I regard this as inevitable, in the case of both whites and blacks. The demand for trained labor is larger than the supply, and we cannot expect these trained negroes not to be snapped up by those who need them in more technical and more highly paid work.

As I started out by saying, the spiritual aspect of the question is all-important. The best industrial schools will amount to nothing if character is not improved by them; but it so happens that training for honest labor is the best introduction to spiritual culture, especially in a race that has not learned the dignity of labor. Many individuals in the South are willing to give the negro industrial education, but balk at giving them the suffrage. In my opinion, such political questions are not important. The suffrage is not a right, but a privilege. Usefulness and happiness do not depend on it. Withholding the suffrage is a matter of social expediency. Real freedom comes through the freedom of spiritual life. Religion frees men from sin, wrong, materialism, ignorance, which are the things that really enslave. The suffrage does not free the real spirit. Onesimus was a freeman of Christ, though he remained a slave.

DISCUSSION

1. Do not civilization, democracy and Christianity include political privileges in their program of freedom?

2. Yes, and these privileges ought to come in time; but they are not now socially expedient.

3. The trouble is that most whites in substance decline to look on the negro as a fellowman in any worthwhile way. This is the crux of the question, and spiritual freedom can hardly come under such circumstances. I see little hope for the negro's advance in civilization when I reflect that the negro enjoyed intercourse with the high civilization of North Africa for generations, but seemed to get nothing from it.

4. We know very little of what they did get. Indeed, white civilization of that region and of many others seemed to get wiped out, leaving very little behind. The average modern Greek bears little resemblance to the free Athenian citizen of the age of Pericles. Besides, African tribes did seem to gain something from the Arabs they came into contact with, for the tribes with Arab blood seem to be the highest. And it may be that environmental influence as well as inherited traits helped to bring these favored tribes up to a higher standard.

5. Ancient civilization had too little spirituality to do much for the negro or any other subordinate people.

6. Perhaps; but, as Bryce and Boas point out, our modern race prejudice seemed to be little in evidence in ancient times; and negroes probably had as good a chance proportionately as had any other subordinate people. We find no ancient records of prejudice against the negroes. But it is precarious to draw any conclusions from a situation that we know so little about, more especially as we find it only too difficult now to draw

any satisfactory conclusions about any present aspect of the negro question, even when prejudice does not blind us.

7.   This whole problem is complicated by the fact that there are very few pure negroes.

8.   There are, I think, very many negroes who are near enough full-blooded to count as pure negroes for all practical purposes. Those extremists who deny that there are any full-blooded negroes should apply their deductions to the whole human race. There are no pure races anywhere. However, it is no doubt true that some branches of the white race amalgamate with the negroes more readily than do others, and there may be biological reasons for the fact. Undoubtedly one of our members was right in saying that the psychology of race prejudice is fundamental in the discussion of the whole question, and another member may be right in holding that there is a biological reason for differences in race prejudice. Some ethnologists hold that the "Mediterranean race" in prehistoric times got an infusion of negro blood. Others think that the Japanese have negro blood in them. If these authorities are right, we should not indiscriminately claim that amalgamation leads to bad biological and psychological results. However, this phase of the question need not concern us practically, for the Southern whites will not entertain the idea of amalgamation, and none of us wants them to do so. Opposition to amalgamation, now and hereafter, and disbelief in the advisability or the practical possibility of it, are two of the planks in the club's platform of assumptions wherewith we begin the study of the negro question.

III.   (Dec. 28, 1911)

No guest present.   The business man discussed informally:

Treatment of the Negro in the Courts

The negro is better treated in Virginia than in Mississippi.   Older traditions and fewer negroes.

In a certain locality well known to me negroes are convicted for the same crimes committed under the same conditions and through the same kind and amount of proof,—I claim, I say, that negroes are convicted under conditions practically identical with those that lead to acquittal of whites.   This is notoriously true of trials for murder.   (Here the business man gave some illustrations.)

2.   But are not whites prosecuted and sometimes convicted for crimes that negroes are not even prosecuted for,—for instance, bigamy?

3.   Yes; but that indicates how little the whites regard the sacredness of family life among the negroes.

4.   I for one cannot help taking up for the negroes on occasions when they are unjustly treated in my own town; but when I go North I am not willing to admit that negroes are *generally* unfairly treated in the South.

5.   Yes, many Southern writers and speakers seem to share your attitude on the subject.   They do not feel called on to tell the *whole* truth, even when telling nothing but the truth.   And when one does not tell the whole truth he is more than likely to tell the truth he does tell in discriminating fashion that may really lead to obscuration of substantial truth.   What we need are facts and figures properly explained, and a belief that the whole truth is best in the long run.

6. I have little faith in facts and figures in such matters as this. White men are declared to be innocent because "whites are not criminal"; negroes are declared to be "criminal in nature," and hence in the interests of society should not have the benefit of the doubt. There is always a precedent presumption of the white man's innocence and the negro's guilt, and hence "facts and figures" mean nothing.

7. True enough, facts and figures may be misinterpreted; but if we had stenographic accounts of trials and all the circumstances of the cases detailed, even a few typical cases would show whether or not race prejudice interfered with true judgments. If we are to give up truth-seeking simply because it is hard to establish the truth, our club has no reason for existence. If truth-loving conservatives will band themselves together throughout the length and breadth of the South, radical public opinion cannot hurt it, provided the conservatives convince the radicals, as they can very easily, that conservatives believe as much in white supremacy as the radicals do, and are as averse to amalgamation and to sentimental philanthropic abstractions. But so long as educated and morally enlightened people stifle the truth and put local patriotism or "economic necessity" before the white light of truth, we cannot hope to have the negro problem studied. Give us a number of actual parallel cases wherein whites and blacks, respectively, are concerned, and let the record speak for itself. If the United States Government did not take care of cases of peonage, Southerners going North on a visit would be ordinarily unwilling to admit the existence of peonage at the South. Even as things are, when Northerners come South we carefully distract their attention from the raw places in our civilization, for they readily re-

spond to our well-known urbanity and hospitality. They
pass by cases of practical peonage right under their
noses, because they do not know where, when, or how
to look for them, unless such cases are very gross and
plainly illegal, so that evidence is well on the surface.

8.   But isn't it perfectly evident from a study of
lynchings that the blacks suffer from race prejudice?

9.   Yes, to us that know all the circumstances. But
how often do we know the circumstances, and how much
better is a case at law where we can obtain accurate
results and can study the phenomena at our leisure?
Moreover, isn't it dangerous for us *to take sides against
our own people* without having a great mass of indis-
putable facts and figures to sustain us? Finally, what
we think is not so important as what we can *prove*. Who
knows that lynchings are due to race hatred rather than
to fear that the negroes will rebel against the whites?
Isn't there much of something akin to hysteria about
lynchings? And should we risk our case on such abnormal phenomena, when we can get accurate facts in
the courts? If the South is to lead in this investigation,
let us begin by telling the whole truth and shaming the
devil. It is not enough to get facts and figures: we
need to get detail, accurately taken and transcribed, with
all the attendant circumstances. Further: we must not
claim that a large humanitarian question concerns us
alone. Such Bourbonism does not fit the twentieth century, and the world will no more admit our claim than
it did in the case of slavery.

Our club members are all Southern sympathizers, and
believe in the substance of the Southern contention. But
are we prepared to give a reason for the faith that is in
us? And are we prepared to study this question scientifically? If so, we must away with suppression of

truth.   If we have a case, let us stand by the facts, all the facts, and nothing but the facts, so help us God. Let us take the lead in this investigation, not only because we are most concerned, but also because we have nothing to conceal and are willing for science to probe to the uttermost.   Covering up yellow-fever did not pay; assuredly attempts to hide any portion of the truth will lead to failure and shame, and will hopelessly discredit us in the eyes of humanity.

IV.   (Jan. 12, 1912)

No one was ready with a paper.   A distinguished guest was fortunately present.   We discovered that he had a paper on the need of more missionary effort on behalf of the negroes.   So we prevailed on him to read his paper.

DISCUSSION

The paper may reach our records ultimately.   But we must content ourselves now with a few notes furnished by one of our number who had been asked to make suggestions with regard to the paper.

1.   I don't think it quite accurate to say that there is any degree of growing skepticism and cynicism among the negroes.   Most of them, even among the higher classes, don't know enough philosophy to be either skeptics or cynics.   They are becoming more careless and indifferent, less docile and reverent, more interested in other things, especially their lodges, as shown by Dr. H. W. Odum in his recent book.

2.   In regard to such an expression as "persecuting the church," I should prefer to say that Episcopalians

among the negroes must run the gauntlet of social criticism and sneering because they are few in number and clearly marked off æsthetically and socially from the great masses of their fellow-religionists. Whether this can be called "persecution" in any sense is a question.

3. When our honored guest says that race culture leads to race pride, and *that* to race segregation, he is speaking of a tendency native to most of us of the dominant race. Our pride is based on belief in our superiority. Does the negro really believe in his superiority as a race? And, on the other hand, is the superior negro trying to claim that his *race* is equal to the white man or superior to him, or is he not rather claiming his own superiority to the majority of the whites that he personally knows, but who pretend to be his social superiors? Do not these superior negroes want to segregate with their spiritual kind rather than with low, illiterate people of their own race? Are they willing to throw in their lot entirely with the lower race? All these questions may conceivably be answered in the affirmative, or in the negative; but I am not willing to state that race culture will have this or that effect when I know that the leaders among the negroes differ among themselves on this question, and when some of them are incensed at being treated as members of a race rather than as gentlemen by the grace of God. Segregation and race patriotism are easy in the absence of physical propinquity, but not so easy in the physical presence of a dominant race that will on no account admit the rights of personality for its own sake regardless of race, color and previous condition of servitude.

4. In this whole discussion what has been said of our duty to evangelize the negro and our duty of practicing Christian love is all right, but we must remember

that neither Christianity alone nor science alone can solve a problem like this. We need the *motive* of the Christian and the *method* of the man of science.

Another member of the club made some trenchant remarks as to the unfitness of the Episcopal church to deal with the emotional negro. But it was pointed out that the English church does deal with them successfully in Uganda, in Jamaica and elsewhere, and that the Roman Catholics know how to deal with them. Besides this, as our guest well said, the Episcopal church need not impose on the negro the exact liturgical and dogmatic culture that it bestows on its white members.

Other worth-while remarks were made by other members, but the scribe was not forehanded enough to get them down.

III. THE NEGRO FROM THE PHYSICIAN'S POINT OF VIEW

(Syllabus prepared at the request of a prominent physician.)

"It would be impossible, as well as unnecessary, in a contribution of this character to review in detail the general physiological peculiarities which distinguish the negro from the white man. The same general complaint must be entered here as in dealing with other phases of the comparative study of the race—viz., the abundance of personal impressions and lack of actually recorded facts."—Rudolph Matas, M.D., "The Surgical Peculiarities of the Negro," in "Transactions of the American Surgical Association," 1896, p. 504.

The following are a few samples of the kind of ultimate questions that need to be asked from the point of view of the scientific and practical physician who believes that the settlement of the negro question is dependent in large measure on the physical possibilities of the negro race:

1. Is the negro becoming adapted to his environment, physical and social? Does he show adaptability superior to that shown by other backward races? Is there any indication in his physiological functions and in his anatomical structure that he is capable of standing the strain of civilization? In his physical nature is there any indication that he will be unable to found an independent civilization of his own?

2. Is he showing physical improvement or is he degenerating? If the latter, is the degeneration due to his inherent unfitness or is it due to preventable causes? Is there any indication that the process of degeneration can be arrested by proper hygienic and sanitary measures?

3. What are the differences between negroes and whites that seem to have a bearing on the general question? (Color and hair, for instance, seem to be more stable than feature.) How far are the differences structural and how far functional? (For instance, cranial sutures and their alleged premature ossification.)

4. Has the negro any strong potentialities as a race? Is it true that he has physical qualities that fit him for some particular phase of the world's work and progress?

5. What are the real effects of admixture of white blood? Is it likely that mixture of negro with Mongolian would have good results? (The Japanese, for instance, are thought to have negro blood.) Can anything really definitely scientific be ascertained as to the stamina of the mulatto? As the mulatto merges into the negro through successive darkenings, does the resultant mixture show improvement or does it show physical weakness or degeneration?

6. Through the processes of natural selection will the negro rise by means of the superior qualities of the minority of the race or will the majority assimilate the minority to itself, with a final result of degeneration?

7. Is there anything in the medical and surgical aspect of the question that will throw light on the negro's educability? Does he stand the confinement and the strain of education as well as the white race does? Does he really show a slowing down of intelligence at the

stage of adolescence, or is this true only of a certain proportion of the race?

SPECIAL QUESTIONS

I. DIATHESIS, TEMPERAMENT, ETC.

1. Temperament. What real facts go to show that the negro has a racial temperament (lymphatic, according to Matas and others)? Is there something of the "peristaltic" about the negro's movements and reactions? Are his apparent indifference and laziness in part due to this peristaltic type of reaction? Is he losing his primitive "temperament"? Has his apparent "fibroid diathesis" anything to do with his "lymphatic temperament," or are both these expressions vague guesses?

2. Characteristic Diseases. Can a connection be traced between the negro's supposed temperament and the kinds of diseases relatively peculiar to him? Is he losing his supposed peculiarities with regard to characteristic diseases? Does he show any peculiarities with regard to stimulants and narcotics? Does his "temperament" show itself in his behavior under the influence of drugs? Has he "favorite medicines"? Is there any indication that he needs to be treated medicinally in a different way from white people?

3. Degeneration. Does he show characteristic abnormalities? Are they in any wise diathetic? Are his stigmata of degeneration as pronounced as in the case of the whites? Does he increasingly show a tendency to develop these stigmata? How does he compare with the whites as to idiocy and insanity? Is there any real indication that the so-called strain of civilization is telling on the negroes? Is there much difference in this

respect between the negroes and the mulattoes? (Comparison of negroes and mulattoes is implied in all these questions.)

4. · Vitality. Is the loss of fertility among the negroes an indication of degeneracy, or simply due to such causes as are normal to civilization? Is this loss increasing, decreasing or stationary? If the negro retains his "lymphatic temperament" (admitting, for the sake of argument, that the race naturally has such a temperament), is it likely to characterize a race that has such a diathesis as the negro has? Is the negro's strong sexuality and the supposed "freshness" of the female genitals a factor in fertility? If so, is there reason to believe that the negro will increase in fertility when he becomes more hygienic?

Is there any relation between fertility and vitality and stamina? Is the negro's supposed loss of stamina due to causes not inherent in his raciality, but rather due to temporary maladjustment to his environment? Is he holding his own well, as to stamina, fertility, etc., considering his handicaps? Would the white race do any better under similar circumstances?

Is the negro's continence increasing or decreasing? Is there any relation between degeneration and incontinence? Is there indication that prostitution is on the increase, and that a measure of the decrease in fertility is due to this cause?

5. Development. Does the negro show any peculiarities with regard to adolescence, senescence, the climacteric, etc.? What are the facts with regard to the supposed arrest of brain development at puberty?

II. VITAL STATISTICS

Will it be possible to study a group of negro households intensively, so that some approximation may be
made to a qualitative explanation of its vital statistics?
Figures often are susceptible of misinterpretation unless
we can check them through intensive study of small
groups.

Some of the data that should be studied intensively:
Birth rate, infant mortality, death rate, mortality of
mulattoes as compared with approximately pure negroes.
See Willcox in "Bulletin of U. S. Census for 1910,"
also in Stone's "American Race Problem."

III. ANTHROPOLOGICAL

Under this head would it be possible to study a small
group of school children intensively, and perhaps a hos-
pital group and a family group? Such data as skeleton,
skull, lung capacity, hair, color, muscular and glandular
development, and the like.

No ethnological and anthropological study of the intensive type has ever been made. Such a study would
prove immensely suggestive, would lead to special studies,
would check the evidence from statistics, and so on.

IV. HYGIENIC AND SANITARY

Here, again, would it be possible to study a group of
homes, so that exact data could be obtained? In this
and other studies could the coöperation of colored physi-
cians be obtained and their statements duly checked?
Could prominent negroes be got to coöperate in some

such investigation, or could the thing be done without their full coöperation?

Here are some of the points: Personal hygiene; diet; clothing; ventilation; disposal of refuse; heat and cold; sleep; sexual habits; endurance in work and play; hygienic treatment of children, especially infants and adolescents.

V.   PSYCHOLOGY

Could medical practitioners collect important psychological data such as come within their scope, such as the self-control, energy, foresight, excitement, emotion, etc., of the negro?   Also such traits as are shown in telling symptoms, obeying directions, nursing, criminality, childishness, hoodlumism, and the like?

The most useful psychological facts are those that are most evidently connected with bodily condition.   Hence the physician's data ought to be the most useful to the psychologist, if they are exact and minute.   Psychological facts are of little use unless they are microscopically exact and are recorded at once.   Experiments show that the memory cannot be trusted in these matters.

The above questions are, of course, intended simply to connect this phase of the study with a general point of view and to indicate some of the things that those of us who have been studying this question a long time want to know.

IV. THE NEGRO AND THE EPISCOPAL CHURCH

(Prepared at the request of a well-known clergyman.)

I.   Nature of the negro.
II.   What the church has done.
III. What the church is doing.
IV.   What the church might do.

I

NATURE OF THE NEGRO

1.   Instinctive Tendencies of the Negro (see paper by T. P. B., read before Southern Psychological Society at Chattanooga, Dec., 1910.) *If* the negro is sensational rather than relational, emotional ("affective") rather than intellectual; if science, law and theology are not his strong points; if he has to be trained to them in a way not necessary with the Caucasian race,—is the ordinary machinery of the Episcopal church likely to do much for him?

Is the negro gregarious, appropriative and expressive, rather than responsive, perceptive and assertive (and so on with higher tendencies)?

2.   Psychological Processes of the Negro. Does the negro show strong affective qualities (pleasure, pain, sensitivity, emotion)? Is he weak in intellect (imagination, imitation, assimilation)? Is his so-called imitativeness nothing but gregariousness? Is his supposed im-

aginativeness only expressiveness? Is his power of assimilation, such as it is, only the mere associative process
connected with innate appropriativeness?

Is he weak in attention power, persevering endeavor,
constancy in pursuit? If so, he is deficient in will.

Does he show the deep character attitudes of interest,
belief and anticipation? For instance, is his "interest"
in heaven a real power of imagination and anticipative
hope, or is it a merely sensuous complex of organic sensations?

If the negro shows unbridled affectivity rather than
intellectuality and volition, is this due to his immaturity
or is it due to innate weakness?

Whatever the cause, if we attribute lack of intellect
and will to the negro, will it be possible to Christianize
him by predominantly intellectual and volitional culture?

In discussing this question must we make a decided
difference between real negro and mulatto? Are negro
Episcopalians nearly all mulattoes? Are negro churchmen prevailingly *low church,* making due allowance for
circumstances, or do they simply "ape" the whites?

II

WHAT THE CHURCH HAS DONE

1.   How much do we know of the real Christianity
and churchmanship of the negroes under slavery? Did
the clergymen of antebellum times use different methods
for the negroes than those employed for the whites?
Was their churchmanship merely personal or was it really
institutional? Was it manners and morals, due to domestic training, or was it in any sense spiritual? Did
the negroes show any tendency under slavery to break

away from the Episcopal church and go to other communions?

2. Did the church change her methods when the negroes were freed? Was change advisable? Have missionary methods been extensively used in the evangelization of the negroes by the Episcopal church? Has the Episcopal church ever been aggressive in work among the freemen? If so, where and what were the results? Has there been any study of negro character on the part of the church which is supposed to adapt her work to the culture state and race characteristics of various peoples?

III

WHAT THE CHURCH IS DOING

1. In considering the needs of the negro—racial bishops, etc.—has any account been taken of the negro's characteristics? Has there been any careful effort made to determine (1) what the negro needs, and (2) what the negro wants? Is anyone suggesting any changes in the church's cult in adaptation to the negroes? Do we really know anything much with regard to the "persecution" of negro Episcopalians by their brethren of other churches? Do negro Episcopalians have any confidence in the adaptability of the church to the negro race? Is any study being made as to the methods of the Church of England in the mission field? What were the methods in Uganda, for instance, and how much real success did they achieve? How about other parts of Africa and the West Indies? When Church of England and other churches have an equal chance at the negroes, which church gets hold of them best, and which

produces most satisfactory results in practical life and
character?

IV

WHAT THE CHURCH MIGHT DO

What might the church do? Make a careful study—
an exhaustive, detailed, expert study of results in one or
two parishes? Try various discreet evangelistic methods
especially adapted to the negroes? Get laymen to champion church work among the negroes? Prove to laymen that the money put into negro schools and churches
is really bringing results that are better worth while than
the results would be if put into some other venture in
behalf of the negroes or of whites that do not know the
Episcopal church?

2. Can any "white" church do anything for the negroes in this country so long as the whites insist on keeping the negroes in a state of spiritual subordination?
Will white churchmen permit the church to offer the
negro full spiritual freedom in the future, a freedom
that applies to the *whole* man,—"privileges," such as the
full ecclesiastical suffrage, included? Do whites regard
the suffrage, social recognition of worthy individuals,
etc., as "privileges" to be accorded by one race to another, when it suits the convenience of the dominant race
to accord them? Are we asking the negro to live in a
fools' paradise that we would not be willing to live in
ourselves? Are we doing to them as we would have
them do to us? If not, why not? Shall we ask of them
a degree of "humility" and "patience" that we would
not ask of whites of similar grade of culture? If so,
why? Do we suppose that we can win the negroes by
segregating them absolutely in the church and then ex-

pect them to obey our bishops and General Convention?
Are we willing to trust them with the espiscopate, which,
in its present form, is a product of Caucasian development?

3.   Will the church leave the study of the negro question to purely secular agencies that care nothing about
the negro's soul? Is the church trying to get more
money for the work among the negroes when she does
not know what she can do for the negro, whether she
is doing anything worth while, or whether more money
is likely to produce better results? Is it better to go on
"blindly" in the old ways, or spend some money studying
results, methods, character, and making a few careful
experiments under proper experimental conditions? Are
the ecclesiastical and scholastic experiments being made
now really supervised so that real results can be studied?
If so, where are the reports that go exhaustively into
the subject instead of dealing in large generalities or
picking out a few "typical" cases?

Shall we do as one of our bishops advises—do as we
are doing and leave "results" in the hand of Providence,
or shall we take it that Providence expects us to be provi-
dent and foresighted and scientific in the Lord's work?
Shall our "faith" lack insight as well as sight? Have
we no faith in God's truth as declared by science? What
results can we plead for the "Episcopalian" brand of
evangelization and education when we ask for money
for the negroes?

D. Negro Education: The Thought and the Thing.

I. EDUCATION AND RACIAL EQUALITY

(Paper read before Southern Educational Association, Dec. 29, 1910, Chattanooga, Tenn.)

Education frees the soul of man. Freedom makes for equality based on personal worth. Worth cannot maintain itself unless its right to the pursuit of happiness is unimpeded. The essence of happiness is social communion. Communion in the social sphere is primarily based on family life. The family rests on marriage. Hence intermarriage of free, equal, worthy social individuals is the natural or generic end of education. The Italian peasant's grandson, educated in free America, and showing himself intellectually, ethically, economically and æsthetically fit, marries the daughter of an old American family. There is none to say nay. But a man of apparently equal character in every respect, except that he has one-sixteenth negro blood in his veins, is debarred from wedding his apparent equal if she belongs to the white race. So long as the man with negro blood in his make-up knows that there is a great gulf fixed between him and individuals of another race that seem to be of equal or inferior character, he is not a free man. He is inferior in spite of his seeming superiority or equality, and such a status is the veriest slavery of the soul. He is deprived of his supposedly inalienable right to the pursuit of happiness. In fine, all our higher life and all our happiness are conditioned by fundamental biological facts. Freedom to marry one's personal equal is fundamental

260

equality. Deprivation of this freedom is relegation to the ranks of inferiority. The educated negro may say, "I prefer the woman of my own race." Yes, but consider the Italian; he, too, naturally prefers to marry an Italian. But make the Italian conscious of impending marital inferiority for his descendants to the fourth and fifth generation, let him realize that his inferiority is not something that can be done away with through time and education, and you are forthwith telling him that he is being unfairly dealt with, for everyone knows that the Italian race is one of the great races of the earth.

How is it with the negro? He cannot claim lineage that is high. He cannot point to the great things that his people are now accomplishing as an independent nation; one cannot tell him that science regards his race as even potentially the equal of the white race. But one does in effect say unto him, "Brother in Black, you are brother only by conventional religious terminology; the prejudice against you cannot be overcome because it has a real biological basis."

And so we come to the nerve of the negro problem. We promise the negro freedom through education, on the one hand, and we take away from him the very basis for equality and self-respect, on the other.

No real man pines because of not having social communion with people that do not welcome him, for he ordinarily knows that the refusal to admit him into a given social circle is but a superficial matter. Let him acquire wealth, or polish, or fame, or something else that so-called exclusive circles value, and he that was once rejected will be welcome.

Many a humble man knows that his educated children will rise to social heights not vouchsafed to him, and he is therefore content with his lot, for he lives again in his children. But the negro's children have no future, except that bound up in their own race. Put him where he will not be subject to *treatment* that brands him every moment as a social inferior, and he can forget the apparent arrogance of the white man. But a definite status of inferiority, felt in daily contact, is one that can be tolerated in patience and equanimity by no free man. Negroes may *say* that they do not want conventional social recognition; but if they mean what they say they are proving their inferiority, and if they do not mean what they say, there is no reason why we should listen to their asseverations.

What I have been saying is, of course, predicated on the assumption that all forms of equality are associated in the free life of citizenship, and that in the long run all depend upon social equality and intermarriage. In order to take a test case, let us ask ourselves whether *political* equality, which is being taken from the negro with a pretense of legal fairness, is organically associated with the general tendencies toward association and fellowship?

No one has studied democracy more fundamentally than did Alexis de Tocqueville, whose great work on American democracy is still a classic. Let us hear him speak from several angles, in order to catch his full thought:

"At the present time civic zeal seems to me to be inseparable from the exercise of political rights. . . . It is impossible that the lower orders should take a part in public business without extending the circle of their ideas, and without quitting the ordinary routine of their mental acquirements. . . . A government retains its sway over a great number of citizens far less by the voluntary and rational consent of the multitude than by

that instinctive and to a certain extent involuntary agreement which results from similarities of feelings and re-
semblances of opinion. I will never admit that men
constitute a social body simply because they obey the
same head and the same laws. Society can only exist
when a great number of men consider a great number
of things in the same point of view; when they hold
the same opinions upon many subjects, and when the
same occurrences suggest the same thoughts and impressions to their minds. . . . Let us suppose that all the
members of the community take a part in the government, and that each one of them has an equal right to
take a part in it. As none is different from his fellows
none can exercise a tyrannical power: men will be perfectly free because they will be entirely equal; and they
will all be perfectly equal because they will be entirely
free. To this ideal state democratic nations tend. . . .
The passion for equality penetrates on every side into
men's hearts, expands there, and fills them entirely. . . .
The great advantage of the Americans is that they have
arrived at a state of democracy without having to endure a democratic revolution; and that they are born
equal instead of becoming so. . . . If the object be to
have the local affairs of a district conducted by the men
who reside there, the same persons are always in contact, and they are, in a manner, forced to be acquainted,
and to adapt themselves to one another. . . . If men
are to remain civilized, or to become so, the art of associating together must grow and improve in the same
ratio in which the equality of conditions is increased.
. . . When a people, then, have any knowledge of public life, the notion of association, and the wish to coal-
esce, present themselves every day to the minds of the
whole community: whatever natural repugnance may

restrain men from acting in concert, they will always be ready to combine for the sake of a party. Thus political life makes the love and practice of association more general; it imparts a desire of union, and teaches the means of combination to numbers of men who would have always lived apart. . . . If at all times education enables men to defend their independence, this is most especially true in democratic countries."

These and many like words of the great student of spontaneous democracy brand our attempts to force democracy with the arm of the law as peculiarly futile. De Tocqueville evidently thought that democracy produced "entire equality" and all that goes with it. And Southern instinct needs only to be translated into philosophic language to say just what De Tocqueville meant and said.

Now, the time for argument about theoretic *racial* equality has passed, not only at the South, where it hardly ever existed even in the minds of the few, but also in other parts of the country, which are rapidly coming to take the Southern view of the whole matter. Under these circumstances it is not surprising that many, if not most, Southerners feel doubtful about the advisability of educating the negro *for an unknown future.* When they say that what the negro needs is industrial education they somehow feel that such education will fit the negro for his "place," which, in their view, is something akin to a status of peasantry. The South has little heart in educating the negro. The North is suffering from moral lassitude as to the whole subject. Some say, both at the South and at the North, "Let the question alone; it will solve itself." Perhaps so, but will it solve itself so as to make the most of the South and at the same time do the negro justice? And *is* it solving itself,

either at the North or at the South? Two headlines
from a recent issue of a well-known metropolitan paper
will reply. The first reads thus: "To Segregate Negro
Homes." But perhaps it is Southern "prejudice" that
makes Baltimore strive to segregate the negro, no matter what his education. Here is an extract from the report to the Baltimore Council that would be amusing
were it not tragic: "No fault is found with the negroes'
ambitions, but the committee feels that Baltimoreans will
be criminally negligent as to their future happiness if
they suffer the negroes' ambitions to go unchecked." A
modern instance is this of the little nursery dialogue:

> " 'Mother, may I go out to swim?'
> 'Yes, my darling daughter;
> Hang your clothes on a hickory limb,
> But don't go near the water!' "

If the Supreme Court of the United States should decide against the Baltimore ordinance, the whites have
plans in plenty whereby their purpose may be effected.
Here is one from New York City, which I introduce as
the second of the two newspaper headings above referred to:

"$20,000 To Keep Negroes Out. Harlemites Sub-
scribe that Amount to Save West 136th Street."

Man's inhumanity to man, we say, until the "am-
bitious" negroes move into *our* street!

We may sum up the discussion thus far somewhat as
follows:

Education is a function of democracy and hence spells
equality of status. To offer education is to offer generic
equality of individual with individual. Equality of opportunity is opportunity for equality of all kinds. If

we deny the possibility of equality, to offer the opportunity that leads naturally to equality is to insult human
intelligence and perpetrate a cosmic joke. For what
else means opportunity without satisfaction except rebellion, or retrogression, or despair? Shall we open the
door of hope to the negro only to usher him into the
outer darkness of disillusion, or else to invite him in
to partake of the feast of citizenship, and then crush
him against the very doorpost of social opportunity?
If we owe the negro an education—and we do—how
shall we give him real, unforced, natural opportunity?

When closely questioned Southern people admit all
the ideal principles of the rights of man, equality of
opportunity and the like. Humanitarianism and democracy are not strange notions to them. But they agree
with the maxim, "might till right is ready," and they
are not convinced that negroes should exercise all their
rights *now*. Nor do they think it self-evident that the
negro should have equality of opportunity *here*. The
Reverend Edgar Gardner Murphy, who has thought
deeply on this subject in his "Basis of Ascendancy," tells
the South to be content with an economic status less high
than that of other parts of the country. But I do not
believe that anyone should ask the South to be damned
even relatively, for its black brethren's sake, unless no
feasible way can be found out of the difficulty.

A man high in dignity and reputation told me only
yesterday, when I confronted him with the facts of human nature as they *are:* "I agree with the saying, 'Damn
your facts!'" But, however much we might like to
damn the facts, it is they that are in the habit of doing
the damning and the blessing. A fact is a sacred thing
from the hands of God, and must find its place in our
practical philosophy of life, even though our "principles"

may refuse to shake hands with it. Until we become
disembodied spirits we must try to square biological and
psychological phenomena with the higher facts of our
spiritual nature as best we can. So long as the world is
wide and the negro question is not studied, *we have no
right to compel a choice between the utilitarian and the
ideal motives of our consciences.* For self-sacrifice is
noble only when ethically necessary. And, until a hurt-
ful necessity is actually known to be such, we are simply
quixotic, if not foolish, in bowing to the alleged obligation to give the negro full equality of opportunity, which
naturally leads to opportunity for all equality, including
social equality, at the expense of the South's development.

The esteemed gentleman just referred to told me,
almost in one breath, (1) that the South is obscurantist,
medieval, and (2) that the South ought to leave the
issue of the race problem to Providence. In other words,
he seems to think it reactionary for one to doubt the
practicality of applying the abstract doctrines of the
rights of man in certain definite temporal and spatial
ways, but *not* reactionary to turn over to Providence a
problem that we have not yet scientifically investigated.
The South may well be pardoned for believing that
everything must be "left to Providence," because not a
sparrow falleth without divine responsibility; and that
nothing must be left to Providence, without effort on our
part, because we are told to work out our own salvation in fear and trembling.

But why this suspicion of biological and psychological
science? Why this pitting of science against religion?
Is there any reason for believing that because Israel was
a "Chosen People" there was no "natural selection" in
her case? Have we failed to realize the implications of

the soul's not being able to express and realize itself in
time and space except through the body, and especially
the nervous system? Have we forgotten that even certain noble phases of the master passion, love, have been
reached by the spiritualization of a natural appetite?

I was not surprised to find that a certain distinguished
New Yorker "didn't know" but that amalgamation might
solve the negro problem if the races remained in contact
long enough. Nor was I surprised to hear him say that
the next great epic poet would have negro blood in his
veins. After all, those who want us to "wait" on the
problem and are not disposed to urge the scientific study
of it may well be suspected either of being deeply logical in their subconsciousness, and therefore dimly expecting and perhaps hoping that the "natural" or biological solution through amalgamation may come about in
time; or else of looking forward to a permanent status of
spiritual, if not economic, serfdom for the negro. The
amalgamationists realize that race prejudice is not primarily instinctive, and that the breaking down of the fashion
that proscribes the negro will leave nature free to solve
the problem in the only way she uses to solve such problems without war, actual or potential; the subordination-
ists know that if they can keep the stigma of inferiority
fastened on the negro the negro cannot rise higher to
ultimate intermarriage.

I have tried to suggest the nature and difficulties of
our problem as fairly and dispassionately as can be
done by one who is a humanitarian and an American
and at the same time a Southerner of the Southerners.
We must not give up our broad American principles.
But we must bring them into contact with the facts of
the situation as well as we can.

We must face the facts, whatever our philosophy, and

thus work out the high designs of Providence. We must study the negro problem, would we educate the negro intelligently. We must find out as nearly as we can what "place" we are fitting him for. Even the broken lights of science are better than a blind faith. For real faith has insight. "We *know* in whom we have believed." And much of our social knowledge, and some of the most usable parts of it, comes from the vigorous scientific method of to-day.

Granting, then, that we as educators should do our best to urge the study of the negro question and help on that study when it shall have been started in a well-organized way, what shall we say about our attitude toward the education of the negro?

1. We must educate him because he is a man, and a man must be educated in some sense, no matter what future lies before him.

2. We must educate him because ignorant men are dangerous, especially to a democracy pledged to educate all men.

3. We must educate him for the protection of our own health and our own moral character, for ignorance spreads disease and vice.

4. We must educate him so that he may help to solve his own problem, for we have no right to impose our "solutions" on the negro without giving him a chance to understand.

5. We must educate him would we have him stand alone; and whatever his fate he must ultimately stand through his own strength.

6. We must educate him because the public opinion of the civilized world demands his education, and if we pay deference to a world view we cannot consistently deny to it some degree of reason and righteousness.

7. We must educate him because he wants to be educated, and we can give him no satisfactory reason for refusing him this boon.

8. We must educate him because he earns his education through his labor and his efforts to educate himself.

9. We must educate him for the sake of the admittedly worthy remnant, and in order that the worthy few may have followers who can be intelligently led and will intelligently follow.

Doubtless there are other good reasons why the negro should be educated: those given will serve our present purpose.

But, while we are educating the negro and assisting him to educate himself, let us tell him and his friends at the North and at the South a few wholesome things.

1. A scientific study, especially of negro character and its possibilities, should be made in order that the education of the negro should have an objective point, and in order that uneasy dread of the future on the part of Southern whites may be allayed as far as possible.

2. Assimilation through intermarriage is not to be considered as a feasible or as a righteous solution of the problem.

3. Northern and Southern opinion are approximating each other. Both tend to lose interest in the negro. The gulf between the races is widening at the North as well as at the South.

4. Unless, or until we know to the contrary, the negro is to be regarded simply as a relatively inferior race, inasmuch as science has not pronounced him hopelessly inferior for all time.

5. The ultimate "peasantry" solution is not to be countenanced, inasmuch as it is un-American and in-

human, and would injure the white people morally and economically.

6. Equality of opportunity should come to the negro somehow, some time, somewhere, provided the white people's supremacy in their own land is not endangered. Let science and the natural course of events determine *where, when* and *how.*

7. In the meantime, while the negro should abate none of his claims to complete manhood, let him, like Brer Rabbit, "keep on sayin' nothin'." Patience now means opportunity in the future. Agitation now may precipitate disaster. There are enough friends of humankind in the country to keep a care of the negro's future if he will prove himself worthy.

8. The negro must develop his own civilization and social self-consciousness.

9. Whatever the final solution may be it must not cause permanent retardation of the South's complete development. This means that the inferior race must never be favored at the expense of the superior race.

10. Conditions will improve when "preternatural suspicion" is allayed by the adoption of a definite policy by the country, whereby generous justice is done the negro without upsetting the rational race orthodoxy of the South.

11. We need to be more pessimistic as to present conditions and more optimistic as to the ultimate future, provided we agree to have a carefully organized, national, non-partisan, coöperative study of the race question.

12. The scientific study may modify some of the above conclusions. Unless we have open minds our study will simply show us what we want to see.

13. As long as the races live together on the same soil, the negro, individually and collectively, will be

treated as inferior, and therefore cannot hope for spiritual freedom.

14.   It would be the part of wisdom to facilitate segregation of the races in as many ways as possible, pending the results of a scientific study of the negro problem.

II. A NEGRO RURAL SCHOOL

(July 1912. Report on two Negro Summer Schools, Tate County, Miss.)

We started, the County Superintendent and I, at half-past eight in the morning on a hot day in August. The school was four miles distant from the county seat. On the way we met negro children of various sizes and complexions wending their leisurely way to school. When we were returning, at about ten-thirty a. m., some of the pupils were still unconcernedly straggling to school. At the schoolhouse I saw several groups come in. None showed the slightest embarrassment. All said, Good morning. Their coming in and their greeting produced no effect whatever on either teacher or pupils. The county superintendent did not seem to think it in the realm of possibility to bring about any improvement in punctuality. The parents are "free American citizens." If hurried or harried on the subject of punctuality, they usually, it is said, prefer having their children quit school to having themselves or their children hurried.

We passed several houses with litters of pickaninnies on their porches. One cabin porch held six children, all apparently under seven years of age. Along the road came several tots of kindergarten age, "going to school." At the schoolhouse I saw a fully developed woman who was one of the pupils. I hope she was in the highest grade—say the "negro" equivalent of the advanced fourth grade of a fair country school. When she dropped her

273

book on the floor and scattered its pages over a considerable area she picked up the leaves without the slightest sign of haste or disquiet.

The schoolhouse is in a pleasant grove, close by a negro church. The County Superintendent told me of its pious name, and then gave the following partial list of some of his negro schools: St. Paul, St. Peter, Paradise, Zion Hill. The church and the schoolhouse were apparently substantial buildings. Although the windows of the schoolhouse were not higher than a tall man's chin, they extended to the floor, and, with the aid of front and back doors, gave fairly good ventilation. There were no desks. The children sat on wooden benches, some of which were grouped in the rear of the room and some placed along the windows. The children "lined up" to recite. Each one had a "number" given him or her. The reason for this could not be discovered, for no reference was made to the numbers after they had been assigned, except that the teacher became rather severe in his language if a pupil could not give his number when called on for it. Perhaps he was trying to teach attention and obedience to command.

I have already intimated that the range of ages in the three or four approximate grades of the school was between four and eighteen. The teacher said that sixty were in attendance; I suppose he meant that there were sixty "a-comin' and a-gwyne"!

Some of the children were atrociously filthy and ragged; others were fairly neat and clean. Most of them were African in color and feature. However, practically none of them looked like the pictures of the lower African type that one sees in popular books on ethnology. Not a few had fairly pleasing, regular features, though of the higher African type. No difference in mental brightness could be detected between the pure negroes and the mixed types. The most intelligent face I saw was that of an apparently full-blooded little negro girl. There was not a harsh voice in the room; the tones were full, soft and musical. The children seemed to pay little attention to the presence of white strangers. Sometimes a child would "study out loud," but seemingly without disturbing the work of others. The children moved around freely, but noiselessly, without asking permission. In fact, they were unconventionally easy in their manners. Apparently not a ripple of interest was excited when a boy came in with a bundle of able-bodied switches which he handed to the teacher, who selected one and used it as a pointer. I could detect no mischievous talking and laughing. Perhaps there had been a letting-off of steam before we entered. And perhaps our presence and the timely appearance of the switches produced the effect of salutary peace.

One of the most noticeable phenomena I observed, one which is constantly to be noted, was the unhurried flow of the children's movements, without sign of articulate sharpness or angularity or self-conscious awkwardness. The thought came to me, How impossible is it to decide how much of the negro's assumed lack of resentment is due to his easy, smooth "Brer Rabbit" manners! How easy it is for us to misunderstand an alien people! There is such a quality as tactful and astute childlikeness.

The teacher was very methodical as to ritual, and absolutely without intellectual method. He lined up the children; he numbered them; he was punctilious in placing the reciter in front of the class and in requiring the rhythmic following of the leader as he sang: "Twenty, twenty-one, twenty-two, etc.; thirty, thirty-one, etc.; forty, forty-one, etc." No attempt was made to count by tens; most of the time was wasted in going over the digits, with which all were familiar. About half the class would make absurd mistakes with the sequence of tens. One put ninety after twenty. Another went back to forty after having safely reached sixty. The class repeated the errors in chorus, after which the teacher allowed corrections. By means of some intuition which I do not understand, the teacher would announce from time to time to the reciter: "That's as far as you can go; that will do." I did not see any blackboard work. There was a very small piece of blackboard of some description in one corner of the room. Here, as in other respects educational, the negro gets his minimum—"good enough for niggers." If the white men of the county were asked whether the schools of the negroes had enough blackboard space, they would be likely to reply —as some have replied: "Enough for the kind of pupils and teachers that use them."

The reading of a "third reader" class was instructive —to me. The seven children had one and a part books. To all appearances, there was not a third enough books in use in the school. The teacher said that "the books had not *come.*" I don't believe that the books had any intention of coming. My friend the superintendent told teacher and pupils very plainly that nothing could be done without at least the reading books. He suggested that a halfday of work by one of the children would buy a book. But why should one work when one doesn't *have to?*

The teacher spent most of the reading period in having the children spell out the new words from the reader as the book was passed from hand to hand. If the teacher himself had a reader, he did not use it, but stood behind each pupil as the child tried to read. However, the chil-

dren *could* read a little. I wonder why! And the superintendent says that this teacher who, with great difficulty,
after several trials, succeeds in getting the lowest (third-
grade) certificate, teaches about as well as the holders
of first-grade certificates. I was told that the teacher
was a reputable, excellent fellow,—and he looked the
part. I want to find out from him how he can dress so
well on less than one hundred and twenty dollars a year.
His shining laundered collar and cuffs, glistening alpaca
coat, striped trousers, well-blacked shoes, would have
passed muster anywhere. Although he came out to
meet us as we arrived, and accompanied us to the
buggy as we were leaving, the superintendent did not
present him to me; nor was any word of farewell ut-
tered.

In some Southern cities the negro principals are called
"Mr." and are duly introduced to strangers; but my
friend, the county superintendent, was natural and logical in making no pretense of departing from the social
facts of the case; who should blame him? And who can
blame him for spending on the negro schools propor-
tionally only from one-tenth to one-twentieth of his time?
His chances for reëlection would be faint indeed if he
"wasted his time on niggers." He is a compassionate,
Christian man; but facts are facts, "niggers are niggers,"
and the belief of the average Southerner in the literary
education of the negro is less than half-hearted. Most
Southerners are perfectly willing to be "shown" that the
negro should be educated; but attempts to prove this by
pointing out the absence of a select class of negroes from
the penitentiary does not convince them. The alleged
existence of a higher percentage of bare. literacy in the
penitentiary of South Carolina, for instance, than exists

outside in that state, more than offsets what one might urge in favor of a crude smattering of literary education for the negroes.

I think that this rural negro school is fairly typical; in some respects (building, for instance) it is superior to most of the negro country schools that I have seen. Now, if you ask me frankly whether the kind of education I see in a school like this is really worth anything, I find it hard to reply, although I believe in the education of every human being to the limit of his capacity. Surely it would be worth while to prove to the Southerner that the education of the negro masses is worth while, and that it would pay the South and the country at large to spend vastly more than we do in training negro rural teachers and in equipping negro rural schools. But I confess that the proof is neither self-evident nor easy.

Why should a believer in universal education feel himself become so unsettled after seeing a few inefficient, grotesquely inefficient negro schools? Well, for several reasons: (1) Because the white people want to "keep the negro in his place," and educated people have a way of making their own places and their own terms; (2) because a Southern man, even if the best type, shows interest in negro education only with bated breath; (3) anything that makes the negro a better competitor of the white man tends to increase race feeling; (4) education is a mockery in the case of people who are fundamentally unfree, who are held in the position of a permanently inferior social caste, who are deprived of the normal accompaniments of citizenship; (5) because, if liberated minds do not claim their due, they are contemptible and are not worthy of education, and, if they do claim their rights and thereby cause interracial strife, they are dan-

gerous to the community.   So thinks the average white
man.

Now, I do not give these reasons as my own convictions, but as thoughts that arise in my mind when I study
a negro school and then note the attitude of its white
neighbors toward it.   Not for one moment do I give
up the belief in universal and adequate education for all
men; but again and again is the conviction forced on me
that education is not a thing apart, but is economically,
religiously, juridically, politically, and, above all, *socially*
conditioned.   Separate education from the normal American principles that should accompany it, and I for
one dare not predict what its result will be.   Here,
as usual, we come back to our primary contention, if
we are disinterested students of the negro question:
until a "solution" is in sight, the Southern whites will
not apply the principles of liberty, equality and fraternity
to the negro; such a solution must not be such as to interfere with the fundamental Southern view of the negro's
social position; a solution that will not attempt to reverse
Southern sentiment, but which at the same time will be
true to the principles of Christian democracy, cannot be
arrived at with the data we have in hand, or without a
careful, long-continued, scientific study.   Nor must it
be forgotten that in a study that is radically psychological
ability to interpret human instinct, habit, custom, usage,
feeling, attitude, prejudice—in a word, ability to interpret subjective, qualitative data, is indispensably necessary, and cannot have its place taken by laboratory experiments, anthropological measurements, economic statistics and historical deductions, important as these are.
Once more, the psychology of the white man's mind and
a psychological knowledge of the negro's capacity and

ability are absolutely essential if the solution of the negro problem is even to be sought intelligently.*

* In this paper and the following actual conditions are portrayed, but these two papers are not intended to suggest that there are no good negro schools. Indeed the author has recently visited negro schools of a fair order of efficiency—mostly in the cities and the larger towns of the South.

III. SHADY GROVE

NOTES OF SHADES AND SHADOWS IN A FIRST GRADE NEGRO TEACHER'S SCHOOL AND A NEGRO INSTITUTE

The school was called Shady Grove, apparently on the well-known principle of "contrary suggestion," for there was neither grove nor shade near the school. But there was a church near by, and there was shade—intellectual and ethical shadow—inside the schoolroom. There were two teachers working in the same room, and apparently in no wise disturbing each other. The principal was loud and the assistant very quiet. This convenient division of labor brought about a popular average. In most respects the school was similar to Zion Hill, the subject of a preceding sketch. No desks, inconspicuous blackboards, etc. Ninety-six on the roll; seventy-one in attendance. We visited the school in the afternoon, hence the phenomena of unpunctuality were not in evidence.

The superintendent tells me that over half the negro schools of his county are in churches. Sometimes the county offers to help build a school, but the negroes invariably decline to deed the building and site to the county, although their local board has complete use of the property. In all cases the local trustees are negroes. The only desks in the negro schools of the county are in the larger towns, except that there are a few rough home-made desks in a few rural schools.

The teacher is of the Bantu type. His face and form

are dignified. He talked for our benefit, and spoke of
us as distinguished educators. He is the holder of a
first-grade certificate and is a teacher of twenty years'
standing. His education showed itself in his greater
facility of speech, which was sometimes of involved
rhetorical nature. Among other things, he called our
attention to the "Tyro Class." I thought he meant a
class from Tyro, one of the villages of the county. When
I expressed surprise that a Tyro class should be there,
he relieved my trouble by telling me that he meant the
primer class. The incident was typical.

The children were black or dark brown in color, for
the most part; but there were two children that might
have passed for white. A year or two previous, when
a negro woman was in charge of the school, the superintendent, seeing several apparently white children in the
room, said to the teacher: "You have some of the wrong
children here, haven't you?" She replied, with the tact
characteristic of her race: "Their mother associates with
the colored folks." This case of concubinage is exceptional—the only one in the county, I am informed. Even
in this instance the association is not open. If it were,
there would be trouble, no doubt. The two "white"
children were the most restless in the room; but seemed
on perfectly natural and intimate terms with the blacks.

Looking very closely for signs of self-consciousness, I
thought, as often before, that the lack of "white" signs,
such as blushing and angular awkwardness, accounts
largely for the apparently easy manners of the negroes.
One black girl in this school suffered a sort of undulat-
ing squirming wriggle that "ran all over" her when she
was embarrassed at missing a question. When the county
superintendent stood up to count the children there was
almost painful silence in the room, though a moment be-

fore the children *seemed* to be paying no attention to the white visitors.

The recitation in physiology consisted of reading the text (one book to every four pupils) and then proving incontestably that nothing had been learned. The only child that seemed to know anything was a lank chap, very black, of the Guinea type, and the perfect picture of good humor and amiability. He was probably the best specimen of a "white man's nigger" in the room: good-natured, docile, respectful and willing. The highest class studied the fourth reader.

On the way back I questioned the county superintendent with regard to a comparison between the country and the town schools among the negroes. Though the town schools are better equipped and have better teachers, often excellent teachers, according to the superintendent, the net result for *character* is about the same. "There is no moral uplift and no relation between the school and life," said the superintendent. And most of the county superintendents seem to agree with my friend's statement.

When the negro teachers talk of practical and moral matters to the children in the presence of the whites their speech has a hollow, unreal sound. Perhaps some of them speak more earnestly when the whites are not around. But I am afraid that the neat and dignified dress of the teachers—for in my experience the two schools we visited in this county are typical so far as the dress of the teacher is concerned—is not the outward and visible sign of priestly helpfulness, for it would seem that the teacher very seldom got close to the hearts of the children. This school, though better off as to teachers than the Zion Hill school, was perhaps even more depressing, not only on account of the presence of the little octoroons,

but also because of the "depressed dignity" of the teacher,
who evidently felt that he had something of the gentleman in him that we whites did not appreciate.

In discussing negro traits the superintendent illustrated the "ingratitude" of the negro by telling me of a
negro girl who had been in his household for twelve
years (from five years old to seventeen) as a nurse girl.
When her people wanted her to go home she wept copi-
ously and took a long time to decide that she *could*
break away. But after she left she seemed to have no
further interest in the family, although at the parting
she had been given additional food and raiment and
money in her purse.

But *was* this a case of ingratitude? The county superintendent, being a careful man and knowing that nobody
understands the negro, would not venture to make a
dogmatic statement.

At a negro teachers' institute next day I asked the
negroes to tell me what they thought about the common
accusation of the whites that the "average" negro lacked
sympathy toward his kind, gratitude, resentfulness and
intellectual curiosity. Most of them would not express
an opinion; nor did I blame them. Those who talked
were afraid that the "lower types of colored folks" did
have the traits attributed to them. The white conductor
of the institute, although he treated these negro teachers
as if they had been sixth grade children, sturdily defended the negroes from the accusation of ingratitude
and lack of sympathy. Nevertheless, though he spoke
of the sympathy and gratitude of negroes toward *him,*
his contention simply bore out the statement of Rev.
Dr. Hedleston of the University of Mississippi, namely,
that negroes are often kind and sympathetic toward
whites in far greater degree than they are toward their

own kind. Their respect for the whites, and their "optimism" (as my friend, the conductor at this institute,
put it), which makes them feel that "there's nothing really
the matter with that (supposedly sick) nigger," may in
part account for the phenomenon. I have authentic information of a negro who faithfully nursed a negro
woman that was sick in a house several miles away, but
who neglected the same woman when she was sick in *his*
house, so that she died. I asked my informant to explain the anomaly. He, too, is a cautious man and
would not commit himself, but suggested that the negro
appreciated the "company" he found at the house several
miles off, and didn't find the nursing interesting or heroic
at his own home. Who knows? How pitiably little we
know about the brother in black. And how necessary
it is that we understand his traits of character if we are
going to educate him, and if we are to solve the negro
problem.

A year of "microscopic" psychological work in Mississippi, if carried on by people who knew what the valuable
facts were and could sympathetically and scientifically
interpret them, would be worth all the books on the
negro question put together, not because some of these
books are not valuable, but because they tell us nothing
internally real about negro character and the psychology
of race prejudice. And these things are the "facts" we
most need to know in solving any human problem that
pertains to racial contact and racial efficiency. The mania
for deductive statement and premature generalization has
prevented first-hand minute study of the *little* things of
character that science has need of. The "little *knowledge*" of the average intelligent white Southerner may
ultimately prove even more deadly to the negro and to
the white also than do even the sentimental vaporings of

benevolent idealists without practical knowledge. First of all, men need and want *justice:* and the first requisite in doing a man justice is to appreciate his common humanity and his capacity for progress. This "justice" the negro seldom gets. Perhaps there is little hope that he can as a race "stand alone"; but dogmatic insistence that he can or cannot do this or that is neither kind nor scientific, though it may be popular and profitable in a political way for some of the "leaders of public opinion in our beloved Southland," who are neither better nor worse than the other politicians of the world.

Wishing, as I do, that there was not a negro on American soil—though there are many negroes whose characters I esteem—nevertheless no "prejudice" can make me or my kind blind to the evident fact that the negro has a right to be understood sympathetically and scientifically before we attempt to declare what education is good for him, or what his fate shall ultimately be. It is, however, even more important that we understand and appreciate the Southern white man's point of view.

When we came out of the institute above referred to my white companion said: "Only one of those negroes was impudent." He referred to the teacher of Bantu type, who evidently resented being treated as a child by saying very deliberately that his reason for not knowing a problem was that he—had—probably—not—given—sufficient—study. I hope that my friend the conductor forgave him for his attempt to express his valuation of his own manhood!

IV. A COUNTY INSTITUTE FOR NEGRO TEACHERS

(Report of the conductor of Negro Institute, Yalobusha County, Miss., held at Coffeeville, Sept., 1912.)

Custom has decreed that, although white people may not teach negroes in the South * without loss of social prestige, one may conduct a negro institute, presumably because there are so few negroes that can do such work, and, perhaps, also because one need have no sort of social contact with the negroes. Apparently the average white conductor of a negro institute seems to think it advisable to "take the negro as he finds him"; pay little attention to punctuality and regularity of attendance; give the negroes copious opportunities to spell and to "work examples" or have them worked by the conductor; and talk to the teachers occasionally in a way that will help the negroes to "keep their places" and teach their pupils to obey this one commandment without which let all negroes be accursed! Intending to do nothing that will alienate from me the entire confidence of my own race as represented by the white people of the South, nevertheless I am fully persuaded that these same white folk have to the full the humanitarian principles and feelings possessed by any other people, and that they wish the negro well, provided he "keeps his place," and provided he and his friends do nothing to endanger "white supremacy." Hence I determined to have this institute

*Except in Charleston, S. C. (?)

make for the betterment of the negro, and at the
same time have him realize even more than he does
that his fate is in the hands of his white neighbors, so
far as any people's future can be under the control of
another people.

The nation as a whole is tired of the negro and the
negro question, and is greatly inclined to leave the whole
matter in the hands of the white people of the South.
So long as the dominant race knows that one who is
working to help the negroes is not simply a "philanthropic" upholder of abstract human "rights," but believes that all rights—at least in their expression—must
be subordinate to the public welfare, no hostility toward
his work need be feared. Many abnormally suspicious
Southern whites are in their heart of hearts inclined to
think that ultimately the race problem will be settled by
"amalgamation"; and this dread of the future unsatisfactory solution makes them look askance on any sort
of relation between whites and negroes that may even
possibly give the negro the impression that the fundamental tenet of the Southern racial faith may in some
wise be relaxed ultimately.

Although I am one of those who believe that intermarriage between the races will never come, and that
illicit admixture is on the decrease, I nevertheless deem
it wise to guard with the utmost care all presumably
possible approaches to any sort of assertion of negro
"equality." Abstract human rights are one thing; the
assertion of them and attempt to have them function
here and *now* are quite other things. The white race is
in control; and hence its welfare must be first considered
when questions of public concern arise. Whatever the
theory of the matter may be, the negro must, under present conditions of racial contact, be willing to be treated

as a people under tutelage, and trust to the real manhood of good men in the South.

Were it not that citizenship in a democratic state is ultimately based on at least *potential* social equality, it would be possible to give the negro all rights of citizenship; but under the circumstances he must ask for a child's right of protection and guidance rather than for adult justice. That such a status bears rather heavily on divers individuals of the negro race is undoubtedly true. But the superior negroes must be content to "die that they may live." Such is the solidarity of race and such the inclusiveness and vigor of the vague instinct underlying "race prejudice" that each negro must submit to be ranked as a representative of his race rather than as an independent man in full possession of individual human rights.

The race platform written by the conductor of the institute and unanimously adopted by the teachers attempts to conserve both the ideal principles of human nature and the real facts of the racial situation at the South. Hence I am here stating my attitude, so as to show the temper in which I conducted the work.

The organization of the institute was substantially the same as that adopted at a white institute held a few weeks before by myself. Three phases of work were attempted: (1) Methods and other professional help given through the lectures of the conductor; (2) round-tables, presided over by some of the more experienced teachers, in which round-table discussions the teachers had an opportunity to exchange views and gain help from one another, and in which the conductor took care that only useful lines of discussion had the right of way; (3) informal talks occasionally by the conductor in which he attempted to show the moral and religious bearing of education in the development of character. Of course, the last-named feature, in the case of this negro institute, was adapted to the actual moral and religious needs of the negroes, and had special reference to their racial status. Each feature of the institute seemed to meet the needs of the teachers. When the conductor offered to devote some portion of the time to text-book work the leading teachers asked him to adhere to his original plan, saying that the teachers ought to "get up their examinations themselves," and not expect the institute to help them get their licenses. In order that the young teachers might have some help in getting ready for examination, some of the older teachers gave them practical help immediately before the morning session, during the midday intermission, and after the afternoon session. The negroes, both teachers and taught, did this voluntary work cheerfully and faithfully.

I was told that it would be of no use to attempt to exact punctuality and regular attendance. Nevertheless, I had the roll called at each session, and was delighted to find that the negroes would practice punctuality and regularity when properly incited to do so. They saw that I wanted to help them and that I was genuinely interested in their welfare. If the teacher is perfunctory, the pupils will be so likewise. But all races and people respond to human kindness if it be judicious, practical and firm.

The attendance increased as the institute progressed, though it was supposed that the negroes would not remain for the full week. All sorts and conditions were represented among the little band present. There were several teachers of long experience—one or two had taught for thirty years. Then there were several who had not taught a day. There were ex-slaves and there were representatives of negro colleges. At least one of the teachers had been prominent in politics during Reconstruction times. But the unity of spirit was remarkable; and no less striking was the dignity of character, the self-control and yet perfect naturalness and spontaneity. All seemed to be fond of fun and laughed heartily at times. They joked one another freely during the round-table discussions. Nevertheless, their docility and their quickness to appreciate the proprieties were very noticeable. I found them entirely frank as to the characteristic weaknesses of the masses of their race. What might have seemed pomposity or bumptiousness proved to be childlike expressiveness, or dramatic make-believe, when more closely observed. It is strange that many of the observers of negro character so easily charge these people with bumptiousness when it is so evident that most of them delight in playing a part and in "showing off" as children do.

They evinced a most interesting combination of unconventionality and politeness. Indeed, the better negroes in the South are really a very adaptable and versatile people, possessed of a certain kind of social tact that helps to explain why they are not "accommodating enough" either to give up in despair or to commit constant errors of behavior toward the white people.

The negroes seem to be a cautious race; hence the whites are inclined to doubt the negro's belief in his own rights. I doubt whether we have a right to call them unrevengeful and ungrateful, and so on. For their apparent lack of resentment is clearly due in many cases to caution, in other cases to amiability, and not seldom to the thorough way in which they have been trained to respect white people. True, they do not as a rule seem to possess the sullen, steady, deep-seated revengefulness popularly ascribed to the American Indian; but, then, the negro, in spite of being so close to "savagery," usually has an eye for results. He may be unthrifty; but he is certainly capable of remarkable self-control, as well as of painstaking thrift. Although I have observed negro character all my life, I find a great difference between the conventional observations of my youth and the more disinterested and discriminating study of the last nine years, during which my observation has been more direct and careful. The negro's lack of dignity of character has always been a source of lack of confidence in the race; but although the teachers in this institute represent a higher grade of negro character, they do prove to my satisfaction that the term negro by no means connotes shallowness and futility in the deeper emotional life. I shall never forget the mingling of constraint, pathetic sense of gratitude, and childlike expressiveness of some of the young women when with faltering lips they strove to express in open institute their appreciation of what the conductor had striven to do for them. The calling down of God's blessings on one's head by these simple folk is an experience that I should like some of our Southern radicals to experience. The young women in the institute evidently felt the strangeness of speaking in terms of gratitude of a white man, but, nevertheless, were not to be deterred from expressing their feelings. The result was pathetic in its poignant humanness.

One night, at the request of the institute, I spoke to the colored people generally at one of their churches. I took two prominent white citizens along with me as "witnesses." Experience has warned me that above all things an investigator of the negro question must avoid even the appearance of evil in talking to the negroes with regard to their relations to the whites. The gentlemen just mentioned avowed sympathy with everything I said to the negroes. Although both men were above suspicion as to their Caucasian and Southern orthodoxy, they nevertheless thought it best to tell no one that they had gone to the meeting. In other words, they avoided the necessity of making explanations.

During my speech I reviewed the disasters of Reconstruction and drew a rather dark picture of the status of the negro at present; but I did not refrain from expressing my firm belief, as part of my belief in God, that the negro folk, somehow, somewhere, in God's good time, would have the opportunity of the fullest development of which they as a people were capable, although they must be content with a subordinate place as long as the two races dwelt together. One of the leading negroes said to me afterwards: "You carried us so deep into the darkness that I was 'most afraid you wouldn't get us out!" This remark is typical. It combines humor, patience, cheerfulness, faith and childlike expressiveness.

As among the whites, discipline proved to be the most popular topic. The discussion of corporal punishment reminded me of similar discussions in white institutes thirty years ago. However, it was interesting to know that some of the oldest teachers, ex-slaves, had found out the dangers and inutility of constant corporal punishment. One teacher put on the board as a recipe for good discipline the single word, "kindness." I amended by prefixing the word "firm." I think that this suggestion, perhaps partly because the incident was a little dramatic, made a deeper impression on the institute than anything else I did. At any rate, several teachers mentioned it at the last, and especially thanked me for showing that kindness and firmness must go together in discipline. I reminded them that sometimes one must be even rigid in order to be kind, and that they must so regard some of the treatment their white friends bestowed on them.   Indeed, it is sometimes necessary to run the risk of hurting the feelings of the whole negro race in order to keep down the foolish and dangerous effervescence of some misguided negroes.   "Whom He loveth He chasteneth" has been said of the Deity Himself.   And the negroes must learn that their true friends are not necessarily those that tell negroes of their abstract rights, but rather those that remind them of their *duties* of patience and self-control and humility.   If ever a race needed to conquer by serving, the negro race is such a one.   No good will ever come to the negroes from their "leaders" speaking of the "so-called negro problem," and so on.   These leaders must learn to realize that there is always a problem, a most serious and deadly one, when one race holds another in spiritual bondage, without intending to give that other the free rights of citizenship, because of the inevitable connection of all human rights with the only worth-while rights of free manhood,—liberty, equality and fraternity.

To assume that the negro's thrift and soberness and the like will make him a citizen and the possessor of freely acknowledged spiritual freedom is a most dangerous error.   There is no observable tendency on the part of the Southern whites to allow the negroes as a race to become complete citizens; nor is there any tendency to treat individual negroes *as* individuals rather than as members of a race.   To suppose that the acquirement of thrifty habits and facility in a trade will spiritually free the negro is an absurd blunder held, I hope, by no one.   Industrial education and the like are good in themselves, but economic and intellectual growth, even along with moral and spiritual development, will not necessarily change one iota the social status of the negro. Although negroes may not *seek* to mingle socially with the whites, they remain unfree as a race just so long as the race barrier is raised against them socially, just so long as higher types of negro individuals are treated simply as representatives of an inferior race. Granted that this will always be so under the general conditions as they obtain to-day, and one grants that there is a most stupendous race problem to be solved,— the problem of spiritual slavery *versus* spiritual freedom. To separate social rights from political and religious and civic rights is to do what nature and historical democracy have never done. The mixing of blood has always solved social problems. Granting that blood is not to be mixed, how is the problem to be solved? I confess that it seems to me necessary for the negro race to be regarded as inferior and subordinate until a more complete segregation of the races is effected. In the absence of a probing investigation, however, this segregation solution must be put forth only tentatively.

The above remarks may seem to go far afield, but the thoughts they convey continually suggested themselves to me as the negroes discussed the discipline of their own children. Must we not treat in general the negroes as children? And do not all children have the same general status, in spite of vast individual differences among them? Can we dare to treat a few children as if they were too grown-up to be called children? And may it not be with a race as with children generally, that a "long infancy" leads to better intellectual results than does a precocious development? I am unable to answer these questions definitely, and most questions with regard to the negro problem; but I think that it is important to ask them, and to put them as variously as possible, in order that we may the better see the problem in all its bearings.

I noticed no "impudence" and very little "servility" among these negro teachers. A few of them showed in their street manners a little exaggeration of courtesy. In all such cases the individuals had been reared under the régime of slavery. Some of the whites seem to like the "Massa" style of politeness in negroes. For my part, I detest it. I can hardly understand how any real American should enjoy the manifestations of a servile spirit. Nor do I think that there is a real humility in this show of "the white man's nigger" *exaggerated* respect for the dominant race; but even sickening servility is safer than social assertiveness and "independence" in demeanor. Most negroes are naturally astute in dealing with the white man, and most of them have a sense of humor that is anything but servile. I doubt whether the negro that always has the word "Boss" on his lips is either especially polite or especially humble; rather he is habituated to the use of servile words, or else cunning enough to know that they serve as a convenient mask. I have expressed this doubt to several representative "polite" negroes, and the look of deep intelligence on their face when the matter was broached was very illuminating. "Playing 'possum" seems to be a device of natural selection in the interests of survival. Many of us who belong to the white race, however, feel nothing but humiliation and shame when we find that we are causing negroes to adapt themselves to our arrogance by the use of pseudo-humble words and a demeanor of pretended servility.

Let me repeat here, what I have often said before, that it is one thing, and an entirely proper thing, to deprecate all social intercourse between the races, and a very different thing to deny the democratic principle that a man's worth depends on his character and not on his race.   Let every white man oppose with all his might anything that may be construed by negroes as an approach to social communion between the races; but let him at the same time take this attitude conscientiously, because it seems best under the circumstances, and not because he wishes to humiliate "niggers."   It is well if our "instincts" go with our conscience in this matter of drawing the color line; but race enmity should not enter into our attitude, and we should not forswear our democratic principles simply because wise and foreseeing expediency, perhaps fused with natural feeling, tells us to block all approaches to "social recognition" for negroes.

However, let me not be misunderstood.   I believe that our attitude in drawing the social color line is distinctly different from that in our minds when we keep certain "undesirable" white persons in *their* "place."   I believe that it is right to let every negro understand fully and clearly that we refrain from giving him social recognition not because he is individually unsuitable, but because he is a *negro,* and it is not wise or seemly to treat even the highest negro as if he were on the same footing with any type of white man whatsoever.   I may be willing to grant that he is *personally* much superior to certain white men; but his social status is one, so far as social mingling is concerned, different in *kind* from that of the humblest white man; for the white man's grandchildren may win our fullest social recognition, and the negro's descendants cannot advance one step toward the welcome that we extend socially to white individuals who have shown themselves to be fit for the higher social

life. I am willing to tell the negro that he is able to
become socially "equal" to anything he may hold up as
a standard; but that admission will not abate one tittle
of my rigidity in contending that all possible social communion between the races must be regarded as anath-
ema. For instance, following the custom in vogue
among the white people of Memphis in school circles, I
called the negro teachers "Mister," etc.; but I was careful to tell them that the title was official only. One may
regret to have to make any such declaration;—but here
again we have a case where apparent cruelty is real
kindness. Not a few negroes put a false construction
on any indication of unusual courtesy. Most whites in
the South realize the dilemma of the Kentucky Colonel
who was at a loss as to what to call Booker Washington,
and compromised by dubbing him "professor"!

After the negroes had unanimously adopted the "platform" that I had prepared at their request, they asked
for permission to express themselves with regard to the
institute. Of course their expressions took the form
of appreciative statements with respect to the work of
the conductor. Their "tongue-tied simplicity" would, as
I have already said, have softened the hearts of various
white radicals had these been present. Practically all
the teachers present were childlike believers in Jesus as
the Christ, the Son of the living God; and as they spoke
in childish accents of their respectful gratitude I could
not but think of the saying of that same Jesus: "Whoso
shall offend one of these little ones which believe in me,
it were better for him that a millstone were hanged about
his neck and that he were drowned in the depths of the
sea." In calling attention to the following platform
which the teachers adopted after debate and reference
to a committee, I do not wish to have it thought that I

attribute any extraordinary value to the document itself; but I do frankly think that it has a typical value in showing how the two racial points of view can be reconciled at the present, pending a full and worthy study of the whole question of the relations between the races.

After a week's work with these colored teachers two impressions were deepened in my mind: First that we white folk, especially those of us that are Southerners, should ever ponder in our hearts the idea of the meaning of such phrases as *"noblesse oblige,"* "chivalry," "the grand old name of gentleman"; and, second, that while we must do all in our power to render ultimately justice and freedom rather than mere pity and condescension, we must do nothing to make the least white man feel that, *as* a white man, he is at a disadvantage as compared with the loftiest type of negro. Let the "higher" negro's life and character shame the "lower" white man, and stimulate him into greater exertion to prove himself worthy of his race; but let not this same white man feel that any of us are *willing* that he should go down beneath the negro because of the latter's superiority in apparent character and prosperity. "The Jew first."

V. PLATFORM OF PRINCIPLES AND PROMISES

(Sept., 1912. Prepared at request of institute.)

We, the colored teachers of Yalobusha County, Mississippi, in institute assembled at Coffeeville, hereby adopt the following platform of principles and promises, and pledge ourselves to put these resolutions into practice as far as we are able, God helping us:

I. Whatever else we may do as teachers, we promise to teach our pupils the dignity of all honest labor and the meanness and dishonesty of idleness and vagrancy; the sense of responsibility, especially staunchness in carrying out their promises and other obligations, and in attention to punctuality, neatness and accuracy in all their work, whether in school or elsewhere; the duty of prompt obedience to parents, teachers and all in authority over them; respect for law and cheerful willingness to aid in the suppression of vice and crime; the value of physical and moral cleanness, and the horrible danger and wretchedness brought about by wild passions and lack of sober self-control. We call upon our ministers and other influential people, including the white people who regard us as God's humble children, to aid us in teaching the children of our race to be self-respecting but modest, patient but hopeful, thrifty but generous. However unfair it may seem to call our race childish and yet expect full-developed conduct from us, we realize that we must be more than usually worthy in order to gain the respect of the world and soften its prejudice against us.

Believing that much crime and misery are due to bad health, and that the progress of our race is endangered by reason of the carelessness of our people as to the health of their bodies, we promise to teach practical hygiene and sanitation as if it were a part of our religion, an aspect of godliness rather than "something next to godliness." We ask our white friends to help us maintain proper health conditions not only because we believe that the white people as a rule wish us well, but also because their health and their children's is endangered by our diseases.

No religious faith is worth while unless it renews our characters and renders our daily conduct purer, more dutiful and more thoughtful. We therefore promise to teach our pupils, and influence others to believe, that the "good ground of an honest and a good heart" is the proper seed-plot for the gospel, and we ask our ministers to help our people always to associate religious feeling with upright, clean and noble conduct.

We pledge ourselves to do our utmost in having home and school and church work together for the practical principles above set forth, and we promise faithfully to teach our young people the sacredness of home ties and home life, and to set them a true example by our own honorable and scrupulous conduct.

II. We urge our fellow teachers to trust in our white friends everywhere, especially in the South, believing, that while our white friends regard it as necessary to treat us as a subordinate race in a state of tutelage, they will use their utmost endeavors to give us, in God's good time, every opportunity for development that all of God's children should have, especially in a democratic country.

To this one end we express the fervent hope that the
race question will be taken out of politics, and *studied
with the motive of Christianity and the method of science.* We hope and pray that God will put it into the
heart of good men somewhere to bring about a dispassionate study of the race question in order that our
white friends may be free from anxiety and in order
that we may look our future in the face intelligently.

Although we believe that the worth of every individual should be estimated in accordance with his character, we realize the dangerous stupidity of making
claims for abstract equality; for some abstract rights
have no practical standing as compared with the welfare of society, and a dominant race must be expected
to interpret the idea of social welfare in terms of their
own success and happiness, first of all. It should be
enough for our race that we practice social equality
among ourselves as far as such practice is feasible. If
the present condition of affairs in the South tends to
stunt our full development as men and citizens, we believe that our Southern friends, noted for their chivalrous
regard for the weak, will sooner or later help us to gain
our full spiritual freedom in some way. For their God
is our God, and our God is their God.

III. Whatever our fate as a race, we need to be
prepared for our future. If the education given us does
not produce right results, let the education be changed
so that it will prepare us for life. Let dispassionate,
scientific men show that all the members of our race
are fitted for nothing but manual labor, and we will
acquiesce in the decision. But so long as men of science
believe that individual differences are as pronounced in
our race as in other races, and as long as our race stands
in need of professional services from our own people,

.

we believe that the more gifted among us should receive an education that will enable them to serve their race in various professional capacities.

Nevertheless, it is the opinion of educational leaders among the whites and among our own people that we especially need industrial education. As teachers of Yalobusha County we therefore promise to carry out the following scheme of activities through our individual efforts, and through our teachers' association, our institutes and in every other feasible way:

1. The formation of corn clubs, tomato clubs, and the like.

2. Attempting to ascertain whether it is feasible for our county colored people to have the services of a teacher of domestic science and art, after the manner of the arrangement about to be made with Copiah County by the Jeanes Fund.

3. Correspondence with the colored industrial schools at Okolona, Utica and elsewhere.

4. Working toward the establishment of an agricultural high school in our county, with the full concurrence and support of the white people of the county.

5. Trying to have at least a few of our more talented pupils of good character enjoy greater educational opportunities than the present educational facilities of the county afford.

Unanimously endorsed September 20, 1912.

E. The Caste of the Kin.

I. SOME SUPPOSED RACIAL TRAITS OF THE AMERICAN NEGRO

(Read before Southern Psychological Society, Chattanooga, Dec., 1910.)

The psychologist of to-day believes in the practical value of his science and desires to see it influential in the affairs of everyday life without losing aught of its dignified belief in itself as an admirable academic discipline. There is thus no need that I should apologize for putting forth a few rough notes of a social-psychological or character-study nature before a body of men who are none the less interested in Southern problems because of avowed interest in psychology. Nor is it necessary to introduce the coming science of psychology of character to men who know full well that the application of psychology to the principles and practice of education constitutes the most important task that the mental and social sciences must set themselves.

The negro problem is in great need of characterological (ethological) treatment, for are we not continually saying that what the negroes need is education that shall cultivate their social, moral and industrial tendencies and talents? And is not the claim often made that the negro's religious and æsthetic instincts are distinctive? Consider, too, how true it is that the race question may be called one of consciousness. Prejudice, pride, enmity —what are these but material for the ethologist to study? I say the ethologist rather than the psychologist, because

304

the former, the student of character, is especially concerned in seeing the national, human and educational
bearings of the study.

If, as seems likely, the apparent drift away from illegitimate amalgamation of the two races is conditioned
by a growing spirit of enmity; if the Southerner's aversion to anything even remotely associated with possibilities of social communion between the races is becoming more and more the fashion in all parts of the country;
if the Southerner is becoming inclined to narrow the
economic sphere of the negro—and all these assertions
are made with some show of reason—an ethological
study of negro traits, even when avowedly based on
prevailing popular judgments by the white folk, may
have some value in stimulating the more careful study
that, in my earnest opinion, is even now the bounden
duty of the people of this country.

Watching the trend of events and discussion, one sees
only two so-called "solutions" of the negro problem that
at present appear to deserve careful consideration: first,
that of a parallel civilization, with more or less segregation locally for the negro people; secondly, that of a
carefully planned organization of a scheme for colonization of the negroes to be carried out during a period of,
say, fifty years. If either of these plans is finally
adopted, the negro must be appropriately educated. Especially necessary is it that those habits and instincts in
him be trained that will develop initiative and pioneer
qualities of every kind. Sooner or later he must cut
himself loose from the leading strings of the dominant
race. His racial self-consciousness must be stimulated.
His race distinctiveness in the psychological realm must
be brought to view. Are his characteristics such that he
he may safely dwell in the future within striking dis-

tance of the white man's masterful arm? Will he be
able to maintain himself, after a reasonable period of
tutelage, without the white man's helpful care? Of
course these questions have already been answered offhand, in opposite ways, by "negro-lovers" and "negro-
haters"—if I may be allowed to disguise these easy gen-
eralizers under uncouth names. But sober men of science ought to set an example of sober statement, without
show of sentimentality and without lack of moral earnestness. I shall therefore be pardoned for a brief discussion of the popular view of negro traits, because of
my strong conviction that the scientific student of character must become a leader in any worth-while study
of America's most imminent and distressing ethical
problem.

I

Allow me, for the sake of brevity, to select six leading
tendencies of a primitive sort from my working ethological scheme. Inasmuch as these tendencies are all noted
in popular appreciation of character, no harm will be
wrought by my use of terms that I cannot stop to explain.

The six tendencies I divide into two groups: the first
group contains three sensational or instinctive tendencies, and the second three relational or habitual tendencies. The sensational tendencies under consideration
are: *appropriative,* tendencies to take, seize, grab, pick
up, acquire, appropriate; the *expressive* tendencies, those
that lead to gesture, vocal expression, garrulousness,
show of feelings, strutting, showing off, fashion, and
the like; the *gregarious* tendencies, hunger for company,
liking for a crowd, sociability of the indiscriminate kind,
mass tendencies in general.

The relational tendencies are the following: the *assertive* are crude manifestations of will, animal initiative, impulses leading to resentment, vindictiveness, and so on; the *responsive*—crude altruism, animal sympathy, the impulse to be *en rapport,* and other impulses of like nature; *perceptive*—impulses of curiosity, observation and so on. These too brief characterizations must suffice to hint at the general nature of the tendency norms of characterization used by popular thought. It will be noted that the sensational tendencies lend themselves to the shallower, more concrete forms of impulse and feeling, whereas the relational tendencies are more intellectual and volitional.

How does popular observation judge negro character with respect to these primitive trends of character?

II

Appropriative. Popular judgment makes a joke of the negro's supposed inclination to "just take" things. He is supposed to purloin after a childish fashion. Southerners never tire of descanting on the "bucket brigade." Petty thieving is practically expected from the servants in many households. Many curious illustrations are given of negroes that "take" little things without showing any disposition toward large thefts. It is freely asserted that the lower grade of negroes show no sense of guilt when detected in these petty pilferings. Many identify the average negro's proclivity to live from hand to mouth with this native tendency to appropriate what he can lay his hands on.

Gregarious. The negro is supposed to have a passion for company. It is thought that funerals and weddings and crowds of all kinds "put him in his element." The whites aver that negroes will follow a leader even to the point of showing much bravery, especially if the leader is a member of the dominant race. The negro's religious fashions are also brought up as illustrations of this propensity. When the negro cares little for his church, it is averred, he more than makes up for his lack of church attendance and religious mass emotionalism by his fondness for all sorts and descriptions of lodges and associations, whose prime attractions are their general sociability and sense of mass solidarity. In his careful study of external negro traits, Dr. Howard W. Odum makes much of the negro's sociability, thus confirming, in a measure, the popular opinion.

Expressiveness. Some say that the negro does not sing and dance as he used to. But nearly everyone calls attention to the negro's boisterous laughter, his love of show, his tendency to strut and show off, his demonstrativeness in greeting and in grief, his garrulousness, his love of big words, his bumptiousness, and so on. Of course, reference is here had to the "natural animal," not to the sophisticated negro on his guard in the presence of whites or anxious to show his respect for social convention. His so-called imitativeness is thought to be largely his love of fashion, which is in part a manifestation of the expressive instinct, when crudely displayed. The negro's method of collecting money in church, as described by Dr. Odum, is apparently another instance of this trait.

Let us now turn to the negro's supposed characteristics with regard to the relational tendencies.

Assertive. Nearly all observers agree that the negro is not resentful. They admit that he may be roused to fits of anger quite easily, but seem to think that he does not cherish vindictiveness and other deeply based passions of the assertive sort. On the other hand, it is thought that he does not show any great degree of initiative; that he lacks the "do or die" characteristics; that his egotism is superficial and childish and not firm and masculine. His vanity is regarded as expressive rather than assertive.

Responsive. Although claiming that the negro is sociable, many observers deny his capacity for sympathy, gratitude, and habitual altruism. It is claimed that he does not look after his sick as he should; that he has little real sympathy for his children; that he has little talent for friendship, though inordinately fond of company. He is said to remember kindness no more easily than injury. His deeds of daring in behalf of white people whose commands he is accustomed to take and to whose circle he "belongs," as an humble retainer of "our folks," are contrasted with his callousness toward his own color.

Perceptive. Popular character study does not take much note of this trait. But those who have spoken about it seem inclined to deny that the negro is observant and full of curiosity about things in general. One observer tested several negroes that worked for him, and claims to have found that they failed to show the natural curiosity that the average white child would have shown. "They don't notice things unless their desire to appropriate or to be like other people, or something of that kind, is aroused," says the observer. Visitors to negro schools sometimes say that the children are likely to observe the external features of the visitor's make-up, but show little interest in what he has to tell them. Some students of negro character contrast unfavorably the negro's mild powers of observation with the American Indian's keenness of perception.

Analogous judgments are expressed with respect to the negro's mental processes that underlie and enter into his character tendencies. Thus it is claimed that he is sensational and affective rather than volitional and intellectual. His emotions are regarded as "peripheral" or sensational rather than as strong in relational and the more deeply based impulsive elements. His imagination is looked upon as merely concrete and sensuous; his assimilative powers as lacking in analysis and comparison, except through superficial analogy; his imitativeness is regarded as mimetic rather than intellectual like that of the Japanese. There is complaint on account of his feebleness of voluntary attention, sustained endeavor, enthusiastic and continuous pursuit of things intellectual. The assertion is made that at adolescence, when the average white child's powers undergo a rapid growth, especially in the intellectual and volitional and deeper affective directions, the negro youth becomes stupid with an access of sensuality, instead of the higher powers of mind.

III

How far are these popular notions scientifically correct? No one, it seems to me, is in a position to reply, for there has been practically no serious study of negro character by the trained psychologist and ethologist. Nor has much been found out as to the negro's nervous system. Dr. Bean's study of the negro brain that appeared a few years ago in the *American Journal of Anatomy* (Vol. IV) goes far to bear out the common judgment as to the average negro's characteristics. He thought that he found the negro brain strong on the sensational side and weak in association fibers.*

* Dr. F. Boas, however, holds that Bean's conclusions have been refuted by Mall in *Am. Jour. of Anat.*, Vol. IX.

Granting that the popular opinion is correct—simply for the sake of argument—does it follow that the usual conclusion with regard to the negro's innate intellectual and volitional weakness is in any deep sense true? Is the negro's trouble simply lack of development? Is his social status such that his character has little stimulus for development? Are the better grades of negro brains that have been examined in any wise the product of education? Must the negro's education be carried on in a fashion to develop his particular kind of brain? Are we stunting him by subjecting him to the white man's system of culture?

These questions, and many like unto them, do not answer themselves. Even Southern gentlemen and ladies who "know all about the negro" are scarcely capable of speaking in terms of scientific accuracy with regard to the immensely complex facts of an alien people. Nowadays the whites very seldom have anything to do with the real negro as he is spontaneously in the setting of his natural social environment. Nor is anything gained by repeating the statement, so weary from overworking, that negro frontal sutures close prematurely, and thus stop brain development. Who knows that the sutures in the negro do, as a general rule, close "prematurely" in *negro* development, even granting the truth of the assertion that they do close at a calendar age earlier than in the case of the whites? And who knows that this supposed premature closing of sutures produces the fearful effects attributed to it? Further, do the sutures close early while active education is going on? These are only a few samples of questions that should be asked and, if possible, answered with regard to the most time-honored of all anatomical statements with regard to the negro race.

To those who claim that the negro is essentially and hopelessly sensational, sensual, superficial, lacking in concentration and initiative, and all the rest of it, we may well say, "Important if true." But popular psychology cannot decide such questions. And, when most important results may depend on our judgment in such a matter, it seems heartless and stupid to neglect the scientific ascertainment of the truth, or as near an approximation to the truth as the scientific methods of to-day will allow. Here is at once home and foreign missionary work for the psychologist. Will he get to work? Will an appreciable amount of money and time and talent be given to the scientific study of a problem that affects the whole theory of modern civilization and the weal or woe of the Southern states, to say nothing of the negro race itself?

We may not be able to solve the negro problem by means of psychological and ethological and other kinds of scientific research. But it does seem clear that such study must contribute to the solution if one is possible. Even though investigation should not be productive of very important results, it is sure to throw some light upon this dark and troubled problem.

When the Greeks were woefully afflicted by a plague that swept off the flower of the youth during dense gloom that hid the animating beams of the sun, this was their prayer: "O Father Zeus, if we must die, let it be in the light!" And this ought to be the prayer of the South to-day in the deeper truth-loving spirit of our twentieth century civilization in this great western land of freedom and democracy.

II. RACE SYMPATHY AND RACE ANTAGONISM

(Based on studies made at Memphis and New York City, 1909-1911.)

"Who was that person that was so abused some time since for saying that in the conflict of two races our sympathies naturally go with the higher? No matter who he was. Now look at what is going on in India— a white, superior 'Caucasian' race against a dark-skinned, inferior, but still 'Caucasian' race—and where are English and American sympathies? We can't stop to settle all the doubtful questions; all we know is that the brute nature is sure to come out most strongly in the lower race, and it is the general law that the human side of humanity should treat the brutal side as it does the same nature in the inferior animals—tame it or crush it. The India mail brings stories of women and children outraged and murdered; the royal stronghold is in the hands of the baby-killers. England takes down the Map of the World, which she has girdled with empire, and makes a correction thus: Delhi. *Dele*. The civilized world says, Amen."—"Autocrat of the Breakfast Table."

Had the babes murdered at Delhi been French, our *natural* sympathies would have been less aroused; had they been Chinese, still less; had they been American, much more; had they been Australian blacks, very much less than in the case of Chinese. We sympathize with the higher race because we are "higher" and sympathize with our like. Our abstract ethical sympathy is far less intense and far less "natural" than our sympathy due to responsiveness to *our* very special kind. We do not on this account discount the worthiness of ethical sentiment; we simply note the patent fact that all our higher faiths and feelings root themselves in natural instincts and tendencies; we realize the truth that the highest morality is more or less factitious, if not fictitious, unless rooted in healthy animal and human sociality. New Testament morality grows out of the ethical norms of the Old Testament, even as the relatively high morality of the prophets grew out of the natural ethnic ethics of the "natural man." "First the natural man and then the spiritual man." To reverse this order is to invite sentimentalism and moral decay that come from unnaturalness of every description. And this principle is not confined to racial sympathies. It is likely that the loss of *normal* sexual sensitiveness in *higher* types of human beings provokes disaster to civilized life, especially when it shows itself in women, who are probably by nature generally far more passive than man in their sexual feelings. So, too, no matter how high a race's morality, a loss of the crude animal fondness for offspring that makes a mother a very panther in defense of her children is a real menace to civilization. Natural appetites for simple food and drink; natural liking for play and vigorous uncomplicated exercise; natural patriotism that would fight for fellows be they right or wrong; natural reverence for the Mysterious Higher in man and nature: these instincts and many like unto them are essential to the usefulness, happiness and success of individuals and nations. We dare not kick from under us the steps that enable us to ascend the steeps of enlightenment. Mere intellectualism has ever meant, will ever

mean, decadence. Even that most recent fetish of
American thought, "Efficiency," must acknowledge at
last that there is an efficiency of feeling and sentiment
that will wreak vengeance on all who subordinate it to
merely intellectual and volitional "results." Pragmatism
is false to the core unless its philosophy of results takes
into account the emotional balance in life.

Dr. W. Cunningham, in his recent little work on
"Christianity and Social Questions," clearly recognizes
the *personal*-social aspect of all morality. Even with
regard to work which the prophets of efficiency are inclined to depersonalize to the utmost, he has this very
old-fashioned but salutary definition: "Work is the active effort to give effect to the will of God" (p. 186).
Realizing the essential unpredictableness of the feeling
side of personality, he says (p. 209): "The attempt to
interpret the ground of other people's actions is only
likely to be an unconscious revelation of dominant motives in our own minds." We are sometimes astonished
at the behavior of those who make a point of minimiz-
ing the personal aspect of public service, and yet at
the same time do not hesitate to make war upon the
work of public servants because of acts committed by
the latter which would be inefficient or insincere if done
by the critic or investigator, but which may be fairly
efficient and perfectly moral to the consciousness of
the actors themselves, whose temperaments and training
may be very different from the critic's.

"A duty changes its character when it is done under
state compulsion," is another of Cunningham's thoughts
that deserves close attention nowadays. There is an educative loss, as he well says, when men are relieved of
responsibility through paying taxes, through compulsory
education laws, and the like. Certainly the present ten-

dency is to *compel* men to be moral through law or system or other forms of "control." Machinery is good and necessary, but it is a doubtful help if it attempts to take the place of personal responsibility or to depreciate the ethical value of unforced, natural, "affective" morality.

Since these things are so, it will be well for us, in discussing the sympathy and the antagonism shown in the contact of diverse races with one another, to investigate the real character values of the primitive impulses of social man. Such a procedure is especially necessary for those that would understand the attitude of Southern whites toward negro individuals and the negro race. Attention has often been called to the claim that Northerners like the negro race but dislike the negroes individually considered, whereas Southerners like individual negroes but are antagonistic toward the race as such. When we consider that Northerners like the negro race *in the South,* and are disposed to share Southern liking for individual negroes that "keep their place," the difference between the attitude of the sections amounts to very little. Northerners whose early Southern experience brings them into contact with negro irresponsibleness are prone to dislike negroes individually *and* racially, for they have not been brought into touch with the more amiable characteristics of the negro and fail to realize that efficiency is a very relative term. And so the phenomena of sympathy are very complex and difficult to understand. Indeed, some of us have seen individuals of tHe white race portray every kind and degree of sympathy and antagonism toward the lower race within the period of a single year. Some of us experience in ourselves all shades of sympathetic or of antagonistic tendencies, in accordance with changes in mood, economic

contact, change of surroundings, and the like. Unless
we analyze the various kinds of sympathy and try to
ascertain the essential meaning of the sympathetic impulse itself, we shall find ourselves in a psychological
tangle that will tend to trip us up continually in our attempts to generalize.

THE KINDS OF SYMPATHY

1. Ethical Sympathy. We sympathize with the oppressed, with those that are making a brave fight against
great odds, with those who are contending for a principle. This sympathy has been felt for people like the
Japanese, the Armenians, the Cubans, the Poles, the
Finns, the Balkan allies. It is evidently based on imaginative construction that is ordinarily rather fragile.
I have known men to change in their sympathies from
the Japanese side to the Russian after forming the
acquaintance of one Russian gentleman. It is doubtful
whether Californians shared the sympathy felt for the
Japanese by the rest of the country. Not a few Southerners grew lukewarm in their sympathy for the "oppressed Cubans" as soon as they were told that the in-
surgents were for the most part negroes. I have noted
that a whole roomful of company disclaimed sympathy
for the Boers when a traveler described how filthy in
their habits many of the Boers were. Northerners very
often become antagonistic toward the idea of "poor,
down-trodden negroes" when these same Northerners
really know the happy-go-lucky blacks in the South.

Underlying this form of sympathy is evidently a kind
of imaginative expressiveness. Most of us have romantic and generous sentiments on tap. The tales of

other people's sufferings or heroism stir our sympathy
or our enthusiasm. We vaguely picture these aliens as
like unto ourselves. When the imaginary bond of kinship is cut away we are apt to lose the verve of our
interest and sympathy; for our imaginative expressiveness seems to depend on our native responsiveness to
our kind for any really permanent tap-root. John Brown
was probably insane, but certainly consistent in his sympathy for the negroes. Perhaps extremes of inconsistency and of consistency are alike pathological!
Brown kissed a negro child, and that kiss indicated that
his ethical attitude, such as it was, and distorted as it
seems to some of us, was based upon vital responsiveness, real sympathy, though associated with lack of sympathy for his own people.

I do not deny that men may experience highly intel-
lectualized forms of ethical sympathy; but with the loss
or the pathological exaggeration of the feeling element
goes much of the instinctive and effective naturalness of
the sentiment. And when a sentiment has become simply
a mildly modulated principle, men cease to die for it or
live for it. Hence one pays little attention to the ethical
sympathy begotten of reading and palace car touring.
In order to be really ethical, a sentiment must have the
ingredients of the ethical impulse. One of these, one of
the most important, is *natural,* spontaneous responsiveness, which at bottom is diffused consciousness of kinship, and is due to psychological and biological likeness.
Some reader will naturally ask the question, "Is there
no truth in the story of the Good Samaritan?" Very
much, I reply. Many a modern good Samaritan would
take care of a wounded dog, which, after all, is an animal with sensitive nerves such as we have. "Who is my
neighbor?" is a question answered in very catholic fash-

ion by the Buddhist. The humanity of the Samaritan is
not hard to understand: the real puzzle is the inhuman
conduct of the priest and the Levite! I believe that
Jesus was trying to call attention to the childlike native
responsiveness to distress shown by the Samaritan as
contrasted with the inhuman ceremonialism of the priest
and the Levite. If a Samaritan can be kind to a Jew,
how much more should a Jew show loving kindness to
his own people.

However, most so-called ethical sympathy is not based
on immediate appeal to childlike instincts, but is, as we
have suggested above, a product of imagination and reflection. You remember the story of the negro tramping
through the Northern states and how he was informed
of his right to "equality," but got neither food nor practical sympathy. The story goes on to say that on one
occasion the negro rang a front door bell and was ac-
costed by the master of the house with this vigorous
command: "You black rascal, why don't you go round
to the kitchen door and get your dinner!" Well, this
would not ordinarily be regarded as a case of "ethical
sympathy," but I doubt not that the negro was sincere
when he replied, with his hat in his hand, "Thank God!
I done foun' a Southern gentleman!" We may eliminate
the implied invidious comparison without losing the lesson of the story. The Southern gentleman made no
pretense of being ethical: he was simply a good, instinctive, childlike, natural, human animal!

The white light of conscience is a blend of ethical colors,
in which the many delicate moral tints all come from a
few primary instincts. Let us take heed that we dogmatically lay no claim to ethicality that does not ground
itself in childlike instinctiveness. There is much truth
in the Socratic statement: "No man does wrong will-

ingly." We sometimes sin against truth and humanity
in our supposed sympathy with "oppressed" people, in
that we fail to sympathize with our own kind whom we
ignorantly brand as "oppressors." Ethical humanitarianism is to be found among all enlightened and not a few
unenlightened people. It is always well to play fair,
to hear the other side—and eminently well to heed Dr.
Holmes' sympathy with the man who "naturally" sided
with the higher race, other things being equal or doubtful or unknown!

2.   Racial and National Sympathy. This form is evidently based on responsiveness of like to like. Make an
American of English descent *realize* that the English are
his nearest of kin among foreigners, and it will be very
difficult to have him take sides with the Russians or the
French as against the English. He may be alienated by
the abrupt or haughty conduct of a given Englishman;
but get him to discount this and appreciate his kinship
to the mass of Englishmen, and you have his pro-Eng-
lish sympathies well in hand. Hence I should like to
insist on the coming inevitableness of the Northern
white man's sympathy for his white brother of the South,
without regard to the metaphysical ethicality of the
Southern white man's cause. The Northerner may not
understand the Southerner's apparent disregard of the
negro's rights, but solaces himself with the thought, "Did
I live South I guess I would act as the Southerners do."
And indeed he would! Should this sympathy for the
Southern whites make the Northerner oblivious to the
black man's welfare? By no means, no more than it
should so affect the Southern white man. Let the Northerner say to himself, "If my Southern brother is so situated as to be compelled to choose between two evils; if
he has to act in an ethically distorted way because of

distorted conditions amid which he finds himself through no fault of his; if people of my own kind are forced to act as if they disregarded the rights of man and the first principles of democracy—then we should all work together so to remedy conditions as to help the black man without injuring the whites. But let me be careful about interfering, or let me avoid gratuitous advice and the assumption of superior sanctity on our part: for the Southerner is doubtless doing as well as he can under the circumstances, and is quite likely to be as good a man as I am." How much more of a "Union" we should have if Northerners were uniformly responsive to their brethren at the South! How much happier we should all be did we realize that the South is humanitarian at heart and that her apparent disregard of human rights is a subject to be patiently investigated, sympathetically pondered and studied, and not simply inveighed against or made the recipient of unbrotherly sarcasm. It stirs a Southern white man's indignation to the depth of his heart to have the Northern brother "take sides" against his own race and nation, without a knowledge of the facts, and therefore without appreciation of the distressing complexity and difficulty of the actual situation.

We may rest assured that, if we love not our brethren whom we ought to understand because of likeness and kinship, we stand a poor chance of loving intelligently an alien people whom we know practically nothing about and who cannot be socially incorporated into the national life. We shall be at least *healthy* in our national morality if we are careful to give free play to our natural responsiveness to those who are most like us. Kinship loads the dice of sympathy. The world would be worse did it not. It is better for love to be blind than to be either hypercritical or hypocritical.

3. Associational Sympathy. We tend to sympathize with those that we "go with." Indeed, we are apt to become assimilated to our company and therefore to sympathize with our like. It is evident that responsiveness and gregariousness underlie this variety of sympathy. Husband and wife, when not ill mated, tend to acquire the same tastes, to use the same sets of concepts, to adopt the same mental attitudes; in truth, they even tend to resemble each other physically. Children attending the same school, members of the same church, partners in business, persons that belong to the same social set; all these and other like social groups tend to acquire sympathy for one another. They respond and go with one another, and the responsiveness and gregariousness in turn bring about greater likeness. In such cases, sympathy gets very deep roots.

4. Utilitarian Sympathy. We say that we sympathize with those that will help us or who are useful to us. But such a relationship, while adjuvant to sympathy and furnishing occasions for its exercise, is not really sympathetic. Labor union men may think that they sympathize with the Southern viewpoint; but such sympathy is shallow unless it has beneath it some degree of native responsiveness and consciousness of kinship. One cannot depend on sympathy for Southern whites at the North when the supposed sentiment is due simply to a desire to retain the *status quo* at the South for economic reasons. However, given some degree of responsiveness and company sense, utilitarian considerations may powerfully aid in the development of sympathy.

THE NATURE OF SYMPATHY AND ANTAGONISM

1. *Responsiveness and Unresponsiveness.* We are ordinarily drawn to our like, provided there is sufficient variety in the likeness; on the other hand, we are repelled by observation of unlikeness in others, especially when we esteem those others to be lower than ourselves. Antagonism becomes amused contempt when the lower race is seen to be slavishly copying the higher and when the higher race believes that the lower prefers the higher to its own race. Responsiveness and antagonism are always more profound when based on connate likenesses or differences, respectively, of physical appearance and nervous structure. When the unlike lower race seems to "fit in" with the life of the higher, and spontaneously and sincerely takes up a station avowedly subordinate, then the consciousness of difference sometimes lends a certain charm to life and a certain dignity and kindly condescension to the behavior of the higher race. This point is well illustrated by the following occurrence which came under my observation in New York City: Two very intelligent young men, both of Northern birth and rearing, were chaffing each other. A said to B— "Whom would you prefer to have as a tentmate during a hunting expedition in the woods, a filthy, low-grade white immigrant or a filthy, low-grade negro?" B replied—"The negro." Then, after a pause, he added— "But I should prefer a dog to either of them." The negro's supposed "humble" subserviency seemed to fit in with B's comfortable sense of dominion, whereas he would have felt that the white immigrant was implicitly demanding some sort of social recognition, or ought to do so. There was no social problem at all with regard

to the dog! B could respond to the dog's overtures for
friendly contact, because there was no implication of
equality nor of competition. Like responds to like of
the lowest degree of likeness, when the principle of the
competitive struggle for existence and the survival of the
fittest does not come into operation. Like responds to
like of the higher grade even with competition and pro-
fession of equality, when both parties acknowledge real
or implicit or feasible equality. One white man of high
grade may listen with equanimity to claims of equality
from another white man of low grade, because he realizes
that his humbler brother *is* biologically and psychologically capable of becoming his social brother, or that the
humbler brother's blood has in it the promise and potency of social equality.

Why is it that so many intelligent people insist that
educated and refined specimens of the negro race should
have accorded them a kind of recognition ordinarily accorded to white men of the same degree of worth and
culture? Do they fail to realize that social recognition
has a biological basis? Do they not realize that even
Jesus the idealist first ministered to His own people?
Was He simply jesting when He spoke of the heathen
as "dogs," to whom the children's bread was not to be
given? Did he not accept racial distinctions in His
social life? In becoming cosmopolitan do we cease to be
national? Can we coerce ourselves into reversing the
law of nature and grace that the natural man precedes
the spiritual man? We may discount our native responsiveness and inhibit antagonistic conduct based on native
antipathy; but we had better be very careful not to interfere too much with even the jots and tittles of the laws
of nature. They, too, must all be *fulfilled*. And he is
least in the kingdom of Heaven that neglects and he

greatest that does them! Lincoln was true to nature and true to his own sincere conscience when he asserted vigorously that he was *not* as responsive to negroes as to whites, that he did *not* believe in anything that would lead to social equality between the races; that he *would* side with the whites did he have to choose between the races. Whatever our attitude toward other races, it behooves us to be true to our fundamental instinct of responsiveness and not attempt to substitute unhealthy sentimentality of self-consciousness for the native childlikeness of unforced sympathy toward our next of kin. The Southerner insists on racial solidarity, and guards all approaches toward it; for he instinctively feels that sensuality on the one hand and sentimentalism on the other are ever threatening race purity, the "conscience" for which is primarily based on habitual responsiveness of the biologically like toward one another.

2. *Gregariousness vs. Exclusiveness.* Responding to our like, we naturally company with them. Feeling no coercive responsiveness to those racially unlike us, equally as naturally we do not "mix" with them socially. Inasmuch as social mingling is intimately associated with all forms of social intercourse, whether economic, political, religious or cultural, our gregariousness tends to confine itself to those whom we feel that we or ours may actually or potentially (through descendants) mingle with. Our exclusion of those "not of the kin" is not unfeeling or cruel. Indeed, when exclusiveness asserts itself in a high-bred gentleman he experiences acute pity for individuals from whom he feels that he must cut himself off. He allows his native instinct of exclusiveness to operate freely because he knows that it is best in the long run to make association with an individual of a lower race a matter of race rather than a matter of

individuality. To make exceptions would be to mistrust nature and science. The Southern gentleman does not wish to inflict pain; but he does wish to be both natural *and* ethical; and his ethicality, in this instance, must be based upon higher utilitarian considerations and not on sentimentality, which is sentiment cut off from its native roots of responsiveness and gregariousness belonging to a certain time and place. One asks, however, this seemingly pertinent question: "Why not graft on the natural stock the shoot of a higher humanitarianism?" The answer is: "We are continually doing that, but only on the condition that the stock has its own natural roots!"

3. *Expressiveness vs. Indifference.* A tap-root of social expressiveness also is responsiveness. We love to talk with our like, to exchange views, on the basis of real or possible social equality. Unless our companions are sufficiently like us to rouse at least incipient admiration, even though it be only reflected qualities of our own that arouse our appreciation, our expressiveness becomes condescending or uncomfortable. Physical differences, when too great, are very likely to counteract any native tendency toward expressiveness. The Southerner likes the negro "in his place," because he does not feel called on to express himself to a *quasi* equal, and knows that the negro, however superior he may be, expects only the kindly and courteous humanitarian treatment extended toward the worthy of his race, and does not expect the Southern white man to relax his assumption of superior status.

Likeness, then, real or implied, is the healthy and natural basis for social sympathy that makes for the common coöperative life of democratic citizenship. It cannot be forced. Lincoln rightly says that we must take into account a universal attitude whether it be right or wrong. Indeed, the question is not one of sentimental morality, but rather one of adaptability, feasibility, congruousness, utilitarianism, naturalness, inevitableness. External forms of sociality imply to the sincere mind certain bases of responsiveness, gregariousness and expressiveness. To make a show of treating a man as a potential equal when one feels that he isn't, or that he ought not to be treated differently from his race, which race one does not believe ought to be assimilated, is to invite hypocrisy in the higher race and dangerous social self-assertion in the lower race.

If an inquirer should ask whether it is healthy and right for two diverse peoples to live on the same soil without becoming assimilated to one another and without the promise of ultimate equality, I should unhesitatingly say, No! The present situation at the South is abnormal, and ought not to be continued. Men ought to be so situated that no one asks questions regarding race. But given present conditions at the South, the Southerner's social attitude toward the lower race is safe and sane, because wise and necessary and *natural*. Every decent Southerner believes in the rights of man and wishes it were possible for the negro to get *all* the development and recognition that he deserves as an individual or as a race. After all, however, the safety of society and the *healthiness* of its social life are of more intrinsic importance than the feelings of certain worthy negroes. Our social actions must always take into account the *tendencies* toward which they lead. Southerners know from experience that it is unnatural, forced and meaningless to pretend that we should treat an individual negro as if we knew nothing as to his racial extraction. We also know that the average low negro regards himself as potentially at least the equal of every cultured negro and entitled to all the recognition that any "nigger" gets. White antagonism at the South, except in the case of negro-haters, whose attitude is of no importance for our present purposes, is not toward the negro race or the negro individual, but rather toward the *pretended recognition of individuality as apart from race,* and toward the unnatural and dangerous policy that would lead the mass of the negroes to claim any sort of equality with the whites, except the equal right to life, liberty and the pursuit of happiness. Even these natural rights are only relative. If the higher race is convinced that *its* right to happiness is endangered by granting the negro the right to the pursuit of happiness, we may be sure, as in case of the "right" to intermarry, that the white man will interpret negro rights differently than in the case of the same rights as claimed by the whites. If a thousand white aliens wished to marry a thousand negroes on South Carolina soil, the South Carolinians would not allow it, even though the alien whites had not become naturalized citizens. The Congress of the United States did not hesitate to interfere with the Mormon elder's right to the pursuit of happiness through marrying several wives. The Southern white regards interracial marriages as inexpedient and immoral. The real question to be asked is not, How to get the Southern whites to treat the negroes as individuals and to give all the negroes their constitutional rights; but rather this, How can we bring about a salutary change that will give the negro what he needs without interfering with the progress of the South in the long run, and without attempting to suppress perfectly natural, inevitable and, on the whole, useful reactions of the Southern whites toward the negroes? The failure to appreciate the meaning of the Southern white's attitude, *his* failure to explain his own feelings properly, *his* tendency to allow people to interpret his conduct in an undemocratic and inhuman sense: these are some of the distressing aspects of the problem that have been largely overlooked even by close students of the subject. Admitting the general rationality of the account thus far given, what shall we say of Dr. Holmes' antithesis, *tame* or *crush?*

The taming process is what the average Southern white means by the sensible "educating the negro for his place." To tame the negro is to make him give up all pretense of ever claiming to be the white man's equal in any respect. What shall we say to such a proposition? Only one thing can be said by true Americans. *There is no "place" in this country for a peasant class: it hurts the lower and the higher race alike, and particularly the higher.*

What remains? A struggle and the ultimate crushing of the negro through violence or through the slow decadence of a race that has lost all hope and self-respect? True Americans will assuredly demur to such a solution as this. We *do* believe in the rights of man; in the preciousness of every human life; in the essential solidarity of the human race; in the fair fight and the square deal. Let Americans generally show their sympathy for their fellow Americans of the dominant race in the South by helping them to cast off *in some way* a fearful incubus, and not waste time, treasure and force in attempting to secure for the negroes supposed rights and blessings that the Southern whites will not allow the negroes to have in a "white man's country." Let us assume that the Southern whites know something of democracy, but must act in the interest of the safety and moral health of society in order that American principles may remain alive long enough to grow and fruit. In fine, let us *study this question* on the assumption that the solution must be such as to injure the dominant race in no serious way, and on the further assumption that the attitude of the better Southern whites toward the negro must not be interfered with unless these men of race conscience are shown that their views are unnatural and wrong, that their fears are foolish, that the negro can become a full-fledged citizen without danger to the South, and so on. But, be assured, no "snap judgment" of the doctrinaire or the politician or the philanthropist can settle these questions offhand. Patient, organized, long-continued research alone will bring out truth that will command the attention of all the people, North and South.

If our popular psychological account is right in holding that Southern white attitude toward the negroes cannot be *naturally* and *fully* consistent with higher ethical insight as long as the races are occupants of a common soil, because natural amalgamation is execrable and colonization is impracticable, what shall we do? We should at least make sure that colonization *is* impracticable, or that there is no other solution possible, before we acquiesce in present conditions of unhealthy moral strain and retarded progress.

F. Freedom Through the Truth.

THE EXPERIENCE OF A STUDENT OF THE NEGRO PROBLEM: THE NEED OF A NEW FREEDOM

(Suggested by various discussions held at conferences with leading Mississippi schoolmen in the summer of 1913.)

I. THE STUDENT'S EXPERIENCE

Born within sight of Southern rice fields, educated wholly in his native state, inheriting from his English blood respect for facts and reverence for tradition, and from his French blood quickness and versatility of sympathy and intuition, the Student began as a boy of nine to puzzle over the Southern interracial situation. The "academy" where he took his high school course had been founded by aristocratic indigo planters in the middle of the eighteenth century. The state university where he worked up from sophomore to professor was a center of purest Southernism. Yet the Student's education knew nothing of sectional bitterness. His father, a Confederate veteran, used to speak of secession as a righteous mistake, of state rights as a geographical incident and yet an eternal principle, of slavery as an economic and ethical blunder that under Providence retarded the development of the South in order that she might become the instrument of ultimate spiritual conservation of the Union.

Brought up during reconstruction times, our Student, as a "red-shirt boy," took part in two political processions in honor of Wade Hampton. He remembers hearing his father say on election day of 1876: "I have told John (the mulatto butler) that he must vote for Hampton if he wishes to keep his place;" and he will never forget his father's look of sadness and discomfort as this remark was made. The Student understood his father's feelings later, when he himself was obliged, on occasion, to chastise "impudent" negroes that disputed the sidewalk with him or made insulting remarks about the white people. But he used to wonder vaguely why white Republicans were regarded as "scalawags" without much hope of redemption in this world or the next, and why "democratic negroes" were always in danger of being "beaten-up" by the rest of the negroes.

In his county, during the eighties, whites and negroes used to "divide up" the county offices. The negroes got the unimportant offices, like that of school commissioner! And the Student has been able to watch the gradual elimination of the negro from politics; the loss of sympathy between the races; the hardening of the hearts of the Southern whites as certain atrocious crimes began to show themselves among the negroes; the rise of the "common people" of the South, coincident with the fall of the negro; the growing sense of white solidarity along with the formation of political factions in each Southern state; transient breakings away from "the Democracy," and subsequent return to the two-partitioned Democratic fold with its guarantee of political independence through the white primary, etc., etc.

The Student can never forget the political rendering of a popular religious ditty: "Hold the fort for Hampton's coming!" And yet he lived to see that same Hampton turned out of the United States Senate by a new political "savior"—this time of the "common (white) people." White supremacy had become strong enough to dare to divide; but so completely coherent had become the racial orthodoxy of the South that not even the bitter factional fights among the whites were able permanently to divide the Democratic party. In the midst of all these movements one thing has remained constant: the passionate dogma of white supremacy.

I need not go into details of the Student's personal history. His six years' sojourn on the Pacific Coast allowed him to look at another set of interracial relations. He was also able to see what the negro problem meant in the great cities of the North.

From the beginning of his graduate university work our Student had concentrated his interest and attention on the psychology of character, and especially the psychology of public opinion and social movements. Hence it is not surprising that his special studies and his contact with racial problems on both sides of the continent should conspire with a conscience somewhat sensitive to Christian-democratic principles to awaken in him a whole-souled desire to do what he could to throw light on a problem that was a constant challenge to men of good will everywhere, and which was evidently interfering with the free development of his beloved South. Perhaps the Student was stupid in thinking that cool science and ethical fervor could work together successfully in one human heart!

When the Student was offered an important post in a Southern state university, under conditions that showed a spontaneous and heartily sympathetic demand for his services on the part of the teachers of the state, he thought that a "call" had come to him. And his resolution to heed the summons was rendered firmer by the advice of an American psychologist and educator of international standing. As soon as he had settled in his new place he began the systematic study of the negro question, and especially an investigation of the psychology of so-called race prejudice. He organized a graduate seminar for the study of the negro question, collected data from all quarters, read widely, and soon had the satisfaction of seeing one of his students devote himself to the same study and publish his doctor's thesis on negro traits under the auspices of two of America's greatest universities.

One morning, immediately upon his return from missionary educational work in his adopted state, after a twenty-mile trip over a wretched road, he was almost overwhelmed with surprise and indignation to find that the board of trustees of the university, by a bare majority vote of little more than a quorum of the board, had turned his department out of the university. The state teachers' association, by a unanimous standing vote, and the entire student body of the university, through a practically unanimous petition, requested the board to restore the department to the university. Soon telegrams, letters, interviews and so on so focused public opinion that the board, four weeks after dropping the department of education from the university, by a unanimous vote, with an almost full board, reinstated the department. The ostensible meaning of the board's first action was the desire for "economy"; but people generally thought that the board's elimination of the department was an attempt to get rid of a student of the negro problem who insisted on holding fast to democratic Christian principles as applicable to all men. Now, our Student had always been entirely "orthodox" in his racial stand as to "social" and "political" equality. He had always stood up for "white supremacy." He had always

insisted that the Southern people were behaving as ethically under the circumstances as any other people would
have done. He had blamed the *situation* rather than his
people. He had insisted on holding open no illusory
"doors of hope" to the negro. But he had nevertheless
maintained, although feeling and professing great sympathy even for extremist views, that the Southern people
should not be complacently *satisfied* with holding another
people in spiritual subjection for all time. Hence he had
advocated careful systematic investigation of the problem, in order that the Southern people and the nation
should be able to look the situation squarely in the face
and take appropriate action. Personally he could see no
solution of the problem except ultimate colonization of
the negro by means of a carefully prepared plan that
would not disrupt economic conditions and would play
fair with the negroes.

Not a single member of the university board had adequate first-hand knowledge of the Student's views and
work; if certain ones had wished to punish the Student
they had acted "on suspicion." True, there was need of
economy at the university; nor would one have the right
to say that some of the "economists" did *primarily* act
on account of the student's supposed views on the negro
question; but it is an assured fact that some of them
avowed their feelings of suspicion toward the Student,
and were willing to restore him to his place only because
his recall was demanded by the teachers of the state, the
students of the university, and the public opinion that
was powerfully influenced by the united teachers and
students.

The Student, believing that the people of his state had
endorsed his work, continued his study of the negro
question, and continued to express his views modestly

and frankly. Although he had opportunities to go
North, he decided to remain South and continue the work
that was so close to his conscience. During several years
ensuing he could at times see some of his friends become
cold and suspicious; he was bitterly arraigned by a prominent newspaper; his friends' timidity "prevented" reports of some of his negro question speeches from being
reported in the newspapers lest such reports might "injure" him; the university authorities confessed that his
race question work was embarrassing to the university.
But time will do its perfect work. Very gradually, first
the leading schoolmen of the state and then the people
generally came to see that our student was the kind of
"friend" that the South needed, because his "defense"
of the South was not special pleading, and was free from
fire-eating, braggadocio, arrogance, side-stepping, involved sophistry, appeals to the gallery, and the like.
Some of the leading "extremists" (including the pictur-
esque and magnetic Vardaman) offered to help the Student with his work when he afterward corresponded with
some of them from New York City.

The Student has had many vicissitudes of fortune.
An accumulation of shocks and crises endangered his
nervous stability during several years. Although several
prominent and influential men attempted to get him the
opportunity to concentrate his attention on the problem
he had at heart, but had failed in their efforts; although
he found apathy or opposition to the study of the question—both North and South; although he still suf-
fers at times from the old canard that had originally
operated against him; although he has seen even men
of limited intelligence and rather mediocre consecration
preferred before him and gain recognition for minor
services in behalf of the South: nevertheless, his faith

in his people's fairness and justice and loving kindness and open-mindedness—yea, faith even in the most narrow-minded and ignorant of them—has grown year by year. At heart these Southern people are tolerant and charitable, frank and sincere.

Without a talent for attracting financial support for his own investigational efforts,—in the face of a prejudice toward the study of race-prejudice,—in spite of the dangerous optimism that wants to "wait" and let things drift,—the Student dares to hope that the South herself, poor as she is, and suffering from anxiety and unrest with regard to the race problem, will help the Student and his friends to organize the investigation of this imminent question. Even now the educational leaders of the state are arranging to utilize over half of the Student's time next year, making him a sort of university extension professor-at-large for the state. And he has already been able to start a little fund that may prove to be the nucleus of an opportunity for a Southern study of Southern problems.

If the Student were asked whether he thought that the investigation of the negro problem should be merely a Southern venture, he would reply most decidedly in the negative. Southern sensitiveness, which has a real reason for being, looks askance toward studies of this problem that are not vouched for by their own trusted leaders; but to accuse the South of obscurantism and bourbonism that she *could* dispense with is unfair and unkind. Indeed, the Student has yet to find a single man in the South, even among professional politicians, that did not sooner or later respond to his appeal in behalf of the dignity of the human soul. Some extremists pretend at times that the immeasurable worth of a negro's soul is an idea not to be taken seriously; but even these, especially when they can be got to take their alleged Christian principles seriously, are compelled to admit that the negro is a true man and has the rights that a real man has, even though under present circumstances, and probably as long as the races are together in the same territory, the negroes must remain completely subordinated in the interests of public peace and the proper pride of race.

Thus the Student is more than hopeful that his Southern compatriots will welcome and support all well-directed efforts to solve the race problem, and in his own person has been able to prove that free speech as well as independent thought is possible at the South. So vitally necessary is the preservation of racial orthodoxy in the South that racial heretics—and all those who insist that negroes must be treated as *individuals* rather than members of a race are racial heretics—should not expect to enjoy their life in the South. Does this mean that Southerners do not believe in the individual worth of the human soul? I have just insisted that they assuredly have such a belief. But they regard their racial treatment of negroes as racial representatives rather than as free men simply as the less of two evils. They are perfectly willing that negro individuals should be *fully* recognized in accordance with their character—somewhere else than on *our* American territory. And they rejoice that the Christian negro can sustain his spirits by believing that God sees his real worth and is no respecter of persons. For they know, nevertheless, that the divine care for each human soul does not conflict with the equally divine course of human history with its Chosen People lording it over the lesser tribes without the law.

II. THE NEED OF A NEW FREEDOM

Since our Southern people are normal Americans, and perhaps the truest American stock, conserving much that the country needs, can we say at the South, "It is well with our souls"? No! The South is not free. Our Student fights for *his* freedom.

I need say little with regard to negro unfreedom. Bad as it is that these "freedmen" (not freemen) should be deprived of political rights; bad as it is that they should have to bear the stigma of imputed inferiority just because of the accident of race; bad as it is that they can have no rational hope of complete citizenship in the United States of America unless public opinion undergoes a change of which I am able to see no "primitive streak"; far worse is it that the white people of the South are not free to develop fully.

After all, much of our sympathy for the negro is wasted. The average "darkey" is perfectly content with being an inferior and with recognizing the overlordship of the whites if people will let him alone and give him a fair share of protection against the sharks among the whites. The small percentage of high-grade negroes and mulattoes that really care for full spiritual freedom, which, of course, includes all the rights of citizenship, can leave the country if they want to, and few will cry about it. Southerners will admire their pluck, wish them well, and help them generously. The masses of the negroes could probably be educated to make a tolerably good peasantry. If the mulattoes would emigrate or breed back into the ranks of the negroes, the unthinking, careless, happy-go-lucky average negro would get along with the whites first rate, provided some machinery be found to supervise them carefully in the interests of law and order, and protect them in their reasonable rights as an inferior race living under tutelage.

If vast masses of white people in Europe have lived for centuries the life of a contented peasantry; if the forces of nature operate in their usual ways and ultimately bring down the rate of negro population so that the "problem" becomes easier as the years go by; then there is no reason why we should weep over the situation. For the upper tenth of the negroes can go where they may obtain true freedom, and the nine-tenths do not need it and do not know what to do with it. True it is that all good men would prefer to have *all* the American negroes lifted up and fully developed. But even if nine million negroes, plus some more millions of the future, should fail to rise, there will be left enough negroes on earth to make a good experiment in African eugenics. The excellent racial traits attributed to negro blood by some of the friends of the child races still have a fair chance in Africa, and perhaps elsewhere, if the friends of humanity will be a little foresighted with regard to them and prevent certain aspects of white civilization from ruining them. In other words, the unfreedom of the negroes, though tragic enough when viewed in the light of the higher ethics, does not necessarily mean the failure of the negro race as such.

On the other hand, how is it with the white man? Many whites seem to be fully satisfied with negro peasant labor, in spite of evidence that white labor is superior, and that it is the glory of free America that her generous life brings out the real man in the European peasant, thus proving the superiority of a peasantless régime. Some go so far as to satisfy themselves with the thought that the South need not, with negro labor, remain hopelessly behind the rest of the country, but will lag—well, just moderately! Does the believer in negro labor, however, pretend that the South would not be better off economically if negroes were ultimately displaced by a higher people? Does anyone suppose that the present economic life of a Yazoo-Mississippi Delta is going to be the typical industrial life of the South? And is the South to trust her hopes of a high economic development to the absurd declaration, long ago worn out, that "Cotton is king"? Even the boll-weevil has done its little best to teach the South some sense in this regard! With white labor in the cotton mills, in spite of its greater expensiveness and assertiveness, how can it be said that the South of the future can hope for good things from negro labor? Science and practical sanitation and hygiene, along with everyday experience, have destroyed utterly the old notion that the "white man can't stand the hot sun." As a matter of fact, he is standing it, and frequently much better than the negro does. Tropical medicine has taught us that there is great hope of a future of the white race even in the tropics—and the South is by no means a part of the tropics.

Every keen observer knows that agricultural, domestic and other forms of efficiency are vitiated by the ways and work of the negro. So much is this the case that in one Southern town—and there are many like it—white ladies no longer speak apologetically because of having to do their own domestic drudgery. The educated negro domestics and other laborers "go North," or set up for themselves—white farms and homes get little benefit from them. Surely one must expect that trained negroes will not submit to the double yoke of "labor" and "race" if they can find some way of escaping the one or the other. And the presence of white student waiters at a number of Southern colleges indicates that the whites are beginning to shake off the shackles of dependence on irresponsible labor and getting rid of absurd lack of respect for "menial" work in itself. Nevertheless the coming industrial independence of the white man is very slow in developing. In some localities, because of the difficulties of keeping white immigrants down South in the midst of a negro population, there may be relapse toward dependence on the negro. The very existence of a lazy, shiftless, incompetent, irresponsible mass of laborers that require the closest supervision all the time necessarily lowers the economic energy and standards of the white people. Many a white man excuses his easy, sauntering way of transacting business by speaking of the ridiculous rush and hurry-scurry of the North. But much of our Southern lassitude is caught from the ways of the negro rather than the wiles of the hookworm. I speak somewhat dogmatically; but I think that investigation will show that the regions of the South with sparse negro populations are as a rule more energetic than are those with a much larger percentage of negroes, other things being equal. At any rate, when a man says to himself, "One cannot expect a negro servant to do more than one-third of what is easily done by a Chinese," he will find himself using a standard of efficiency below his best. In a thousand ways negro economic inefficiency retards the development of the South. And this constant doing of less than our best, this easy-going lack of regard for time, this willingness to put up with inefficient service and to overlook small pilferings because one "expects that from a negro"—what is all this but an insidious form of psychological economic unfreedom?

We are no better off in politics—rather worse. The existence of a "Solid South" is a form of political slavery for the South itself. Southerners say—and rightly

—We dare not divide. But when supposedly free men say that they dare not act politically as they want to; when they suffer even socially if they do not vote the Democratic ticket; when they are driven to vote for men rather than measures; when discussion of national issues on the stump often sounds like a solemn and tedious joke; when political thinking has nothing to stimulate it, because Southerners must think alike on the main issues —what have we but political unfreedom? Last fall I heard dozens of men say that they would like to have an opportunity to vote for Roosevelt, but that it "wouldn't do"; some of us who had no yearning desire to vote for the Colonel felt nevertheless a perverse sensation of protest because we were "expected to" vote for Wilson or not at all. While Wilson was our choice, we did not want to be obliged to vote for him. Is such a feeling unreasonable?

Naturally, Southerners are independent in politics. Like other people who live in warm climates, they would ordinarily tend to split into small groups rather than to vote in solid ranks. But who would suppose that Southerners had any sense of political independence? Shall Southern children be brought up to believe that independence in voting is disloyalty, if not treason? Such is the lesson of things as they are. Why should I have to teach my children that at the South the terms white, Democratic, gentleman and Christian meant pretty nearly the same thing in popular parlance? Remember, I am not railing at the South. I share all the limitations of her citizens in my own conduct. I blame a wretchedly anomalous situation, and not our sane, broadly democratic and Christian people.

Even in religion does the black blight of unfreedom appear. To say nothing about the existence of denominations with "South" or "Southern" tacked onto them, and the straying apart of religionists. that should be growing together in the general trend toward Christian unity, how absurd it is that even those whites who wish to help the negroes in their religious life are likely to do more harm than good in their efforts. Who can blame a negro for not desiring the help of a people who allow so much "arrogant indifference toward the feelings, to say nothing of the rights, of human beings"? Let a preacher in a Southern pulpit begin to plead for the negroes, and he at once endangers his popularity if not his support. Preachers do thus plead, on occasion, and are generously called "courageous" by some of their friends. Why should a minister of the church be "courageous" when he reminds his parishoners of the fundamental principle of Christianity, the priceless value of every human soul? And yet I should personally advise nine out of ten clergymen to leave this negro question severely alone. If he wants to correct injustice or arrogance or cruelty, let him work with the individual. Yet I know that I am advising a man to act slavishly—in the interest of peace and because he cannot hope to do good by his exhortations unless he has remarkable tact or wonderful powers of mind and heart. If a special student of the negro question must submit to being called "brave" because he gently insinuates that, according to Christianity, negroes have immortal souls and that Christ died for those souls, although he has prefaced his remarks with a stiff statement of his adhesion to "Southern" principles, is it surprising that the people should want their ministers to keep clear of a subject which they ordinarily have not studied? On the other hand, I have heard esteemed and godly ministers make heartless remarks about negroes, remarks so cruelly harsh and unsympathetic that they aroused my indignation that alleged ambassadors of the Most High should speak so slightingly of any of God's children.

It is needless to insist that healthy theological thinking is difficult in a land which finds itself *compelled* to use thought fashions of a bygone age. In my judgment, the theological conservatism of the South has been in many respects a good thing for the country, and has acted as a sort of national religious balance wheel; but it is humiliating to listen to much of the childish ignorance and rabid narrowness that one still hears in the South after it has long departed from other parts of the country. When men *must* use certain thought molds in politics, and *must* fear the effects of disturbing a bristling racial orthodoxy, it is natural that they should not be free in religion. The amount of underground "heresy" in the South is remarkable. I find it in numbers of young collegians especially, even in those coming from denominational institutions. These young folk have got into the habit of weighing the social and political results of differing from the common opinion: the result is that they suppress doubts that ought to be aired and sunned. I speak not as a so-called "liberal" Christian, but as one to whom the Nicene Creed is still the best expression of the highest Christian theology, making due allowance for historical differences in modes of speech. Again I am not blaming the Southerners—my people—but an untoward situation.

Shall I go on? What is the use? We need a new freedom in the South. We need freedom to vote as we please without accusation of disloyalty. We need freedom to work as we please, even though our work be "nigger's" work, without being in danger of losing caste; we need to discuss religion and churches as we please, even to the extent of expressing our preference for "Northern" rather than "Southern" Presbyterian, Baptist or Methodist forms of belief or worship or government. We even need freedom to use our own enlightened judgment as to how we treat our racial inferiors without being accused of preaching or practicing "social equality." We need freedom to teach the truth without fear or favor in our universities, without having our official heads endangered because some people are displeased with a second-hand account of our belief in the value of American principles and the reality of the Christian faith in its application to *all* men.

Now, for myself I can say that I do not value very highly the subjective subtleties of German higher criticism; that I am a Democrat in politics from reasoned preference; that I prefer running no risk of displeasing white extremists in racial matters just in order to make a few superior negroes feel the dignity of their souls a little more acutely; that I conform to our Southern traditions and manners because I like many of them and believe that most of them are the best for the present situation. But I for one want freedom—relief from the "situation" itself. The Southern people are good enough for me. The situation is atrocious in that it prevents the Southern people from developing freely as they would like to and deserve to.

But the worst has not been told. The veriest slavery of the spirit is to be found in the deep-seated *anxiety* of the South. Southerners are afraid for the safety of their wives and daughters and sisters; Southern parents are afraid for the purity of their boys; Southern publicists are afraid that a time will come when large numbers of negroes will try to vote, and thus precipitate race war. Southern religionists are afraid that our youth will grow up to despise large numbers of their fellow-men. Southern business men are afraid that agitation of the negro question will interfere with business or demoralize the labor market. Southern officials are afraid of race riots, lynchings, savage atrocities paying not only for negro fiendishness but also for the anxiety caused by fear of what might be.

Then, too, there is the whole wretched brood of *hates.* The humble white hates his negro competitor. The white woman hates a race that is a constant temptation to the lustful passions of white men. The uneducated white hates the negro "upstart" that struts around with an "education" not vouchsafed to the white man's children. And so on.

Yes, we Southerners need a freedom from suspicion, fear, anxiety, doubt, unrest, hate, contempt, disgust, and all the rest of the race-feeling-begotten brood of viperous emotions. If I speak strongly it is not because of either lack of self-control or because of fondness for rhetoric. To me Christianity and democracy are eternal realities. Liberty, equality and fraternity are still of the substance of my aspirations. I want my own people to have the chance to show the world their really splendid qualities of head and hand and heart. At present they are so often tempted above that they are able, and God's grace seems hardly sufficient for them!

This is the lesson of our student's history and this the lesson of the papers collected in this book: Since our democracy and our Christianity are fettered in their exercise on account of an abnormal and unnatural situation, we of the South, at least those of us who see the situation clearly and see it whole, are asking the help of science, of study, research, investigation—call it what you will. We have not solved and are not solving our problem. Whoever you are that love mankind and *your* fellow citizens of the South, come over and help us, not with bayonets turned in our favor rather than against us; not merely with your money to educate the head and hand without helping the situation that enervates the heart!—but come with the agencies of truth, with that scientific method which is transforming the earth; with the scientific temper that keeps the brain clear of clouds; with scientific facts that no one can honestly doubt. And when you come or send let your coming or your sending be in the spirit of brotherly sympathy toward your fellow Americans. Do not treat Southerners as foreigners or as curious psychological specimens.

We Americans need freedom from corporation dominance; we need freedom from the professional politics that binds all grafters together in a "party" without a name; we need freedom from unsettled and cumbersome financial systems or lack of systems! And so on. But let us never forget that the greatest slavery is that of fear of the future and fear of the fullest and freest discussion of all questions whatsoever. The worst slavery is spiritual unfreedom.

Give this naturally open-hearted, genial, loving, generous, free-spirited South of ours freedom to be her own true self. Thus should the South call on generous men of this country and elsewhere. But we can, perhaps, best have our plea listened to if we begin the effort of unraveling our own difficulties for ourselves. True, the Pacific Coast begins to understand us; and the Northern cities are catching a glimpse of a race problem at their doors. And we should gladly welcome all honest, sympathetic help that comes to us.   Let us, however, begin the work of understanding our own situation for ourselves; and we may be sure that we shall not lack the coöperation of our fellow Americans and of the civilized world in general.

APPENDIX

I. ANCIENT ROME AND THE SOUTHERN RACE PROBLEM: AN HISTORICAL PARALLEL

(Prepared for graduate seminar in the University of Mississippi.)

Coulanges' "The Ancient City."	Southern States, U. S. A.
Social state controls ideas. From Ethnic r e l i g i o n came law and institutions, pp. 11 and 12.	All "equalities" ultimately based on social equality, actual or potential. Southern "religion" is race solidarity and prestige.
The past never completely dies for man. Much time needed even to modify belief, 13.	Idealized past ever present to the South. The overt h r o w of "Reconstruction" strengthened faith in past.
H e a r t h - fi r e and Divine Dead, 30, 32, 35f. Domestic religion of blood-kin, 42. Religion propagated only by generation, 45. Marriage the most sacred institution, 53, 55, 62.	Southern home and Southern h e r o e s. States' Rights, patriarchal society, faith of fathers. "This is a White man's Country." Sanctity of home. Rural life.
Religion, family, property, 72, 89, 105. Ancestors—family—posterity.	"This is a White Man's Country." South is solid. Declines to break with past.

350

Family did not receive its laws from the city, 111.

The alien cannot receive the cult, 124.

Piety the all inclusive virtue, 125, 129b.

The *gens* is an enlarged family, etc., 136, 140f., 144.

Taking nourishment prepared on an altar brings about indissoluble bond between co-partakers, 157.

We cannot modify belief at will. It tells us to obey and we obey, 174.

Religion regulates every act of life, 209, 220f.

Religion binds all things together, 222-231.

He who has no *family* worship can have no *national* worship, 247.

Law born of religion, not of j u s t i c e. Different religion, different law, 24.

If a citizen renounced his religion, he renounced his rights before the law, 24. Special tribunal for alien,

Essence of S o u t h e r n "States' Rights."

"You weren't born and raised in the South."

All inclusive race-consciousness.

"We, the people of the United States," means enlarged "home folks."

A home-meal is racially sacramental and typical of all equalities. Other meals so by association.

Belief in race is coercive b e c a u s e fundamentally vital.

Race feeling pervades all life. The "Solid South" is religious dogma. Our fathers not theirs, our government n o t theirs. Nationality u l t i m a t e - ly based on kinship.

Only citizens *equal* before the law. Others may be protected *by* the law, especially when *p a t r o n s* stand sponsor for them.

R i g h t s — including f r e e speech—only for the adherents of Southern orthodoxy. Heretics dan-

cause not of the kin, 303-305.

Laws in behalf of plebeians not respected, because not religious, not of the kin, 311.

Touch of plebeians was contaminating, 312f.

Without patrons, no justice for clients; no recourse against patricians, 345.

Plebeians held back by a habit of respect. No leaders, 361.

Plebeians gained religion of their own and self-respect. Equality followed, 367f.

Man of noble family marries with plebeians. *"Marriage confounds the races,"* 370.

Thought of the plebeians just before they brought the patricians to terms: "Where we find liberty there our country is. Rome to us is nothing." 389.

Plebeian and Patrician had apparently nothing in common. Could not live together; could not live

for negro's "imitations" of whites.

Treatment of the 15th Amendment.

Touch of "free nigger," especially contaminating.

So to a great extent in Southern trials. Negro must be vouched for by patron.

So negroes in the South. This has warded off catastrophe.

South inclined to ridicule negro pride of race and assumption of self-respect. "Keep your place, and don't put on airs. Be humble." Otherwise equality creeps in .

Senator Tillman avers that this will occur if anti-amalgamation laws are repealed.

Some few of the negroes so express themselves. Others, who feel thus, keep their feelings to themselves.

Is this what some astute friends of the negro hope for? Ultimate amalgamation?

Aristocracy of wealth honors labor and intelligence and destroys religious distinction of blood, 433.

Public interest of *all* leads to democracy and equality, 437.

Suffrage must come *organically* and impose obligation, 444, 449.

Plato says *laws are just only when they conform to human nature*, 478.

Stoicism, by enlarging human *association*, frees the individual, 479.

Conclusion—Loss of Religion of the kin changed all things and brought on assimilation.

Booker Washington's advice to the negroes is most astute, if history is to be trusted.

Hence the South will not admit the negroes as citizens and declines to grant interracial democracy. Whites very democratic among themselves.

Because of the lack of this principle, "reconstruction" failed.

So the South believes, assuming the *single standard* of race-valuation.

Hence to free the individual is to superinduce association. The individual can not be emancipated apart from the race.

Southerners decline to have assimilation of the negro race and hence stand resolutely by the religion of the kin, even though the finer parts of morality may have to suffer.

[Comment Appendix 3]

COMMENT ON PARALLEL

Coulanges' "Ancient City" may lay undue stress on the religion of the "ancient city." But most competent authorities agree that kinship and respect for ancestors are basic principles in early civilization.

Are these principles outworn creeds?[*] Has "contract"

taken the place of "status"? Recent writers on social, economic and political subjects seem to be less enamored of Sir Henry Summer Maine's "Status to Contract" theory than were writers of a generation ago. The contract theory of marriage, for instance, has not produced the best results. And it is significant that one of the most progressive of the Southern states of to-day, South Carolina, goes so far in its allegiance to the *status* idea of the marriage relation as to prohibit remarriage after separation. This same state has no law requiring marriage licenses.* The religious ceremony is paramount. And yet this state of affairs produces no legal tangles. It is also significant that South Carolina is said to have a larger percentage of church members than any other state in the Union.

Is South Carolina going to set an example of moral secession from the prevailing *mores* of the United States? Will she show to the world that there is precious worth in the status theory of the *caste of the kin?*

These questions may be fanciful, but South Carolina and the Southern states generally are well worth studying in the light of the study of the "Ancient City."

Evolution may yet be shown to be conservative of the fundamental attributes of the past. It may be that the principle of biological kinship must be steadfastly adhered to by the nations (*natus*—born). We may find that democracy dare not reject the fundamental principles of aristocracy—kinship is the basis of assimilation. We may yet find that territorial common occupancy does not constitute a nation.

Some men are becoming cynical about the claims of "democracy." The present writer is not one of their number. He has a passionate belief in the *rule of the people.* But *who are* the people? Laws and institutions and constitutions do not make a nation. 'Tis the nation that makes these.

---

* Law since passed.

Caucasians of Teutonic-Celtic descent were the citizens who made the laws and institutions of this country. The "people of the United States" were born such bodily and psychically and have subsequently added to their number others who could be biologically assimilated. The doors are shut against "Mongolians" and open to "persons of African descent." Why this strange discrimination? Would it have occurred had there not been negroes by the million who had to be "called" citizens?

Now, in the light of the foregoing study and comments, let us ask ourselves the question: Are Christianity and the Moral Law and Humanitarianism to be regarded as forces working in a psychological vacuum? Or must we admit that the most sacred principles are conditioned in their application by time, place and circumstance, and especially by the Laws of Life? Practical men believe in Newton's Laws of Motion, but, in applying them to the practical affairs of life, do they not take into account the resistance of the air?

At this time of the world's history when the consciousness of race is becoming more acute; when race-friction is increasing the world over; when men of science are discovering the immense sweep of the principle of heredity; when the unity and solidarity of all social institutions are becoming more and more evident—I say, at such a time as this, is the South's radicalism as to race a phenomenon entirely out of touch with modern life?

II. NEGRO TRAITS AND THE NEGRO PROBLEM

(These notes embodied suggestions based on a collection of data pertaining to negro character. The facts were gathered by Doctor H. W. Odum, who was at the time doing graduate work at the University of Mississippi under the guidance of the author. The most important collection by Dr. Odum were the negro songs. Inasmuch as Dr. Odum's subsequent book on Mental and Social Traits of the Southern Negro did not include some of the material outlined in this paper, I have thought that the suggestions involved in this outline might prove interesting, especially since they are related to other papers in this book, as well as to portions of Doctor Odum's book where reference is made to the present writer.)

OUTLINE OF ARGUMENT ON THE RACE PROBLEM IN GENERAL:

Negro life is now, and will be, determined by the negro's *character* tendencies, psychical and social; by his *environment* (including all the forces that make or mar civilization), and by that special *correspondence* between his character and his surroundings involved in the relations between whites and blacks and their attitudes toward one another.

Hence the proper *interpretation* of negro life depends upon an estimate of negro character as it *is* under present circumstances and as it *tends to become* if the *present forces* affecting it remain essentially unchanged. But the negro's *future* is so largely in the hands of his *white* neighbors that we must understand the significance of so-called *race-prejudice* in order to *forecast* the scope of the negro's development. Having grasped the meaning of the forces at work *in* and *on* the negro, it is proper to enquire into the fitness of *education* to develop him within the *limits set by the whites* as well as the *limits set by the negro's own nature.*

It thus happens that we must not only ask the pregnant question: What is to become of the negro? but also, For what kind of future shall we educate him?

The study of race-prejudice will show that the whites, while admitting the *abstract righteousness* of the various forms of *equality*—social, economic, political, religious, legal—admitting that character is not to be judged by such external accidents as color, in *practice* refuse to grant to the negro an actual right to equality of *treatment* based on character. We shall find that this affirmation of the *right* of equality carries with it a *check* in that the whites implicitly and instinctively hold that all forms of equality are at bottom based on at least the possibility of social *communion,* and that social communion holds out the possibility of intermarriage. Now *intermarriage* between the races is held to be taboo, and hence all that tends toward it is likewise under the ban. Therefore all forms of social recognition are withheld from the negro and in proportion as they tend to connect themselves with social communion ("social equality"). *Individual* negroes, however excellent in character, are also members of a race that cannot *share* the community life of the whites, and hence, though respected for their character, they are *"outside the kin,"* and must socially, politically and in other modes ultimately connected with social communion be treated as *negroes* rather than as excellent *characters.* There seems to be much *historical justification* for this implicit theory of the dependence of all forms of social communion on the implied right of intermarriage. (Plebeians and Patricians, Normans and Saxons, etc. Negatively: Jews, Gypsies, Turks or Greeks.)

Shall we, then, counsel the negro to submit to his fate as an *"outcast,"* and become educated to *fill his place* in our civilization as a *subordinated* race? Shall we educate him for a *maimed citizenship?* Is the present order, which seems to be the only *feasible* one just now, the best possible for *either race ultimately?* Such a situation is *unamerican* and indefensible before the bar of the civilized conscience, unless we are sure that the negro is *incapable* of exercising the rights of developed human nature. And even if the negro cannot rise by *his own efforts* to any great heights of civilization, it can hardly he said that the presence and work of a race of *serfs* will be good for the economic and moral development of the *higher race.*

If the negro is to *develop freely,* though *not* at the expense of the *whites,* shall he have a *civilization of his own,* parallel to that of the whites, tho' not touching it at any point? This is the *present tendency.* Such an outcome is, of course, not practicable unless the negroes are *segregated,* perhaps under a *separate state* government with full rights of citizenship. Even then the federal relation would still remain and open all the doors to the evils that now exist. Moreover, the cry of the whites, North and South, would soon be: The territory is ours. *This is a white man's country."* (Compare attitude toward the Indians.)

What remains? Life for the negro under his *own national* government, or *colonization* in various parts of the earth where he can secure free development, or *emigration* by individuals to lands where they will be welcome, or *all* of these movements combined.

The question, can he *maintain himself apart* from the *white* race, is hardly relevant. He *has done so* in Haiti and Liberia for several generations. If he has escaped absolute failure under such *untoward conditions* as in the case of the above unfortunate experiments, he stands a far better chance of success if future experiments are *scientifically carried* out after careful and long continued planning and education. At any rate we cannot do more than our *best* for him and for the whites. *Nor should we do less.*

If the negro is to remain we must make the most of him for the sake of the *whites* if not for the sake of the colored man himself, granting him such political privileges as will not endanger white supremacy. If the negro is to *leave* this country, however gradually, his *education* should prepare him for the pioneer life that is before him. The *older* negroes, as a rule, need not be considered, they will stay where they are. But if the people of this country once decide on this solution of the problem, the *younger* negroes can be *compulsorily educated* and forced to "go where they are sent," though it will be far better to secure their free consent and enthusiastic co-operation.

The vital necessity of *studying* negro life and character now becomes apparent. What we shall do with him depends upon what he *is*, what he *may* be, and whether he is in *any sense assimilable* as a man and as a citizen. If, as urged here, all forms of assimilation depend on social communion, and that in turn on intermarriage, and if—as seems certain—amalgamation will not be permitted; and if, finally, the negro cannot remain in this country without endangering his own and the white man's future, then all the more does our *study* of this unfortunate people become our bounden *duty*, for we cannot help them establish himself unless we know his capacities and potentialities. In any case we must *educate him*, and this we cannot do without *understanding* his nature.

The crux of the question is "the *physical* presence of the negro." Once we decide that his presence is *temporary*, we shall all, in South and North, work together not only to educate the black man for his destiny, but also to prepare the South gradually for a monoracial rather than a biracial civilization.

GENERAL PLAN OF STUDIES

I. Negro character as related to the present surroundings of the negro and as influenced by the attitude of the whites.

II. Race Attitude (Race-prejudice) and its effects on the negro's probable future.

III. The education of the negro, scholastic and institutional, as dependent on a knowledge of his character, actual and potential.

IV. Comments on the concrete studies. Suggestions for further study.

I. *Traits, etc., as shown in negro songs (mostly secular).*

Considered psychologically and sociologically (processes and tendencies). Traits depend on psychical processes. Data on *Songs* gives psychological material as well as sociological. Superficial glance shows an apparent contrast between songs and the tendencies sketched in the rest of the material. Fuller study shows unity. Folk-ways and Folk-mind.

1. a. *Tendencies.* Expressiveness: Abuse, "bluff," indecent language, love of display, music, inactivity and superficiality, lying, care for churches, emotionalism, exaggeration.

Appropriativeness: Love of money, desultory work, (taking whatever comes along). Gregariousness: Sexual morality, sociality, law-abidingness, imitation and originality, honesty. More inclusive traits, spontaneity as shown in expressiveness, gregariousness and appropriativeness working together. Vagrancy, wandering, sense of dependence, lack of restraint, provincialism, childishness, moral earnestness (lack of).

b. *"Weak" tendencies.* Assertiveness. Competition with whites, lack of resultfulness. Responsiveness (sympathy) not gregarious. Irreverence to age (ingratitude charged by many).

Perceptiveness. Curiosity and observation power—not indicated by data, but probably characteristic.

2. *Psychological Processes.* Analysis of "sporting" songs.* *Feeling.* Sensuality.—If I get drunk, who's goin' to carry me home? Brown skin woman, she's chocolate to the bone. Learn me to leave all women alone. Clothes all dirty and ain't got no broom. Ole dirty clothes all hangin' in de room. Satisfied (women, whisky and brag). Don't you let my honey catch you here. Wonder where my honey stay las' night. Got a baby; don't care whar she goes. Biscuit, gravy an' potato pie.

Sensuous feeling.—If this ain't the Holy Ghost, I don' know. It just suits me. You have hurt my feelings but I won't let on. Good mornin', judge, done killed my man.

Intellect. Imitation.—Dere's one little, two little, three little angels (from the whites, but adapted). If I git drunk, etc. (adapted from similar songs of the whites). I wouldn't have a yaller gal (original from the whites, but much changed). Slow train run thro' Arkansas (partially from the whites). (Probably many other instances, but in all cases adapted and changed by the negroes.) Fatalism.— 'Taint no use o' me a-wukkin' this mornin', cause I ain't goin' to work no mo'. Good mornin', judge, etc. (Probably others.)—Concreteness.—Dere ain't no gamblers in heaben. R. R. Songs. Joe Turner and the chain-gang. Song of the "hand-out." Ev'y since I lef' dat country farm, ev'ybody been down on me. (Train song with mimicry.) Obscene songs in general.

Humor.—Ole satan weah a i'on shoe. Adam an' de rooster had a fight. Stagolee. Good mornin', judge, done kill my man. Joe Turner and the Chain-gang. When you think I'm workin', I'm walkin' the street (pun?). Ev'ybody been down on me. Greasy, greasy, Lawd! I killed a man, killed a man. Nobody to pay my fine. Goin' to

* The titles are first lines of negro songs collected by Mr. H. W. Odum.

raise hell roun' de pay-cab do'. Went up-town on Friday
night, went to kill a kid, reached my han' in my pocket,
nothin' to kill um wid. Wonder whar my honey stay las'
night. Watermelon smilin' on de vine. Chicken, don't
roos' too high for me.

Will. Inertia, etc.—Take yo' time. I ain't bother yet.
When you think I'm wukkin' I ain't doin' a thing. "Hand-
out" song. Still I ain't bother none.—Elasticity of spirit.—
Slide me down, I'll sho slide up again.

Irresponsibleness.—Went up-town to give my trouble
away. Got a baby; don't care whar she goes.

General character attitude, temperament. Bumptiousness.—'Taint nobody's business but my own. Goin' to
raise hell around de pay-cab do'. My pahdner fall sprawl-
in'. I ain't goin' to tell how he died. Went up-town to kill
a kid, etc. Coon songs. Stagolee, etc.

Irresponsibleness (under will, add the following): I
ain't bother yet. Still I ain't bother none. Good mornin', judge, etc. Wonder whar my baby stay las' night.

Anthropomorphism.—Ole satan weah a i'on shoe. O
God, don't talk lak a natchral man. Do, Lord, remember
me. Religious songs in general. (Songs concerning animals.)

SUMMARY OF TRAITS.

From the sociological study in general: *provincialism*
(lodges, churches, songs, fashions, etc.), *dependence* (religion, attitude toward whites, gregariousness in general),
lack of restraint (religion, social and family life, sexual
morality, etc.). From the psychology of the songs:
Bumptiousness, anthropomorphism, irresponsibleness.
Sense of humor seems to be a katharsis for all of these
characteristics. The traits go in pairs: Bumptiousness and
provincialism, the *hoodlum* characteristics; anthropomorphism and dependence, the *savage* element; irresponsibleness
and lack of restraint, the *child* ingredient. Tends to be

hoodlum in his *pleasures*: savage in his *intellectual* processes; child in *will*. Hoodlumism the danger. Child and
savage normal; hoodlum abnormal and criminal.

Restlessness, loafing, love of excitement, sensuality—be-
setting sins. Hoodlumism the refuge of the submerged
tenth.

Bodily traits. Not specifically dealt with in data.
"Peristaltic" in bodily temperament. Use of fundamental
rather than finer accessory elements. Not jerky, smooth
and flowing, animal gracefulness even when awkward.
Body not degenerate. Large death rate mostly due to
ignorance, carelessness, filth and poverty. Probably not yet
adapted to high pressure city life.

Brain undeveloped rather than deficient. Associative
systems meager. Bean's investigations show a fair number of negro brains up to and beyond lower level of whites.
Frontal suture idea overworked and without sufficient
authority. Closing of frontal suture may be largely functional and hence easily affected by development of the
brain.

Negro not an aberrant form of white; nor a hopelessly
arrested form of anything. His character shows great
plasticity and not a little promise. His most exploited
fault, sensuality, seems to have been a common one among
the Corinthian "saints" to whom St. Paul wrote. Shakespeare's day seems to have been quite sensual, etc. Fashion
and custom in sexual morality. Negroes develop a system
of conventions, and are beginning to practice social ostracism for sexual irregularities.

Another fault often referred to is laziness. Compare
Prof. Barrett Wendell in Boston *Transcript* for Feb. 5,
1908, where he describes the work of certain white laborers in the north. Laziness is human, especially when
climate is languorous and one knows nothing, is regarded
as nothing and has nothing to live for.

Their religion is often spoken of as peculiarly savage.
Perhaps so, but compare the older revival scenes, love

feasts, class-meetings and the like. Nevertheless, tho' the negro's hope of development as a race is by no means to be sneered at, he differs from the white not only in development but in kind. The lowest whites have the defects of whites, not negroes; the highest negroes have the good qualities of negroes, not whites. Many of these differences are indefinable; but a consideration of the songs (for instance) of low grade negroes will show at once characteristic differences in temperament that will keep whites and blacks apart for all time.

PSYCHOLOGY OF RACE-PREJUDICE

Will follow the lines indicated in "Outline of Argument." Race-enmity, race-pride and race-conscience will be distinguished. The relation of political, religious and other forms of "equality" (communion) will be shown and their connection with intermarriage. The ground will be taken that the whites will never permit any form of equality in practice (communion). Whites are beginning to withhold land from negroes. As soon as the idea takes root in the mind of the white masses, this is a white man's country! will become a reality in a still greater degree than it is to-day. Present status of negro only feasible one if he remains in South. Race feeling spreading rapidly all over the English-speaking world. "Nation" has ever meant "birth" to the Teutonic consciousness. And social utility as judged by the ruling population is the supreme test of the moral rightness or wrongness of a people's attitude toward putting abstract humanitarianism into practice among people who can never be "of the kin."

III. Education, etc.

Interest on the part of whites will hardly increase unless it is decided that negroes are ultimately to go. In such case all the latent humanitarianism of the South and the whole country will be aroused. At present, the tendency is: Hands off; let the South settle its own problem.

The whites could do a great deal for the negroes and for themselves by training negro servants. Such efforts will increase when once it is believed that negroes will not remain and that whites must become self-dependent. White doing of "chores" is now rapidly on the increase, as well as doing of all work on small farms by whites. Negroes will learn to respect chores when whites show the real nobility of honest handwork of any kind.

Whites can help negroes in education by church and lodge only on condition that negroes are believed to be no permanent part of population. Negroes show the germs of social coöperation in their management of their institutional affairs. Social settlements among negroes by better class of colored folk ought to be organized on a scientific basis. If the negroes are to be here only temporarily, the social help of whites will not be put under the ban as at present, inasmuch as it will be seen that only humanitarian motives and results are in evidence.

The mulattoes present the hardest educational problem, for they tend to desire human (white) education. But the better ones can be led to coöperate when they see that a solution of the difficulty is in sight. If the negro is to have an independent future, the apparently opposing views of Washington and DeBois will really prove to be complementary.

IV. STUDY OF THE NEGRO QUESTION

General comments on method and special comments on the concrete studies with suggestions for future studies.

III. THE RACE QUESTION AND SOUTHERN DETERIORATION

(Part of letter to the author from a North Carolina gentleman)

. . . . . There (in the South) is the White Lamb to lie down side by side with the Black Dog, and the Puritanical Pharisee (always from afar off, however) is to bless the Union. Unlike Christ, they think it is only meet that "the children's bread" should be cast to "Dogs."

Only fifteen or twenty years ago, despite the orgies of reconstruction, a majority of the blacks (it is safe to except Beaufort, S. C., and Asheville, N. C., not to mention Washington, D. C.), when addressing white people, would, as a rule, use those old terms of courtesy,—"Sir" and "Mam"; and now and then, though rarely, even touch the cap; but now these outward signs of deference are nearly always *positively omitted*. If words of this sort are ever now employed by blacks, it is when one of your servants announces that a "gentleman" or a "lady" wishes to see you. We all know now perfectly well when these words are used it means a negro man or woman; but if, instead, they said simply "man" or "woman," we are never in doubt as to the *color*, that always designates a white person, not a black. Evidently, the intent is to assert that the black is not only the equal, but the superior of the white; and tho' I have overheard this sort of thing a thousand times, I cannot recall a single instance in which the servant was reprimanded.

Indeed, the whites, on the other hand, are, either

368

through policy or fear, so anxious not to antagonize nig-
gerdom, that one rarely hears them speak of the blacks
(that is, *in their presence*) save as "colored people," "nigger" is tabooed. This implies a certain deference towards
their pretensions of at least an approximation to social
equality; a claim that even in Reconstruction Days would
have been resented. Some might insist this is really a very
unimportant matter, but it very clearly indicates not only a
change in conditions, but what is more important by far, the
direction in which we are drifting; and such movements
are characteristic. . . . .

In the South to-day, as of old, the *inside* of the sidewalk
was always accorded to the fair sex; at least in communities where the New Woman and the Suffragette have not
abundantly satisfied us that she isn't a bit better or more
refined than a "Mere Man." Stand to-day on the pavement
of any street in a Southern town, that is, where it is *not
crowded* (then "to the right" as mere matter of necessity,
has to be the custom), and watch the passers, blacks and
whites. In nine cases out of ten, the negroes, both men and
women (more especially the latter) will very persistently
endeavor to monopolize the *inner side;* even the negro
children show what are their home teachings by their efforts *in this direction.* There is, it is true, a very considerable difference in this, even in towns not very far apart.
At least, less than ten years ago, the negroes in Greenville,
S. C., accepted the white man's "right of way," but at the
same time, in Spartanburg, S. C., hardly over 30 miles
further east, time and again, I have seen negroes forcing—
practically—even "ladies" to take the outside.

On the other hand, while the whites, say some twenty
years ago, would have resented this, they now usually
acquiesce without the faintest protest (the *men,* too); as
they do in ignoring intentionally many other little imperti-
nences on the part of the blacks; none of very aggressive
character, but always very evidently intended, not only as
assertions of independence, but of racial equality, and per-

sonal, too. It is quite sure that when they effect this without any resentment being shown by the whites, it inspires the average negro with the conviction that he has got the better of his betters; and this is not calculated to make him as satisfactory a factor in the labor problem. Your darkie who is continually striving to show truculently his independence, as a "dependent" (and in vast majority of cases he cannot hope to rise above that) makes usually a very unsatisfactory sort of laborer.

No doubt millions of New Englanders would laugh at my contention, and insist that such negroes were only showing a praiseworthy and manly spirit,—yet the better classes, at least, at the North would never dream of permitting a *white* servant to take the liberties that black servants at the South insist on as one of their privileges. I have seen Yankees in Florida who would address a *white* laborer as an inferior, and yet in intercourse with the commonest blacks would use the deferential titles of "Mister" and "Mrs." . . . .

There is no race of people more prone to personal vanity than the negro; none more certain to grab an ell if you grant them an inch: therefore when the whites yield in what would be usually called "trifles," they may some day discover that little by little these trifles have grown into "thunder-bolts." The serious part of all this is the sense of a *moral victory* that the negro feels and believes he has won over the—at least nominally—superior race: all this is a two-edged weapon that cuts both ways; it encourages that truculent vanity, which is one of their wily racial traits, and at the same time it lessens, fraction by fraction, that sense of self-esteem which really helped of old the Southerner to be what he pretended—a *man* of the *highest race.*

That *faith in ourselves* is made up partly of conceit there can be no doubt, but in practical affairs in real life it has often effected greater results than some of the noblest virtues. And when any race loses faith in its own powers of achievement, when it begins to even only suspect that its "superiority" is merely a sham, that people will never win the prizes of this life, however much their humility may entitle them to "many mansions" in Heaven.

On the other hand, what of the whites? In 1861—if the South could have placed equal numbers in the field as the Northerners, is it not manifest that in a year or two almost the war would have been decided in our favor? Yet, were "Yankees" really more deficient in courage than Southerners? Not a bit of it. But the Southerner, just because *he was master of an inferior race,* had come to feel and honestly believe that he was of the highest type of mankind; and this conviction (conceit you may call it) helped at any rate to make him a nobler being, certainly, than had he felt that he was only posing, an empty pretender to virtues he did not possess.

But under present conditions, and conditions that have persisted for over forty years, the race, in all its nobler qualities, could not fail to deteriorate. When we have to truckle to a people that we *know* are our inferiors, whether it be from policy or as a matter of necessity, it cannot but fail to weaken our moral fiber.

And we do truckle to the "Heroic Hottentot," and its influence is even worse, because, as a rule, it is done less from fear than from *policy.* The larger *land-owners* (not the one-horse farmer), the employers of labor, want to keep on good terms with that class on whom they must depend largely to cultivate their crops. Any able-bodied negro, however ignorant or brutal, is an important factor in the cotton-patch; and if another man's tenant this year, next year he may be mine. Then there is the country *merchant,* the "storekeeper," who really makes the best of his profits— not out of the whites, who are shrewd and given to saving, but out of the blacks, who are gullible, who forget the past, never give a thought to the future—and what they make this month is next either on their backs or in their bellies. He is really the *Tradesman's Treasure-trove,* and without him they would rarely climb up, as they often do, to the position of "leading citizens." They are our "Captains of Industry," and in all these the "acquisitive instinct" is the one great virtue under the Commercial Code. The highest development of *some* of the *higher* faculties gives us a genius; the highest development of the *lowest* faculties gives us a Morgan and a Rockefeller.

Now then two influential classes, the large landholders and the country merchants, the one needing the negro for what he calls (I think mistakenly) his "cheap labor"; the other, really depending on him, as his "best customer"— these two, I say, were an exodus of the black race inaugurated, would be the first to bitterly oppose any such course. In such an event, the lordly landlord and the lucrative tradesman would grow eloquent in their declaration of devotion to the darky. This is his country as well as ours (except on "Election Day," of course); it is our duty ("duty" comes in so conveniently as a substitute for the omnipotent dollar) to encourage and help them. Back to Africa? Never. Our "colored people," no, they must never leave us! The Devil, you know, is never seen canvassing openly "on the stump," but always dodging—*behind it*. Satisfy the landlord and the merchant that as blacks go out whites will come in, and that with this immigration of a better class of people, land values will enormously increase, and "business" steadily advance, then, I am quite sure, even these two classes will help to "speed the parting guest."

Now, here at the South to-day, nearly every State, in fact, I think all of them, are spending liberally to educate the negro; that is, to *increase the negro vote* (which is and always will be a Republican asset) in this section. To effect this, too, as compared to the North, though poor, we are taking the pennies out of the pockets of poor whites, whose own children are very imperfectly educated, to educate the blacks; though it is very evident the more highly we educate them the less likely they are to remain contented with a subordinate position racially or individually. Indeed, if we really intend to persist in exacting this racial subordination, it is an injustice to the negro, because by reënforcing his discontent, we, of course, lessen his chances of happiness. It is true, here and there, by this method, we may evolve a "Booker Washington" (that is out of the mongrelized portion of the negroes), but surely the vast majority of them, if never to be accepted as equals of the whites, had much best remain fairly contented plowboys than thoroughly disaffected, disgruntled professors or parsons; all the more so—as there would be, in any case—probably not one "Dubois" to a thousand laboring darkies. It is both foolish and unfair to encourage methods that benefit (even if that be not doubtful) a very few, and practically punish the many.

No doubt even many Southerners believe that the very liberal assistance given to educational institutions for the blacks in the South is an evidence of honest philanthropy; but this, as a rule, is altogether a mistake. Instead of being an evidence of the deep interest the Yankee takes in the negro's welfare, it very clearly shows their shrewd recognition of the fact that the best way to protect the Northern States from an undesired and undesirable class of colored citizens is to make them better satisfied with their conditions in the South. Of course, just as the Southern planter, who is really after "cheap labor," prates about his friendly interest in his black hirelings, so the wealthy and far-sighted Pharisee of New England covers his "exclusion policy" with the broad mantle of philanthropy. Nor can I blame him. Everything, including, of course, too, the "other fellow" should be sacrificed to maintain the racial purity of the white man. That once lost, there can be no hope of regeneration.

. . . I have no hopes of getting rid of *all* of our "brothers in black"; the "poor we shall have always with us," but the swollen swells, the "gentlemen of color," who are haughty, and the "ladies of color," who are very generally naughty, these, and the really discontented, it is safe to say, would avail themselves of free tickets to a show where the whites, at any rate, would have no "showing." . . .

. . . Depriving the negro of his vote by tricks can never prove a really satisfactory triumph. It is now only winked at because the lesser of two evils. . . .

Even the Indians, a much nobler race than the Africans, recognized the white man's primacy. They have a saying—even to this day—among the Cherokees in western North Carolina: "First, white man; next, Indian, then Indian dog, then—nigger !"

As I have explained, the changes from year to year are so very slight that those who live in the "Black Belt" fail to recognize them at all; nor perhaps should I, but as for some twelve years past I have lived—at least usually from April to November—in the mountains of western North Carolina, where the blacks in rural neighborhoods are hardly ever seen; and in winter usually far south in Florida, which is less infested by "colored gentlemen" than by Yankees, just because only at comparatively long intervals am I brought in contact with conditions here, I can perceive the changes which the resident flatters himself *haven't occurred.*

But they "have occurred," and when the drift is always and steadily in one direction such changes will eventually entirely revolutionize conditions. The negro will never—as a pure blooded black—dominate, it is true; but the white man will deteriorate and become mongrelized.

A summer boarder who occupied one of my two cottages near Hendersonville last season, spoke in almost eulogistic terms of a "colored" doctor in their little town; and she mentioned that a cousin of mine (now dead), also a doctor in same place, often called on him for "consultations." Though of old Southern stock, she held this quite right and proper.

A wise and witty Frenchman has said: "It is only the first step that costs." Once you stoop, whether it is from necessity or policy or convenience, you will find that the oftener you do it the less you will feel its degradation. The big planter who objects to any negro exodus, because it will lessen his supply of labor, knows perfectly well that if socially he and his escape to a large degree the racial contamination, his poor neighbors do not. This now may concern him very little, but in the next generation the sons of that very poor neighbor intermarry with his own, and sooner or later the deterioration of one class will affect imperiously a higher and better one. Try as we may, we can never in this country build up a really "privileged class" who will not suffer for the sins of those nominally below them.

IV. SYLLABUS OF TENTATIVE AND SUGGESTIVE SCIENTIFIC STUDY OF THE NEGRO AND NEGRO PROBLEM

I. *Anthropology*

(See Haddon. Study of Man, Appendix A: The Anthropological Sciences—Brinton's Classification.)

1. *Somatology.*—Craniology (celebrated frontal suture hypothesis, which keeps on getting stated uncritically in book after book); myology; "peristaltic" action of negro muscles (T. P. B.); splanchnology (peculiarities of sexual organs, etc.) (Broca).

2. *Anthropometry.*—Data collected by Hoffman taken as a basis and greatly extended. School children, white and black. Experimental building up of children of both races with physical culture and proper dieting.

3. *Psychology* ("Laboratory").—Sensation, reaction-time, etc., effects of emotion, etc. (See later for Psychology of Character.)

4. *Developmental and Comparative Heredity.*—Traits running through negro families—how far biological and how far "social" inheritance. "Spontaneous variations." "Rapid mutations." Ethnic anatomy, physiology, pathology. So-called pubertal arrest of development. How far is it associated with bad sexual and other habits? Comparative nosology and medical geography (immunity, susceptibility, adaptability to climate, etc. See references by Tillinghast, et al.). Hookworm, pellagra, etc. Vital statistics. Fertility and sterility. Causes and tendencies. Zones of fertility and zones of morbidity. Mulatto and black. Habits and hygiene. Artificial sterility. Concubinage *vs.* prostitu-

tion (Hoffman). Criminal anthropology. (Native or environmental. Consciousness of being outcasts.)

II. *Ethnology*

1. *Social.*—Government, African, American. Tutelage in African colonies and West Indian negro states. Ethical standards: morality *vs.* religion (a hoary contrast that needs critical examination: the indications are that the most religious negroes are the most moral, and *vice versa*).

Marriage relations. (How much due to slavery, how much to white prestige, scorn and lust.) Women working for men (Cp. S. Africa).

Social classes and institutions. Negro aristocracy, how far imitative, how far does it draw color line between mulattoes and blacks?

Development of societies, lodges, etc. (H. W. Odum).

2. *Technological.*—Tool-making. (Study of "natural" artisans and their devices—not much "necessity" to stimulate technological invention in the jungles of Africa).

Music, how far spontaneous; what are its differentiæ? Games—variations from those of whites. (Place to study latent possibilities of inventiveness. See Groos: *Play of Animals* and *Play of Man.*)

3. *Religion.* Is it emotional or is it excitable? Moral, immoral or non-moral? Are there many temperamental types, as among whites? Negro Presbyterians, Episcopalians, Congregationalists, Roman Catholics, "Northern" Methodists, etc., as compared with independent negro churches.

Peculiarities of theology. Idea of a "Saviour." "Justification." "Heaven and Hell." Religion, rhythm, and sex.

4. *Linguistics.*—Vocal peculiarities. Africanisms. Labials *vs.* gutturals. "Gullah" (coast of S. C. *Sewanee Review*, 1909). "Negro laugh." Poetry and rhythm.

5. *Folk-lore.*—"Uncle Remus" variations: Georgia, Virginia, Carolina, Mississippi, Louisiana. How far do negroes live in folk-lore stage?

(6.   *Æsthetic.*)

(7.   Moral.)

(8.   Institutional, etc.)

III.   *Ethnography*

1.   *General.*—Migrations toward alluvial regions, toward cities, etc. Town *vs.* city families and individuals. Is Stone right in calling negroes migratory? Is this necessarily a bad trait?

2.   *Special.*—Relation of African to Mediterranean race. Japanese and mulattoes. (Ripley, Sergi, et al.)

IV.   *Archæology*

Why is there no tropical African archæology? Heredity *vs.* Environment. Is there a jungle archæology anywhere? Primitive Negro Industries (Bras, Ripley's bibliography.)

A.   *Psychology of Character*

I.   Negro as (1) child, (2) savage, (3) hoodlum, (4) tramp, (5) criminal. Consciousness of being an "outcast."

II.   Tendencies, instinctive and habitual: Gregarious, Appropriative, Expressive, etc. (Ethological system of T. P. B.)

III.   Character in Song (see notes in Odum's materials).

IV.   Temperament. Is there a typical negro temperament? E.g., are all negroes "emotional" in any sense of the word? Are there sub-racial types of temperament?

V.   Psychological phases and stages (assimilation, imitation, imagination, attention, endeavor, pursuit, interest, belief, anticipation, etc.) (T. P. B.'s Psychology of Character). Do the psychological phases square with the impulsive tendencies?

"Stock traits": Unresentful, ungrateful, sensual, lazy, unobservant, shiftless, emotional, shallow, patient, etc. Great need of critical working over of concrete cases. (E.g., Is the negro usually unresentful because of his amiability, his shallowness, his caution, etc.? Does he *control* his anger better than the American Indian does? Is the Indian as resentful as he used to be? etc., etc.) Collect "stock traits" from farmers, merchants, housekeepers, writers like Hoffman, Tillinghast, Stone, Thomas, Keane, Ratzel, etc., and compare with collections of concrete cases critically and "biographically" studied.

B. *Psychology of Race Prejudice*

1. Plebeian *vs.* Patrician. "Blood."
2. Slave *vs.* Freeman.
3. *Unlikeness:* (a) physical; (b) social; (c) intellectual; (d) moral, etc.
4. "Rights," "Equalities."
5. Biological and psychological bases of democracy.

C. *Study of Suggested "Solutions" of Race Problem*

1. Amalgamation. (White and Negro, Mongol and Negro, Indian and Negro, etc. South America. Cp. Teutonic *vs.* Romanic amalgamation with negroes.)
2. Peasantry. (A. H. Stone, et al.)
3. Parallel civilization. No geographical segregation.
4. Segregation, local and sectional.
5. Colonization: commercial, benevolent, etc., *vs.* prepared and scientific.
6. Degeneration. Dying out.
7. Race War. Extermination, etc.

AA. *Some Reasons for Studying the Negro Problem*

1. Understand the past and then do justice to slave-holder, abolitionist, etc.
2. Seeing things as they are and thus allay bitterness; discourage dilettante dogmatism; inhibit senseless agitation; remove anxiety.
3. Prepare the way for a solution and mark out plans for carrying it into effect.
4. Scientific spirit of the age taking hold of all such problems. Correlation of scattered data obtained by the biological, anthropological, psychological, and social sciences. Coöperation of students of Race Problems.
5. Bringing North and South together in a non-sentimental, intellectual, moral, scientific and humanitarian study.
6. Duty to the negro.
7. Saving the South's best self from anxiety, arrogance, etc.
8. Utilizing the South's resources by removing doubt and suspicion, etc., encouraging white immigration and discouraging white emigration.
9. Direct education: physical, mental, moral, industrial.
10. Prevent amalgamation.
11. Prevent strife.
12. Help solve the world's race problems.

BB. *Some Questions That Need to be Answered*

1. Does the negro show potentialities evincing high possibilities *as a race?* Can these possibilities be made kinetic under present conditions? Is the negro really adaptable, or is he parasitic? Is his slowness of development due to deep-lying anatomical and physiological causes or to environmental causes?

2. Is the negro deteriorating? If so, why? Is civilization killing him, or is it neglect, ignorance, slum life, etc.? Is his peculiar proneness to certain diseases connate? If so, why did it not develop in slavery? Is the progress of the few a permanent gain correlative with a stable, physical basis, or is there physical deterioration going on in the "best families"?

3. Is the negro developing his own civilization? Can it stand alone? Has he enough talented individuals? Can the few save the race? Is his morality deeply based, or is it merely conventional?

4. Where does he fit in? Will the Southern whites allow him to develop freely? Should they do so, and be content with a lower efficiency than might come to a purely white population? If the negro should develop a worthy parallel civilization, can it stand permanently without biological assimilation of the races?

5. Are the "equalities" all based on potential social equality? Is social equality possible or advisable in a democracy without intermarriage? What would happen if race enmity could be put out of the mind of the Southern masses? If the gap between the races is growing, should we expect the problem to "solve itself"?

6. Should people be educated in the dark without reference to their future? Will the Southern whites give the negro "industrial education" at the expense of the white children? Should the negro *élite* be as well educated as the superior individuals among the whites? If education gives freedom and initiative and calls for liberty, equality, and fraternity, shall we expect negro education to act in some exceptional way? Is there any probability that Southern whites will ever grant the negroes all the equalities that free human souls ought to have?

7. Is there greater danger in *drifting* than in organizing a national study of the question? Is *now* always the day for foresight as well as "salvation," or is the Southern situation sufficiently satisfactory for all practical purposes?

Shall our Southern children of the dominant race be allowed to grow up in an atmosphere of contempt and arrogance and hatred and our men and women suffer from chronic uneasiness and anxiety and a divided conscience, or is the present situation morally and economically satisfactory?

V. TENTATIVE SUGGESTIVE SYLLABUS OF STATISTICAL STUDY OF THE NEGRO

Method

I. *Comparative* data as to whites, negroes and mulattoes.

II. Following leads indicated by *cross-classification*. For instance, in studying number of rooms in houses, follow up suggestions as to biological effects (disease, maldevelopment), social conditions, economic bearings, moral results and the like. Reduce qualitative data to quantitative and explain quantitative by qualitative.

III. *Many observers* to study *one topic,* and *one* observer to study *many topics.* Check off results of one observer by those of another; one locality by another, etc. Fresh study of Philadelphia to compare with Du Bois'; of Columbia, Mo., to compare with Elwang's; of Covington, Ga., and Oxford, Miss., to compare with Odum's; and so on.

IV. *Concrete* studies of localities to be compared with *general* census and other statistical results.

Topics (*Divisions Not Mutually Exclusive*)

I. *Biological and Pathological.*—Vital statistics. Number of rooms and persons in room. Articles of diet, and methods of food preparation. Amount and kinds of exercise. Amount of sleep and rest. Consumption of liquor, tobacco, etc. Diseases. Use of drugs and patent medicines. Insanity and feeble-mindedness. Strength, vitality and physical efficiency tests. Care of bodies; teeth; bathing. Efficient children of inefficient parents and inefficient children of efficient parents. Longevity. Negro types: Senegambian, Guinea, Bantu, "Arab," etc. Percentage of negroid characteristics.

II. *Economic and Industrial.*—Per capita taxes, due, collected; poll-taxes; relation of tax to income. Ownership of land and homes. Mortgages and liens. Savings accounts. Kinds of expenditure. Relative amounts spent for food, clothing, amusements, and the like. Buying on installment plan. Hours of work and play. "Basket brigade." Vagrants. Tramps. Length of engagements of servants and laborers. Care of stock, tools, utensils, implements. Insurance: fire, life, funeral; companies, societies, fraternal orders. Investments. Farming arrangements: advances, interest paid, crop-sharing and the like. Peonage: "moral" cases not reached by law. ("Inside information—not for publication," except statistically.)

III. *Social and Ecclesiastical.*—Churches: Number, membership, real and nominal, finances, money spent on buildings, charities, missions, converts, backsliders, "repeaters." Societies: fraternal, social, economic, and so on. Marriages and divorces. Migrations: time, place and circumstance (a typical illustration of cross-classification). Men supported by women. Memberships in labor unions. Exclusions from labor unions and fraternal orders. Keeping rules of church and society. Number attending institutions supported by whites; shifting of membership. Preferences in song, story, jokes, Bible texts and the like. Collection of songs, proverbs, etc. Spontaneous *vs.* adapted or imitated. Social circles due to shades of color. Segregation in cities, towns, and country. Servants living in servants' rooms or servants' houses *vs.* number living at homes—preference shown. Composition of households. Comparison of numbers as to childlike, savage, hoodlum, vagrant, tramp, criminal. Giving and receiving presents. (These are only a few samples of topics.)

III. *Psychological and Moral.*—Crimes. Prostitutes and concubines. Illegitimate births. Abortions. Infanticide. Social and religious taboo for immorality. Ideas of moral turpitude in crimes, sins, wrongs, mistakes. Gambling. Rape: black victims and white victims. White rapists and negro women. Amalgamation: city, town and country. Classification of crimes by motive, kinds, etc. Recidivants. Kinds of criminal temperament, disposition, etc. Cruelty to animals and children. Neglect of old people and children. Pilfering. Instances of usury, especially ratio of mulattoes to blacks. Kindness to whites. Gratitude *vs.* ingratitude. Revenge. Preference for money *vs.* preference for playtime. Relative preference in attending funerals and weddings. Average wait between first and second marriages. Payment of debts. Proportion of those progressing as compared with those retrograding or standing still.

IV. *Legal and Political.*—Verbal accusations *vs.* written preferment of charges. Litigation. Voters; public officials (increase and decrease in proportion to population and literacy). Owning and carrying weapons. Kinds of weapons. Proportion saved from arrest or jail by white people. Poll-taxes paid by whites and relation to votes. Negroes killed without notice being taken by law. Convictions and acquittals in cases of blacks against whites and *vice versa*. Numbers deprived of votes illegally.

V. *Intellectual and Educational.*—Illiterates and unlettered. Mental arrest at puberty. Scholastic data, especially ebb and flow of attendance. Number and kinds of school houses and playgrounds. Manual training, music, physical culture. Methods of discipline, corporal·punishment. Efficiency of graduates. Consulting palmists, astrologists, mediums, etc. Classification of superstitions, magical practices, etc.

Percentage who pass examinations as teachers, lawyers, doctors. Number of newspapers, books, magazines in proportion to literacy. Percentage of talent in music, art, science, etc. Pioneer qualities.

Relation of illiteracy to crime.

Favorite phrases and expressions. Characteristic grammatical, and rhetorical and logical and observational errors.

ImTheStory.com

Personalized Classic Books in many genre's

Unique gift for kids, partners, friends, colleagues

Customize:

- Character Names
- Upload your own front/back cover images (optional)
- Inscribe a personal message/dedication on the
  inside page (optional)

Customize many titles Including
- Alice in Wonderland
- Romeo and Juliet
- The Wizard of Oz
- A Christmas Carol
- Dracula
- Dr. Jekyll & Mr. Hyde
- And more...

CPSIA information can be obtained
at www.ICGtesting.com
Printed in the USA
LVOW10s2111091017
551752LV00010B/921/P